The Family Album

Portraits of Family Life through the Centuries

OTHER BOOKS BY RUTH A. TUCKER

From Jerusalem to Irian Jaya: A Biographical History of Christian Missions

Daughters of the Church: A History of Women and Ministry from New Testament Times to the Present,
   with Walter Liefeld

Private Lives of Pastors' Wives

Guardians of the Great Commission: The Story of Women in Modern Missions

Christian Speakers Treasury

Another Gospel: Alternative Religions and the New Age Movement

Stories of Faith: Inspirational Episodes from the Lives of Christians

Women in the Maze: Questions and Answers on Biblical Equality

Multiple Choices: Making Wise Decisions in a Complicated World

The Family Album

Portraits of Family Life through the Centuries

Ruth A. Tucker

VICTOR BOOKS

A DIVISION OF SCRIPTURE PRESS PUBLICATIONS INC.
USA CANADA ENGLAND

Scripture quotations in this book are from the following: the *King James Version*; the *Holy Bible, New International Version*®. Copyright © 1973, 1978, 1984 by International Bible Society. Used by permission of Zondervan Publishing House. All rights reserved; the *New American Standard Bible*, © the Lockman Foundation 1960, 1962, 1963, 1968, 1971, 1972, 1973, 1975, 1977; and *The Living Bible*, © 1971, Tyndale House Publishers, Wheaton, Illinois 60189. Used by permission.

Project Editor: Greg Clouse
Cover Designer: Joe De Leon
Interior Designers: Paul Higdon & Thomas A. Shumaker
Production Coordinators: Kristine Smith & Myrna Hasse

Library of Congress Cataloging-in-Publication Data

Tucker, Ruth A., 1945—
    Family album / by Ruth A. Tucker.
       p.   cm.
    ISBN 1-56476-236-X
    1. Family—History—Miscellanea. 2. Family—Quotations, maxims, etc.
3. Family—Religious life. 4. Family—Biblical teaching. 5. Christian life. I. Title
HQ503.T83   1994
306.85—dc20   94-11857
                                              CIP

---

1 2 3 4 5 6 7 8 9 10 Printing/Year 98 97 96 95 94

In Loving Memory

of

George Young

(1919–1990)

and

to

Wilda Young

in appreciation for

a quarter century of friendship

and for being

a very special mother to me

after I had lost my own

CONTENTS

Introduction

When we think of a family album, a dusty old leather-bound volume of dimming photos comes to mind—or perhaps a floral-covered book with clear plastic pages filled with snapshots of fun vacations and smiling faces. But very often this book of memories and happy times serves as a shiny veneer that hides the decaying wood underneath.

What would an authentic family album look like? Of course, there would be fun vacations and picnics and happy faces of cousins and aunts and uncles all standing around Grandma and Grandpa seated in the lawn chairs. But would there also be shots of angry brothers and weeping mothers and a fourteen-year-old cousin who's pregnant? The coffee-stained snapshots would reveal dirty little secrets that are often hidden from neighbors and church folks.

Families were created by God, but ever since that first family in the Garden of Eden, family life has not always matched the paradise portrayed in the albums. In albums of life there are families who have struggled to maintain healthy relationships and have often failed. The Bible presents these families with brutal honesty, and so does a behind-the-scenes look at church history. It is a fascinating story that has been overlooked by historians, and as such has been a great loss to Christian families who are shortchanged in their understanding of their heritage.

Why do we need a history of the Christian family? Mary Stewart Van Leeuwen addresses this issue in her book *Gender and Grace*:

> *It used to be a feminist truism that all disciplines were concerned with men's studies—for example, with "history" rather than "her story" and that was why women's studies were so desperately needed to balance the account. Now we realize that so-called androcentric scholarship has short-changed men as well. It has concentrated on the public activities of elite, powerful males, effectively ignoring all other groups as well as life in semi-public and private realms. A visiting Martian anthropologist doing research in our earthly libraries would hardly guess that human males did other things besides wage wars, draft treaties, or make advances in art, business, science and technology. That they also played, worshiped, married, parented, joined service clubs or had identity crises has hardly been acknowledged outside of the writings of novelists and playwrights....[1]*

A look back at family life can be inspirational. We see continuity and traditions from every era: parents' love for children, husband-wife devotion, children's concern for parents in old age, holiday celebrations, leisure-time activities, church rituals, and spiritual renewal. There are lessons to learn and models to follow. But of even greater significance, there is that profound discovery that we are not the first generation to endure hard times.

Today the family is threatened on all sides. We wonder sometimes whether the family as we know it will survive into the twenty-first century. But it is comforting to know that families before us have faced similar uncertainties, and we can draw strength and encouragement from our Christian heritage. Parents who are inconsolable on learning that their son is charged with murder—and in their heart they know he's guilty—can identify with Adam and Eve, who on that fateful day were suddenly faced with a double sorrow of discovering one son dead and the other a murderer. A woman who is enduring a rocky marriage can identify with and draw strength from Susanna Wesley and her marital breakdown. A mother or father with a wayward son can take counsel and encouragement from Ruth Graham, who found the Bible her source of strength during difficult days of child rearing.

The underlying thesis of this book is that Christian families of bygone generations have much to offer today's families by way of inspiration, instruction, and advice. May we accept this gift from the past with gratitude and pass it along to our children and through them on to future generations.

Adam, Eve, and the Boys: God's First Family

1 The account of Adam, Eve, and the boys is the most familiar story in the Bible. It sets the foundation for family life for all generations by showing the priority God placed on the family, but it also illustrates the fragile nature of family relationships due to our fallen natures. Indeed, here we have a "dysfunctional" family setting an example down through the generations that seems to have become a norm rather than an exception to the rule. The only difference in this case is that Adam and Eve had no one to blame. They were not adult children of alcoholics; nor had they been psychologically damaged by death or divorce. They had no victim status to claim—no physical abuse, no sex addictions, no drug dependency.

Assessing Our First Parents

Adam and Eve had no one to blame but themselves for their failures, and perhaps for that reason their example as marriage partners and parents is often brushed aside when we look to the Bible for guidance. It is sometimes assumed that there is nothing positive to say about them.

History too has judged our first parents harshly—singling them out for bringing down the human race. Bible commentators through the ages have focused almost exclusively on one brief moment in the Garden when Adam and Eve put their own interests ahead of obedience to God. But before the Fall they lived together in sinless perfection—or did they?

A Timeless Drama with a Message for Everyone

Because of the lack of biblical narrative covering this period, there has been endless speculation. For those who insist on the facts and only the facts, there is a limited amount of material from which to draw. Consequently, the story has been interpreted and reinterpreted a thousand different ways through the centuries—and not just by Bible commentators and theologians, but by literary figures and popular culture in general. It is a timeless drama that has something in it for everyone—especially if a little imagination is called forth.

Adam longing for a companion

The biblical account of this first family is truly a unique one. It begins with a solitary Adam—the only human being on the face of the earth. What was it like to be so utterly alone? Did Adam talk to himself? Did he fantasize? Did he long for the woman not yet created?

Did Adam Stumble Before He Fell?

If God created a perfect universe, how could it be that it was not good for Adam to live alone? Did God miscalculate, or did the solitary Adam stumble in such a way that God relented and gave him a mate? This is the view of Jacob Boehme, a seventeenth-century German mystic, who believed,

> *there must have been something of the nature of a stumble, if not an actual fall, in Adam while yet he was alone in Eden. Adam ...was pronounced to be "very good." There must therefore ...have been some sort of slip or lapse from his original righteousness and obedience and blessedness before his Maker would have said of Adam that he was now in a condition that was "not good." And thus it was that Eve was created to "help" Adam to recover himself.... Adam had somehow altered his first state and had brought some beginnings of evil into it, and had made that not to be good which God at one time had seen to be very good.[1]*

The Legend of Adam's First Wife

Many legends about Adam and Eve have arisen over the centuries, including those contained in the Jewish commentary on the Old Testament known as the Midrash. Here Jewish scholars speculated that Adam may have been married before Eve was even created.

> *One Midrashic text...tries to make us believe that...Eve was not the first woman in creation; she had been preceded by Lilith, mother of demons, but Adam didn't love her, couldn't love her, for he had been present at her creation. She therefore held no mystery, no attraction. And so God introduced Eve, and Adam found her to his liking. Indeed, it was love at first sight.[2]*

Eve in All Her Splendor

We can only imagine what Eve may have looked like. Was she a tall and slender version of a contemporary fashion model, or was she voluptuous and earthy? Since ancient times, artists have sought to capture her beauty in their minds and on canvas.

Poets too have sought to capture her beauty, and no one described it more eloquently than the seventeenth-century English poet John Milton in *Paradise Lost*.

> ℰ *O fairest of creation, last and best*
> > *Of all God's works, creature in whom excelled*
> *Whatever can to sight or thought be formed,*
> > *Holy, Divine, Good, Amiable or*
> *Sweet.*[3]

Eve's Diary

What was it like for Adam and Eve during their first days together? The biblical story is tightly condensed, allowing for the imagination to run wild as Mark Twain's did when he contemplated Eve's first days together with Adam in the Garden:

Eve

> *SATURDAY: I am almost a whole day old, now. I arrived yesterday. That is as it seems to me. And it must be so, for if there was a day-before-yesterday I was not there when it happened....*

> *NEXT WEEK SUNDAY: All the week I tagged around after him and tried to get acquainted. I had to do the talking because he was shy, but I didn't mind it. He seemed pleased to have me around....*

> *WEDNESDAY: We are getting along very well indeed, now, and getting better and better acquainted. He does not try to avoid me any more, which is a good sign, and shows that he likes to have me with him....*

> *THURSDAY: My first sorrow. Yesterday he avoided me and seemed to wish I would not talk to him. I could not believe it, and thought there was some mistake, for I loved to be with him, and loved to hear him talk.... I went away and sat lonely in the place.... But when night came I could not bear the lonesomeness, and went to the new shelter which he has built, to ask him what I had done that was wrong and how I could mend it and get back his kindness again; but he put me out in the rain, and it was my first sorrow.*

> *SUNDAY: It is pleasant again, now, and I am happy; but those where heavy days; I do not think of them when I can help it....*[4]

No Sex in the Garden?

The Church Fathers drew many lessons from the story of Adam and Eve. For example, Tertullian warned against the sin of gluttony because "eating led to Adam's fall." He likewise exhorted Christians to abide by God's standard and marry only once, since God created for Adam "only one wife." Jerome held that they were created to be virgins, and were permitted to marry only after they had sinned and were banished from the garden—"from the Paradise of virginity."[5]

The Honeymoon in Paradise

In *Paradise Lost*, John Milton offers a glimpse of the garden paradise through Adam's good-morning song to Eve:

   Awake
My fairest, my espous'd, my latest found,
Heav'ns last best gift, my ever new delight,
Awake, the morning shines, and the fresh field
Calls us....let us to our fresh imployments rise
Among the Groves, the Fountains, and the Flours
That open now thir choicest bosom'd smells
Reserved from night, and kept for thee in store.[6]

Enigmatic Eve

It all started with Eve. Man slept through her creation and has been puzzled by woman ever since.[7]

Nancy Tischler

First Family Squabbles

Think of all the squabbles Adam and Eve must have had in the course of their 900 years. Eve would say, "You ate the apple," and Adam would retort, "You gave it to me."[8]

Martin Luther

Adam and Eve
in the Garden

Eve Created as a Partner

Peter Lombard, a twelfth-century churchman, was probably the first to proclaim "that God did not make woman from Adam's

14

head, for she was not intended to be his ruler, nor from his feet, for she was not intended to be his slave, but from his side, for she was intended to be his companion and his friend." [9]

Prescription for a Good Marriage and Sex

"The Gospel on Sex" began in the Garden with God's instructions to Adam and Eve and continues to be relevant today—so much so that Adam and Eve captured the cover story of *U.S. News and World Report* in 1991. But through the ages Bible commentators have debated how the words of Scripture should be applied.

> *Therefore shall a man leave his father and his mother, and shall cleave unto his wife: and they shall be one flesh.*

Genesis 2:24, King James Version

Some early Jewish teachers took the passage as a prohibition against incest. Not only was a man not to marry his mother, but neither should he marry "her who is related to his father or mother." Rabbi Akiba, a Talmudic sage writing around A.D. 135, interpreted the phrase "and cleaves to his wife" to mean "but not to his neighbor's wife, nor to a male, nor to an animal" thus disposing of adultery, homosexuality, and bestiality. And Rabbi Issi, another Talmudic writer, took "and they become one flesh" to mean that the man "shall cleave to the place where both form one flesh"—one flesh being a child. Thus the passage was read as a prohibition against sexual acts that might inhibit conception. [10]

Feisty Eve and the Zoo Baboon?

What can we deduce from the first chapters of Genesis about our first parents' personalities and intellects? The few clues we have lend themselves to interesting speculation, but they are easily misinterpreted, according to Gilbert Bilezikian:

> *Adam's conduct throughout the encounter between Eve and the tempter remains a source of bafflement. Some scholars compare the feisty, brainy, confrontational involvement of Eve to the lethargic presence of Adam and draw disparaging conclusions about him. They point out that his sole activity consisted of grasping the fruit offered to him and eating it without raising questions, as if he were in a state of moronic stupor, like a zoo baboon....*

Bilezikian goes on to emphasize that this picture of Adam is unfair and without warrant. Not only was he created in the image of God unlike the zoo baboon, but also, as a man who had talked with God, he had good reason to avoid direct dialogue with the serpent. He let Eve do the talking "in the hope that the blame would fall upon her." [11]

**Message on a
Church Marquee**

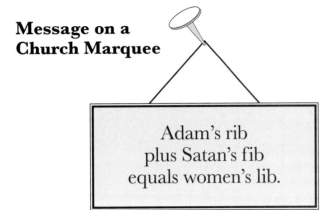

Adam's rib
plus Satan's fib
equals women's lib.

Adam, Eve, and the serpent

Role Reversal in the Garden?

It is often tempting to view the relationship between Adam and Eve in contemporary terms, and to see in their behavior issues and struggles that we are concerned with today. Elisabeth Elliot, who laments the loss of femininity among women and masculinity among men in modern Western culture, traces this transgression right back to the Garden:

> *Eve, in her refusal to accept the will of God, refused her femininity. Adam, in his capitulation to her suggestion, abdicated his masculine responsibility for her. It was the first instance of what we would recognize now as "role reversal." This defiant disobedience ruined the original pattern and things have been in an awful mess ever since.*[12]

Eve's Confession

One way to single out Eve for bringing sin into the world is by putting words in her mouth, as in this heartrending confession penned by a medieval Irish poet:

> *I am Eve, the wife of noble Adam; it was I who violated Jesus in the past; it was I who robbed my children of heaven; it is I by right who should have been crucified…. It was I who plucked the apple; it went past the narrow of my gullet; as long as they live in daylight women will not cease from folly on account of that. There would be no ice in any place; there would be no bright windy winter; there would be no hell, there would be no grief, there would be no terror but for me.*[13]

All Women Are Flawed by Grandmother Eve

Eve was repeatedly rebuked by the Church Fathers for her manipulation of Adam, causing God's perfect man to sin. In medieval times the censure was no less stinging. Eve was portrayed as the temptress, who like all women seek to bring men down through sexual enticement or any other means available to them. And she fared no better in the hands of Protestants.

Indeed, in some respects, Eve has been a more significant figure for Protestants than for Roman Catholics. Protestants—especially Puritans—spurned the notion of venerating Mary. "So Protestant womanhood was left with Grandmother Eve alone—that fearful guilty ancestress—to represent them. There was no chaste heroine in their pantheon: Grandmother Eve being very much a wife and mother, in her own guilty way, as all women in the seventeenth century were supposed to be."[14]

If a wife sought to control her husband or to get uppity in general, she was deemed an "Eve." So it was with Argula von Stauffer, a Reformer whom Martin Luther praised as "a singular instrument of Christ." But in the eyes of her Catholic opponents, she was "an insolent daughter of Eve." A century later when Anne Hutchinson challenged the Puritan hierarchy in the American colonies, she and her women followers were feared, because "as by an Eve" they might "catch their husbands also."[15]

Sometimes women themselves, in moments of self-depreciation, confessed to their own "mental and sex deficiency" inherited from Eve. In her pamphlet, *Spiritual Thrift*, Elizabeth Warren, a seventeenth-century writer, lamented the fact that "we of the weaker sex, have hereditary evil from our grandmother Eve."[16]

Adam and Eve cast out of the Garden

Adam's Responsibility for the Fall

The husband-wife "blame game" that began in the Garden has continued down through the generations. The first two stanzas of this poem, which blame Eve for the Fall, were published anonymously in 1891. The following stanzas, printed in 1905, offer a response, by an individual identified only by the initials, N.B.C.

Who hailed the first appearance of pride, And listened while the serpent lied, consented to be deified?

'Twas a woman!

Who by the tempter first betrayed, Infringed the laws that God had made, And all the world is ruin laid?

'Twas a woman!

Who failed to tell his new made bride How Satan basely, foully lied About their being deified?

'Twas Adam!

Who joined his wife in sinful pride, Altho' he knew the serpent lied About their being deified?

'Twas Adam!

Who tried to charge upon his wife The blame of his own sinful life When God and men were set at strife?

"Old Adam!"

Who ever since has laid the blame Of his own follies, sin, and shame Upon the wife who bears his name?

"Old Adam!" [17]

Adam and Eve cast out of the Garden

Eve, Our Spiritual Mother?

Churchmen from the early centuries to modern times have blamed Eve for bringing down the human race and for infecting womanhood with the tendency for evil and deception. Tertullian urged the Christian woman to dress and behave appropriately "in order that by every garbe of penitence she might the more fully expiate that which she derives from Eve.... Do you not know that you are an Eve?" Cotton Mather, the great Puritan preacher, viewed Eve's role very differently, suggesting that Eve had a positive effect on women.

Tho' both Sexes, be thro the Marvellous Providence of our God Born into the World, in pretty AEqual Numbers, yet in the Female, there seem to be the Larger Numbers, of them that are Born Again, and brought into the Kingdom of God.

His explanation for this was that the difficulties in childbirth women endure as a result of Eve's punishment increased their spiritual sensitivity:

The Dubious Hazards of their Lives in their Appointed Sorrows, drive them the more frequently, & the more fervently to commit themselves into the Hands of their Only Saviour. They are Saved thro' Child bearing; inasmuch as it singularly obliges them to Continue in Faith, and Charity, and Holiness, with Sobriety....[18]

A seventeenth-century portrayal of Grandmother Eve

Grandmother Eve and Women in Childbirth

The pain women suffer in childbearing and Eve's culpability as well as their own has been a frequent theme in the history of Christianity. The following excerpt from a seventeenth-century prayer is an example:

The smart of the punishment which thou [Lord] laidst upon me being in the loins of my grandmother Eve, for my disobedience towards thee: Thou hast greatly increased the sorrows of our sex and our bearing of children is full of pain.[19]

The Trials of Eve

Here sits our Grandame in retired place And in her lap her bloody Cain new born, The weeping Imp oft looks her in the face, Bewails his unknown hap, and fate forlorn; His mother sighs, to think of Paradise, And how she lost her bliss, to be more wise.[20]

Anne Bradstreet (1660s)

19

The Birth of Cain

And Adam knew Eve his wife; and she conceived and bare Cain, and said, "I have gotten a man from the Lord."

Genesis 4:1, King James Version

    Cain's mother mistook Cain for Christ. As soon as Eve saw her firstborn son, she no longer remembered the anguish. What a joyful woman Eve was that day! For, what a new thing in the earth was that first child in the arms of that first mother! Just look at the divine gift. Look at his eyes. Look at his hands. Look at his sweet little feet. Count his fingers. Count too, his toes. See the lovely dimple in the little man's right hand. What a child....The Garden of Eden, with all its flowers and fruits, was forgotten and forgiven from the day that heaven came down to earth; from the day on which Eve got her firstborn son from the Lord God. Nor, if you think of it, is it at all to be wondered at that little Cain's happy mother mistook him for Jesus Christ....The Lord God had come down to Eve in her terrible distress, and...promised her that the seed of the woman should bruise the serpent's head, and should thus redeem and undo all the evil that she had brought on herself and on her husband. And here, already, blessed be God, is the promised seed! [21]

Alexander Whyte

Eve, a Model for Breast-feeding Mothers

Elizabeth Knyvet, a seventeenth-century English noblewoman and mother of eighteen children, wrote a book urging mothers to breast-feed their babies. The book, printed in 1622, was entitled *The Countess of Lincoln's Nursery.* Here she cites Eve as an example for mothers who might be tempted to have their babies fed by a wet-nurse. Eve most certainly nursed her children, she argues, because there were no other women to fill that role for her. Suckling one's own babies was God's plan for all women beginning with Eve.

    We have followed Eve in Trangression. . . . Let us follow her in obedience.[22]

The Faces of Eve

The pain and anguish and disappointment that is a mother's experience in child rearing were felt most poignantly by our first mother Eve.

    Eve becomes the mother of the first murderer. And she worships him. She calls him Cain, which means "to get" or "to possess," a name that pictures her hugging the small child to her heart in the fierce joy of maternity. And her second son is Abel, which means "a breath," "a vapour," something that is doomed to fade; for Abel, unlike his brother, was sickly and weak. There is an unwritten chapter in the life of Eve. She is the mother who sees her favorite firstborn branded with shame, while the pitiful Abel becomes a martyr. The idyllic garden vanishes. The streets of London or Paris might surround her, for, in the knowledge of good and evil, she is all the women who have ever lived.[23]

Adam the Tailor and Eve the Seamstress

Andrew Johnson, who became President after Abraham Lincoln's assassination, defended his trade as a tailor by citing Adam and Eve.

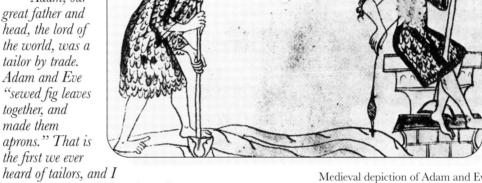

Medieval depiction of Adam and Eve

 Adam, our great father and head, the lord of the world, was a tailor by trade. Adam and Eve "sewed fig leaves together, and made them aprons." That is the first we ever heard of tailors, and I do not see that—without intending to be personal—anyone need be ashamed to be called a tailor, nor any young lady need be ashamed to be a seamstress, for her mother Eve, it seems, handled a needle with some skill.[24]

The Good Old Days

Parents are notorious for telling their children how it was in the "good old days." Adam and Eve were probably no exception. How many times did they hark back to the days gone by and the good life they had once enjoyed in the Garden. But there was another story to tell as well—one of pain and hardship. Did Cain and Abel ever hear their parents say, "If you think you've got it bad, you should have been around when we were young"?

Around the fire and smoke on damp, chill evenings Adam and Eve would rest and tell Abel and Cain about how life used to be in the garden. They made no secret to their children of their disobedience. For centuries, word of mouth, the record of their trespass was to be passed down through elders to children, until with the invention of writing the whole story could be put down on dried sheepskin and so preserved. But in the beginning, the tale was recounted to Abel and Cain by its two human actors, told under the stars, in the warmth of the blazing cedar boughs and the pungent incense of smoke.[25]

Abel's Faith

> *By faith Abel offered unto God a more excellent sacrifice than Cain, by which he obtained witness that he was righteous, God testifying of his gifts: and by it he being dead yet speaketh.*

Hebrews 11:4, King James Version

Cain's Crime

> *And Cain talked with Abel his brother: and it came to pass, when they were in the field, that Cain rose up against Abel his brother, and slew him. And the Lord said unto Cain, "Where is Abel thy brother?" And he said, "I know not: Am I my brother's keeper?"*

Genesis 4:8-9, King James Version

Cain's Jealous Rage over Property or a Woman?

Was the first murder really commited because "the Lord accepted Abel's offering, but not Cain's" as the Genesis account says? Some would argue that this explanation is merely symbolic, and the real reasons lie in a struggle over property—or perhaps over a woman. The Talmud offers both of these explanations:

> *First hypothesis: Cain and Abel quarreled over strictly material possessions, two brothers at odds over their parents' heritage—but what a heritage: the whole world. Cain appropriated all the real estate while Abel took everything else. The conflict broke out when the older of the two, greedy and dissatisfied, wanted to expel his brother from his domain.*

> *The Talmud advances a second theory: cherchez la femme. Yes, a woman must be responsible, the question is, "Which one?" Again, there are two theories.*

> *1. The brothers quarreled over the woman in their life: Adam's second wife and their mother, Eve....*

> *2. The woman was none other than Abel's twin sister, whom one source describes as having been the world's most beautiful woman....*

Adam and Eve
find Abel's body

Thus, whether mother or sister, woman would be responsible for the first fratricidal war in history; because of a lover's disappointment, Cain lost his soul, Abel his life, and we, their fellowmen, our good conscience.[26]

The Family in Jeopardy

When Cain slew Abel, Adam probably turned to Eve and said, "The future of the family is in jeopardy."[27]

Patricia Harris, former Secretary of HEW

Abel's Destiny

Abel was the first man who went to Heaven, and he went by the way of the blood.[28]

D.L. Moody

Two Sons and the Curse of Death

Abel, the second son of Adam, pleasant and beloved of God and man, was found dead, slain by the hand of his brother, her firstborn Cain, who was henceforth to be a wanderer on the face of the earth. It is impossible for us…even to imagine the feelings of the first pair as they looked on the lifeless body from which the animating soul had departed….

Cain slays his
brother Abel

Then for the first time they realized to some extent what they had done in bringing sin, and death through sin, into the world…. It is doubtful if the murderer ever again revisited his childhood home, or looked again on the faces of his parents. He too, as well as Abel, was dead to them, and in a sense far more painful to endure….[29]

S.T. Martyn

Where Did Cain Get His Wife?

An "old chestnut" of a question, and one which agnostics and hecklers are fond of hurling at defenders of the authority of the Bible is, "Where did Cain get his wife?"…Because they lived long before the Sinaitic Laws were given, there was no moral difficulty involved in the marriage of near relatives. With Cain, the course was obviously a necessary one, as it was with his brothers—they married their sisters…. Whoever the sister was who chose to go into banishment with her branded brother, she deserves credit for her willingness to share Cain's curse and wanderings. It is significant that they call their first child Enoch, which means "dedicated."[30]

Herbert Lockyer

23

Seth and the Aftermath of the 1992 L.A. Riots

> ℰᴀ *Cain and Abel have always gotten the headlines. Only in the quiet and the fine print do you discover God's grace in giving Adam and Eve a third son, Seth. A beaten-up America needs to look right now for the quiet where the significance of Seth can be heard.*[31]

Joel Belz

The generations of Adam and Eve

Legends of Adam and Eve in Christian Literature

There are many apocryphal traditions about the first family that date back to the Middle Ages, including the Greek *Apocalypse of Moses*. It opens with Cain's murder of Abel, and an angel's message that Seth will replace Cain as their firstborn son. But Adam is ill and overcome with grief. Thus begins a quest by Seth and Eve to obtain oil from paradise that will relieve Adam's pain—but to no avail. They return to Adam who is on his deathbed and still blaming Eve for their awful dilemma. Eve responds more positively. To her children she admonishes:

> Listen…and I will tell you how our enemy deceived us…. Now then, my children, I have shown you the way in which we were deceived. But you watch yourselves so that you do not forsake the good.

In the end, both Adam and Eve repent of their sin, and Adam dies, is taken to the heavenly sanctuary, and is fully pardoned.[32]

An Extended Family

> Adam had more children than the three that are mentioned in the Bible. The reason why particular mention is made of Seth, is the genealogy of our Lord Christ, who was descended from that patriarch. Adam, doubtless, had many sons and daughters, full two hundred, I am persuaded, for he lived to a great, great age, nine hundred and thirty years. It is likely that Cain was born thirty years after the fall of his parents, as they were then comforted again. I believe they were often comforted by the angels, otherwise it had been impossible for them to enjoy each other's society, by reason they were filled with great sorrows and fears. At the last day, it will be known that Eve exceeded all women in sorrow and misery. Never came into the world a more miserable woman than Eve; she saw that for her sake we were all to die. Some affirm that Cain was conceived before the promise of the seed that should crush the serpent's head. But I am persuaded that the promise was made not half a day after the fall; for they entered into the garden about noon, and having appetites to eat, she took the apple; then, about two of the clock, according to our account, was the fall.[33]

Martin Luther

The Generations of Adam and Eve

We can easily imagine Adam and Eve as the parents of Cain, Abel, Seth, and their other children, but they were also grandparents—and great, great, great, great, great grandparents.

> After the birth of Seth, Adam lived for another 800 years, and died at the age of 930. When Eve died we are not told, but if she lived as long as her husband, and she was able to continue procreation through the centuries, then the family of earth's first pair must have been

large indeed. . . . Adam lived for over 100 years after the birth of Methuselah, and the latter would have been over 300 years old when his grandson, Noah, was born. There is little room for doubt that Enoch, the seventh from Adam, had the privilege of conversing with earth's first man.[34]

Medieval Legend of Adam's Death

Illustrated Bible stories were popular in the late Middle Ages, just prior to the Reformation, but they often embellished the truth as is evident in this extract:

> *When Adam was dying, he sent Seth into the garden to get medicine. The cherub gave him a branch from the tree of life. When Seth returned, he found his father dead and buried. He planted the branch and in 4000 years it grew up to be the tree on which the Saviour was crucified.*[35]

Father Knows Best: The Old Testament Patriarchal Family

2

The term *family* in Old Testament usage did not mean what it means today. It was not a nuclear family made up merely of parents and children, but rather a household that might incorporate dozens of multi-generational related persons, in addition to servants and friends and perhaps even visiting foreigners. The father headed the home, and next in authority might be his widowed mother. His own wife (or wives), though considered property by law, were far more than mere servants. They were frequently managers of large households, and as such, wielded power and influence that might overwhelm a modern-day homemaker. Nevertheless, the Old Testament family structure, as it developed among the Hebrew people, was thoroughly patriarchal. In theory, the husband dominated the household while the wife's primary function was to bear children. The curse in Genesis 3 specified that the wife would bear children in the midst of pain, and that the husband, in addition to toiling by the sweat of his brow, would rule over the wife. In this sense, the curse overturned the creational ideal of marriage and family. Never again would there be perfect harmony as there was in the Garden.

Paradise Lost

The ideal for marriage and family that God instituted in the Garden was badly damaged by the Fall. Adam and Eve were created as partners, and there is no hint of male domination before the Fall. Together they were to be fruitful and multiply and have dominion over the Earth. Never are those admonitions separated by gender, nor is Adam commanded to have dominion over Eve. There is perfect harmony in Eden. But because of their sin, all of humanity is affected by God's curse, not just Adam and Eve. No longer does the son leave his father and mother and cleave to his wife, but rather the wife joins the family of her husband and in the process she loses that perfect partnership that was instituted in Eden. The creational harmony and equality is tempered by laws and regulations that set forth a double standard for women and men, wives and husbands. This double standard is seen most clearly in the treatment of women as inferior to men. Wives were regarded as property of their husbands along with children and cattle. In the best of situations, this arrangement was workable.

Indeed, in many instances the husband showed great love for his wife, as in the case of Jacob and Rachel and Elkanah and Hannah; and the wife often behaved as fully her husband's equal, as in the case of Rebekah and Isaac.

The Woes of Womanhood

In the worst of situations, the wife as "property" could be treated very badly, as when Abraham turned Sarah over to the lustful Egyptian Pharaoh, or even more deplorably when the old man of Gibeah gave his own daughter and another young woman to vile strangers, rather than letting his male guest become the object of their bestial lusts (Judges 19:22-26). Such treatment of women was a result of sin—and became part and parcel of the world after the Fall.

Ancient metal vessels that might have been found in "kitchen" of an Old Testament home

> *As we all know only too well, the Fall has introduced distortions into all aspects of creation, including the relationship between women and men. And the Old Testament is quite unsparing in its documentation of the results. It presents us with accounts of rape, adultery, incest and polygamy gone wild. (King Solomon had seven hundred wives and three hundred concubines!) It adds accounts of further sins aimed at covering up sexual sins, such as King David's plot to murder the husband of the woman he impregnated. And it presents such events not primarily as the acts of pagans trying to undermine Israelite society, but as the acts of God's own people…. None of this, of course, is meant to portray God's intentions for marriage and family life.[1]*

Israel, the Unfaithful Family

The sin of disobedience that corrupted the first family continued to corrupt the family of Israel—a family that was very often rebellious and far from God's creational ideal. In many respects, Old Testament family life is a fascinating microcosm of society as a whole and serves as a picture of our communion or lack of communion with God. It is a picture of the family that God uses to convey his message to Jeremiah. God, in speaking to the prophet, compares his unfaithful people to a family unit:

> *So do not pray for this people nor offer any plea or petition for them; do not plead with Me, for I will not listen to you. Do you not see what they are doing in the towns of Judah and in the streets of Jerusalem? The children gather wood, the fathers light the fire, and the women knead the dough and make the cakes of bread for the Queen of Heaven. They pour out drink offerings to other gods to provoke Me to anger. But am I the One they are provoking? declares the Lord. Are they not rather harming themselves, to their own shame?*

Jeremiah 7:16-19, New International Version

An Old Testament family at work

Israel, the Rebellious Child

> *The early chapters of the book [Jeremiah] show an offended parent trying to reason with a hopelessly rebellious child…. God's conversations with Jeremiah express the anger and futility, and behind them the pain, every parent feels on occasion. Suddenly, a lifetime of selflessly given love seems wasted, scorned. Deep family hopes wither and die. The child, bent on twisting a knife in the belly of his parents, defies them with shocking behavior.[2]*
>
> Philip Yancey

Israel, the Adulterous Wife

The husband's relationship to his wife was often used as a symbol of God's relationship to His people. When the Israelite people were unfaithful to God, they were behaving as harlots. In Ezekiel, Israel is seen as the lover and bride, wooed by God—only to become a prostitute. The description of this courtship and marriage cannot be viewed as the usual Hebrew pattern, but it does indicate how marriage and family represents the very fabric of society and society's relationship with God.

> *You grew up and developed and became the most beautiful of jewels. Your breasts were formed and your hair grew, you were naked and bare. Later I passed by, and when I looked at you and saw that you were old enough for love, I spread the corner of my garment over you and covered your nakedness. I gave you my solemn oath and entered into a covenant with you, declares the Sovereign Lord, and you became Mine. I bathed you with water and washed the blood from you and put ointments on you. I clothed you with an embroidered dress and put leather sandals on you. I dressed you in fine linen and covered you with costly garments. I adorned you with jewelry. . . . But you trusted in your beauty and used your fame to become a prostitute. You lavished your favors on anyone who passed by and your beauty became his.*
>
> Ezekiel 16:7-11, 15, New International Version

Israel, the Secure Infant

The very negative portrayal of Israel is balanced by God's love for His people—again viewed figuratively in the family relationship. In Isaiah, God is a comforting mother:

For you will nurse and be satisfied at her comforting breasts; you will drink deeply and delight in her overflowing abundance. . . . You will nurse and be carried on her arm and dandled on her knees. As a mother comforts her child, so will I comfort you.

Isaiah 66:11-13, New International Version

Marriage and Singleness

As God's family, the ancient Israelites took very seriously the command to be fruitful and multiply. But even closer to their hearts was God's promise to Abraham that his descendants would be as numerous as the stars in the sky and the sands on the seashore. Marriage and family were celebrated. There was no place for career-minded singleness.

 Marriage and the production of a family, in particular the production of male heirs to carry on the name and the family inheritance, were of major importance to Israelites of both sexes. If a person should remain single, it was viewed as a disaster. Men who could not gain wives and women who were given no husbands considered themselves deeply deprived. It is, therefore, not surprising that we find very few unmarried persons in the Old Testament.... A woman who had given birth, especially to a son who could carry on the family name and inheritance, had a special place of honor. Without children she lamented her fate, and was sometimes scorned.[3]

Marriage at an Early Age

There have been very few cultures in all of history that have placed a higher priority on marriage than did the ancient Hebrews. Marriage and procreation were God-ordained and the very essence of Hebrew existence.

Egyptian wall painting from time of Abraham showing a caravan of people ever on the move

Every man and woman was expected to marry at an early age, even priests. The importance of children, repeatedly stressed in the Bible, was undoubtedly due to high infant mortality, ceaseless wars and the rigors of an ever-mobile people. Marriage took place shortly after puberty for both men and women, and most widowers and widows who had not reached menopause usually married.[4]

Marrying in the Family

The "Children of Israel" were just that, and in order to remain pure and free from outside contamination, they often arranged the marriages of their daughters to close kin. But they had less control over their boys, who sometimes ran off with the girl "on the other side of the tracks."

The Hebrews generally favored endogamous marriages: Abraham married a half sister; his brother Nahor married a niece; Isaac, Esau, and Jacob married cousins; and Amram, the father of Moses, wed his aunt. Marriage with foreigners (usually women) took place from time to time. Judah and Simeon took Canaanite wives, Joseph espoused an Egyptian, Esau married a Hivite, and Moses was wed to both a Midianite and a Cushite. The plaint of Samson's parents seems to have been the forerunner of the modern Jewish parent's plea: "Are there no Jewish girls around that you have to marry a Gentile?" In King James English they ask, "Is there never a woman among the daughters of thy brethren, or among all my people, that thou goest to take a wife of the uncircumcised Philistines?"[5]

Arranged Marriages

It was the practice in Old Testament times for parents to negotiate the marriage plans for their children. Children did take matters into their own hands, as in the cases of Esau and Samson. And young women apparently had some say in the matter, as is implied when Abraham sent a servant to find a wife for Isaac: "If the woman will not be willing to follow thee, then thou shalt be clear from this my oath."

The father, having selected a bride for his son, paid the bride price, or mohar, generally consisting of 50 shekels of silver. There were alternate forms of payment. Jacob, for example, was too poor, and in lieu of the traditional mohar he contracted to work for his beloved Rachel's father, Laban, for seven years. Unfortunately, the wily Laban, true to another ancient custom of marrying off the oldest daughter first, slipped the veiled Leah into Jacob's tent. After the consummation, there were no marital refunds, and Jacob had to toil yet another seven years for Rachel. Happily, because Jacob loved her, his earlier seven years had "seemed unto him but a few days." One may presume that the second seven years passed almost as quickly.[6]

"We're moving to someplace called Ur. It's an entirely new concept in group living."

Drawing by W. Miller © 1989 The New Yorker Magazine, Inc.
All Rights Reserved.

Testing Faith in Family Matters

God wanted faith, the Bible says, and that is the lesson Abraham finally learned. He learned to believe when there was no reason left to believe. And although he did not live to see the Hebrews fill the land as the stars fill the sky, Abraham did live to see Sarah bear one child—just one—a boy, who forever preserved the memory of absurd faith, for his name Isaac meant "laughter."

And the pattern continued: Isaac married a barren woman, as did his son Jacob. The esteemed matriarchs of the covenant—Sarah, Rebekah, and Rachel—all spent their best childbearing years slender and in despair. They too experienced the blaze of revelation, followed by dark and lonely times of waiting that nothing but faith would fill.

A gambler would say God stacked the odds against himself. A cynic would say God taunted the creatures he was supposed to love. The Bible simply uses the cryptic phrase "by faith" to describe what they went through. Somehow, that "faith" was what God valued, and it soon became clear that faith was the best way for humans to express a love for God.[7]

Philip Yancey

The Ultimate Dowry

In cultures throughout history and today, the issue of the dowry can be a source of contention and hard feelings. The amount is often negotiated after long hours of bartering back and forth between relatives on both sides, and sometimes includes large sums of money, cattle, and land or, as in the bride price for King Saul's daughter, flesh and blood.

> *The question might be asked: What do you give as a mohar to the man who has everything? When David requested the hand of Michal from King Saul, the monarch had no need of the petty sum of 50 shekels. He did, however, perhaps as a function of his incipient schizophrenia, have a strong desire for David's death and requested "not any dowry, but an hundred foreskins of the Philistines, to be avenged of the king's enemies." Despite Saul's hopes of seeing his prospective son-in-law slain in battle, the victorious David delivered twice his required "pounds of flesh" to his king.* [8]

The Wedding Celebration

As the marriage tradition developed among the Israelites, it was the custom for the bride to leave her father and mother and cleave to her husband and become part of his family.

> *With the acceptance of the mohar, the couple was considered betrothed, a state that was legally binding. The next step was the departure of the bride from her father's household and the move to the home of the groom. If the groom's family was wealthy, an extensive celebration was held at their home. If his family was poor, he would simply lead her to his tent to consummate the marriage. When evidence of the bride's virginity (i.e., a bloodstained cloth presented by the bride's parents to the elders of the city) was forthcoming, the bride became a recognized member of the married women's community.* [9]

The "Father's House"

So important was the father in Old Testament times that the common term to designate the family was the "father's house," which was often an extended family. The father held dominion in the home. By law, he was the undisputed ruler, whether he exercised wise and loving authority or whether he abused his power, which was frequently the case. Indeed, all too often the "father's house" was anything but a happy home, and women sometimes exercised more authority than the man. The story of Judah and his extended family in Genesis 38 is an example. When his oldest son died, Judah demanded that Onan, his second son, take the widow Tamar as his wife so that they might have

A father teaching the law to his children

a son to receive the deceased oldest son's inheritance. Onan dutifully "went in onto his brother's wife," but knowing full well "the seed should not be his…he spilled it on the ground." For this act of rebellion, God struck Onan dead, and Judah sent Tamar to her own "father's house" to live, promising his next oldest son when he came of age. It was a hollow promise, and when her mother-in-law died, leaving Judah a widower, Tamar dressed up as a veiled prostitute and made herself available to him. He took advantage of her, thinking she was just another prostitute, and she conceived and bore twin boys. So it was that she tricked her father-in-law into complying with the levirate obligation. Ancient biblical times were not the "good old days." Too often, family life was anything but happy and tranquil behind the closed doors of the "father's house." [10]

Polygamy in Ancient Israel

Polygamy was widely practiced in the Old Testament—never in happy circumstances. Sarah fought with Hagar; Hannah with Penninah, and David treated his wives and concubines miserably. But polygamy was by no means the universal custom. Indeed, some of the most noted Old Testament patriarchs had only one wife: Adam, Noah, Lot, Isaac, Joseph, Job, and the prophets.

The Family and Food

Wherever we find biblical narratives relating to family life, there is typically some reference to eating.

> *Food, glorious food, is everywhere to be found in the Bible. From the description of the fruit in the Garden of Eden to the importance of the Last Supper in Christian theology, nearly every major biblical account contains a description of food.*

Unfortunately, there are no biblical recipes unless we include Abraham's very general instructions to Sarah a recipe: "Quick, three measures of choice flour. Knead and make cakes." But the meal consisted of more than cakes. Abraham "ran to the herd, took a calf, tender and choice, and gave it to the servant boy." Actual recipes on clay tables dating back to 1750 B.C. have recently been discovered. These are "the world's oldest cookbooks" that contain dozens of recipes, most of which are stews. The main ingredient was meat—gazelle, deer, mutton, pigeon, and wild dove. Some recipes were very simple: cook meat in water, add onions and garlic. A vegetarian dish called for "choice" or "cultivated" turnips. [11]

Children—A Blessing from God

> *As arrows are in the hand of a mighty man; so are children of the youth. Happy is the man that hath his quiver full of them.*
>
> Psalm 127:4-5, King James Version

Fruit of the Womb

The blessing of a newborn baby

For the Jews, children had always been considered as a blessing and as the highest form of wealth. One psalm said "Fatherhood itself is the Lord's gift, the fruitful womb is a reward that comes from him," and another compared the father of a large family to a man whose table is surrounded by young olives (Psalms 126 and 127). A common pun turned the word banim, *children, into* bonim, *guilders. Barrenness, then, was a standing shame…and the rabbis went further, stating "that a childless man should be thought of as dead." As for voluntary sterility, it was so grave a sin that the Prophet Isaiah came to call King Hezekiah to account for it, telling him that death was the just penalty for such a crime. The desire for children was so great that in the early times a legitimate wife would agree to her husband's begetting them with one of her maids, as Abraham did, and Jacob after him.[12]*

Henri Daniel-Rops

Family Devotions in Ancient Israel

Fix these words of mine in your hearts and minds: tie them as symbols on your hands and bind them on your foreheads. Teach them to your children, talking about them when you sit at home and when you walk along the road, when you lie down and when you get up. Write them on the door frames of your houses and on your gates, so that your days and the days of your children may be many in the land that the Lord swore to give your forefathers.

Deuteronomy 11:18-21,
New International Version

Stubborn Moses?

We now know why Moses wandered in the desert for 40 years. Like most men, he was too stubborn to ask for directions.[13]

Miriam guarding Baby Moses

35

Romance in Living Color

The Bible—specifically the Song of Songs—contains some of the most powerful romantic images contained in any literature of any age. The fact that the song contains the interaction and mutual expressions from both partners makes the demonstration of love even more powerful.

Kiss me again and again,
for your love is sweeter than wine. (1:2)

How beautiful you are, my love, how beautiful!
Your eyes are soft as doves'.
What a lovely, pleasant thing you are,
lying here upon the grass,
shaded by the cedar trees and firs. (1:15-17)

His left hand is under my head and with
his right hand he embraces me. (2:6)

My darling bride is like a private garden,
a spring that no one else can have,
a fountain of my own. (4:12)

Many waters cannot quench the flame of love,
neither can the floods drown it.
If a man tried to buy it with everything he owned,
he couldn't do it. (8:7)

The Living Bible

Naming Children

Eve: *life, mother of all living*	**Adam:** *red, earthy man*
Sarah: *princess of a multitude*	**Abraham:** *father of a multitude*
Rebekah: *portly and fair*	**Isaac:** *laughter*
Miriam: *judgment*	**Jacob:** *the supplanter*
Ruth: *satisfied*	**Moses:** *drawn out of water*
	Joshua: *savior*
	David: *well beloved*

The Hebrew people placed great meaning on naming their children—the names signifying something memorable about the occasion of birth or a characteristic of the child or perhaps an expectation for future greatness. Sometimes the names signified circumstances in which the parents endured, as in the case of Moses who named his first son Gershom because "I have become an alien in a foreign land," and his second son Eliezer because "my father's God was my helper," *Eli* meaning "God"; *ezer* meaning "helper." Some of the more familiar biblical names have similar significance.

A frieze from Ur showing an ancient dairy

A Mother's Broken Heart

When Sarah heard that she was to conceive and bear a child at the age of 90, she laughed. She simply could not believe it. Isaac's birth was her most cherished dream come true. But when Abraham took him away to offer him as a sacrifice to God, she could not endure the pain—according to the Jewish tradition of the Midrashim:

> *When Abraham returned from Mount Moriah to Beersheba he found the door of Sarah's tent shut…. Abraham went to the neighbors and asked: "Have you seen my wife Sarah, and do you know where she is?" And the neighbors replied: "While you were gone an old man came to Sarah's door and told her that you had taken your son Isaac to Hebron to be sacrificed on the altar as you would sacrifice a lamb. And Mother Sarah remembered that you had left with wood for a fire and the sacrificial knife, but without a ram for the altar. Then she left for Hebron to seek her son—her only son Isaac." Abraham rushed to Hebron and there he learned that when Sarah came and could not find her son, her soul fled…. As Abraham was bowing over the body of his dear wife, he heard the loud laugh of the angel of death…. "Wherefore dost thou weep," mocked the angel of death. "The blame of her death is thine. For hadst thou not taken her son from her, she would certainly be alive now."* [14]

A Mother's Love

One of the most memorable Old Testament stories of a mother's love is the story of Rebekah and Jacob. Rebekah was a remarkable young woman who became Isaac's wife. They had twin sons, and the rest of the story is familiar. Isaac favored Esau; Rebekah favored Jacob—so much that she manipulated her husband into giving Jacob the blessing that should have been given to Esau, the older of the twins. But Rebekah paid for her deceit when Esau turned on Jacob, and Jacob was forced to flee.

And must thou go, my darling son?
Light of thy mother's eyes;
Her brightest hope of future bliss,
Her dearest earthly prize?
How many thoughts at this sad hour
Are thronging on my mind;
To draw more tight the cords of love
Around my heart entwined.
For thou wast ever at my side,
A comfort and a stay—
Thy brother, like a roaming deer,
A wanderer far away.
And I had thought in death's dark hour,
To know that thou wast near;
To have thy soft and soothing tones
Fall sweetly on my ear:
To cheer me through the darksome road
Which leadeth to the grave,
And that thy hands would lay me low
In dark Machpelah's cave. . . .
What though I may not see thy face,
Or hear thy loving tone,
One comfort still is left to me—
I bear the curse alone.[15]

Advice for Youth

Remember now thy Creator in the days of thy youth, while the evil days come not, nor the years draw nigh, when thou shalt say, I have no pleasure in them.

Ecclesiastes 12:1, King James Version

Why Families?

God sets the lonely in families.

Psalm 68:6, New International Version

Ruth, A Model Daughter-in-Law

Ruth's love for her dead husband's aged mother is as pure as gold and as strong as death. Many waters cannot quench Ruth's love. And her confession of her love when she is constrained to confess it, is the most beautiful confession of love in all the world.[16]

Alexander Whyte

Marriage Vows

Ruth's confession of her love to her mother-in-law is truly one of the most profound professions of love ever offered—so much so that it has become tradition in wedding ceremonies.

> *Entreat me not to leave thee, or to return from following after thee: for whither thou goest, I will go; and where thou lodgest, I will lodge: thy people shall be my people, and thy God my God.*

Ruth 1:16, King James Version

Ruth and the Generations to Jesus

"The Gleaners"

I like to think of gentle Ruth
⠀⠀⠀⠀As beautiful indeed—
The love of God within her heart,
⠀⠀⠀⠀The Golden Rule her creed…

Naomi begged her to return
⠀⠀⠀⠀With Orpah…but she said
"Entreat me not to leave thee,
⠀⠀⠀⠀But go with you instead…."

Perhaps she longed to see the land
⠀⠀⠀⠀Her husband knew in youth,
But Naomi's heart was very glad
⠀⠀⠀⠀For loving, trusting Ruth.

Now Boaz was a kinsman,
⠀⠀⠀⠀A wealthy man and good,
So Ruth went forth into his field
⠀⠀⠀⠀To glean her daily food….

Then for his wife he took her,
⠀⠀⠀⠀And Obed was their son—
Thus, through David's generation,
⠀⠀⠀⠀Christ's lineage was begun.

In one of the greatest dramas,
⠀⠀⠀⠀With connecting, vital roles—
Ruth, the gleaner of barley and corn
⠀⠀⠀⠀And Christ, the gleaner of souls! [17]

Ruth Ricklefs

Ruth gleaning

The Legacy of Orpah and Ruth

The Jewish Talmud embellishes Old Testament accounts offering details or explanations that are nowhere found in the Bible. Concerning Orpah, the legend censures her for not insisting she follow her mother-in-law back to Judah. She was less noble than Ruth, and this flaw in her character was passed on from generation to generation—on to her great-great grandson…Goliath. For Ruth, the legacy is very different, but not without pain and sorrow. In one Midrashic source… Boaz is eighty when he marries Ruth. He dies on the day of his wedding. Ruth [apparently already pregnant] is once more a widow. Alone. And yet, at the end, we are called upon to think not of her solitude, but of our happiness; we must think of her descendant, David. [18]

A Little of Eli in All of Us

Alexander Whyte, the great Scottish minister, often preached on Bible characters. He personally identified with them, especially with their weaknesses and struggles. Eli was one such character. He was the priest who questioned Hannah's sobriety when she was praying at the temple, but beyond that he was a permissive father who had no control over his sons and their contempt for things holy. His dereliction—as a priest and as a father—is a lesson for all ages and for all people, as Whyte testifies:

Hannah giving Samuel to Eli the priest

I am filled with shame for myself and for my order as I see Eli sitting on a seat by a post of the temple, and as I see Hannah's lips moving in prayer, and then hear Eli's rebuke of Hannah. "Put away thy wine," said Eli to Hannah. If he had said that to Hophni and Phinehas twenty years before, and had, at the same time, put away his own, Eli would have had another grandson than Ichabod to bear and to transmit his name. "How long wilt thou be drunken?" said Eli to Hannah. I do not wonder that Hophni and Phinehas became prodigals. What else could they become with such a father? When the blind lead the blind, what can you look for? That temple post, and that doited old priest sitting idle in the sun, and Hannah drunk with sorrow, and the way that Eli looks at her, and the things he says to her—Rock of Ages, let me hide myself in Thee! Only to Thy cross I cling—as I see Eli, and myself in Eli, and my children in Hophni and in Phinehas and in Ichabod. I see in Eli my idleness, my blindness to my own vices, and to my children's vices…. O my God…let me have the grace to preach to them out of Hannah's song, as I have never yet done. To preach to them, and to tell them that there is none holy as the Lord….[19]

"Spare the Rod, Spoil the Child"

One of the most often quoted Old Testament proverbs on child rearing is taken from Proverbs 13:24: "Those who spare the rod hate their children, but those who love them are diligent to discipline." Charles Swindoll emphasizes that the message from Proverbs is "disciplining with dignity," which involves *yahsaar* and *yahkaag*—two different facets of discipline. *Yahsaar* refers to correction, as in disciplining with the rod. *Yahkaag* refers to reproof through instruction. "*Yahsaar* has to do with the outside, the outer activity, the outer wrong, the outer overt disobedience. *Yahkaag* deals with the inside. It supplies information and direction." When the two are combined—correction and instruction—parents have a model for "disciplining with dignity." [20]

Children Lost in History

Elie Wiesel, the award-winning Jewish writer and Bible commentator, reflects on the Book of Daniel and its message and perspective on family life:

> This story, beautiful and disturbing, is about children, Jewish children. Their fate, majestic and tragic at the same time, will sound familiar to us. Exile, separation, suffering, endurance, fidelity: it has everything…even ferocious lions. Right from the beginning, we sense danger. These Jewish children have been uprooted from Judea, their homeland, by a powerful, relentless enemy. Transported to Babylon, they are seen taking compulsory courses in…assimilation…. Apparently, such was the custom. The victor seized illustrious children of vanquished nations. In wars, it is always the children who lose. Grown-ups fight with each other and it is the children who die. The lucky ones are deported…. Far from their families, far from their people, they had to confront events in which the lives of kings and their nations were at stake. Unfortunate Jewish children, tossed about in history. Innocent Jewish children, attached to their faith, their tradition. Daniel was the most celebrated among them—perhaps because he was the best student in his class…. What ultimately happened to Daniel? He leaves the Book without a trace. In what circumstances did he die? Where?… Having survived so many dramatic events, so many threats, so many perils, he disappeared into the night of history. [21]

God's Ideal Family

There is much in the Old Testament that reflects negatively on family life. Israel as a nation could be described as one great big "dysfunctional" family, and individual families were no better. But the Old Testament does offer a glimpse of the ideal family in the Book of Proverbs where admonitions for family living are plentiful. Parents are charged with child discipline, and warnings are given to wives who agitate their husbands and upset the household. "It is better to dwell in a corner of the housetop, than with a brawling woman in a wide house." But the true model for a happy home is Proverbs 31. Although this passage is generally interpreted as referring to the ideal or virtuous woman, it more accurately describes the ideal family, given in a family context—a mother's advice to her son. The central figure in this extended family is the wife and mother, as is so often true in families. She is the one who holds the family together:

11 *The heart of her husband doth safely trust in her, so that he shall have no need of spoil.*

12 *She will do him good and not evil all the days of her life.*

23 *Her husband is known in the gates, when he sitteth among the elders of the land.*

26 *She openeth her mouth with wisdom; and in her tongue is the law of kindness.*

27 *She looketh well to the ways of her household, and eateth not the bread of idleness.*

28 *Her children arise up, and call her blessed; her husband also, and he praiseth her.*

King James Version

A picture-perfect Old Testament family

Beyond the Nativity Scene : Mary, Joseph, and a Growing Family

CHAPTER

3

The engagement and marriage of Mary and Joseph and the birth of Jesus—apart from its incredible spiritual significance to Christians—is one of the most captivating family stories in all of ancient literature. It is a story that offers lessons for every era and for all cultures. Mary is the leading character in this drama. She is the one who was granted the privilege of fulfilling Isaiah's prophecy:

> *Behold, a virgin shall conceive, and bear a son, and shall call His name Immanuel.*
>
> Isaiah 7:14, King James Version

Mary's role in Scripture has been contrasted with Eve's. Eve, the "first lady" of the Old Testament—the mother of all living, who brought death and destruction to the human race; Mary, the "first lady" of the New Testament—the mother of the Messiah, who brought forth life and redemption through her Son. With such a significant place in the redemption story, it is not surprising that Mary has become not only the object of adoration but also the center of controversy. For many theologians and Bible scholars, the nativity scene and beyond is much more than a family story of our Lord. It is first and foremost the story of the Blessed Virgin—Mary the Mother of God, the sinless saint. So exaggerated is the significance of Mary, that the simple story of the family itself is sometimes forgotten.

The Real Mary and Joseph

Who actually was Mary, if she was not some sort of sinless, deified immortal? Scripture itself does not portray Mary as anything other than an ordinary human being—a pious young virgin engaged to Joseph when her story begins. The New Testament opens with the genealogy of Jesus through Joseph, and then goes on to tell an extraordinary story of how Jesus was not actually the son of Joseph. Mary, a young woman—most likely a teenager—is pregnant and her fiancé Joseph— "a righteous man"—is not the father. When he becomes aware of the situation, he faces the dilemma of how to deal with it. Jewish law regarded betrothal as legally binding, and the only way the relationship could be

43

severed was through divorce. Joseph plans to do this with as little public fanfare as possible, but before he takes any action he is informed by an angel that Mary is supernaturally pregnant by the Holy Spirit and that he should not hesitate to go through with the marriage.

St. Anna and St. Joachim looking on as Mary takes her first steps

Mary, the mother of Jesus, and Joseph, her husband are without doubt the most famous couple in all of history, equaled, perhaps, only by Adam and Eve.[1]

A Lowly, Obscure Heritage

In the poorest, most sordid, most despised village of Judea dwelt, unknown and neglected, two members of the decayed and dethroned royal family of Judea— Joseph the carpenter and Mary his betrothed.

Though every circumstance of the story shows the poverty of these individuals, yet they were not peasants. They were of royal lineage, reduced to the poverty and the simple life of the peasants. The Jews, intensely national, cherished the tradition of David their warrior and poet prince; they sang his psalms, they dwelt on his memory, and those persons, however poor and obscure, who knew that they had his blood in their veins were not likely to forget it.[2]

Harriet Beecher Stowe

Holy Family Hagiography

The biblical story of Jesus is simple and straightforward. Apart from the incredible miracle that occurs at His conception, there are no other miracles associated with His family or early life. But for many writers in the early centuries and the Middle Ages, the story was not good enough, and the temptation to embellish it called forth their creative energies. Yet these embellishments give a fascinating perspective on the Holy Family and prompt us to wonder again about all the Bible fails to tell us about this obscure first-century family from Palestine.

Legends of Mary's Family

During the Middle Ages, as the cult of the saints—and particularly the cult of Mary—gained popularity, there was intense interest in the stories of their lives. Apocryphal literature flourished, among them *The Nativity of Mary* that offered details about the mother of Jesus that were not found in the Bible, including a description of her parents. They were pious people who practiced celibacy—a pattern prescribed for the truly spiritual of the Middle Ages, though surely not for Jews living in the generation before Jesus.

> *The blessed and ever-glorious Virgin Mary, sprung from the royal race and family of David, was born in the city of Nazareth, and educated at Jerusalem in the temple of the Lord. Her father's name was Joachim, and her mother's Anna. The family of her father was of Galilee and the city of Nazareth. The family of her mother was of Bethlehem…. Their lives were plain and right in the sight of the Lord, pious and faultless before men…. In this manner they lived for about twenty years chastely, in the favor of God and the esteem of men, without any children….*[3]

Mary's Birth an Answer to Prayer

The story goes on to say that when Joachim went to the temple in Jerusalem, the High Priest Issachar despised his offering and cursed him because he had not born a male heir. Joachim was so distressed that he went out into the desert and fasted for forty days and forty nights. Anna was distraught: "I shall bewail my widowhood; I shall bewail my childlessness." But then she went into the garden and poured her heart out to God: "O God of our fathers, bless me and hear my prayer as thou didst bless the womb of Sarah, and didst give her a son Isaac." Soon her prayer was answered:

> *And behold an angel of the Lord stood by, saying: Anna, Anna, the Lord hath heard thy prayer, and thou shalt conceive, and shalt bring forth, and thy seed shall be spoken of in all the world.*

While in the desert, Joachim received a similar angelic message. He went back to the temple with an offering, and then home to Anna.

> *And her months were fulfilled, and in the ninth month Anna brought forth. And she said to the midwife: What have I brought forth? And she said: A girl. And Anna said: My soul has been magnified this day. And she laid her down. And the days having been fulfilled, Anna was purified and gave the breast to the child, and called her name Mary.*[4]

St. Anne, the Grandmother of Jesus

Despite the very questionable nature of the stories about Mary's parents, Anna became a great saint of the Roman Catholic Church. During the Crusades, knights returned with relics to honor the Mother of the Virgin, and soon there were churches and hospitals dedicated in her memory. She was the patron saint of women in childbirth and also of copper miners. Martin Luther was one of her ardent devotees, and she was the one he called forth to save him when a bolt of lightning struck him to the ground—the incident that drove him to his monastic vows.

The Immaculate Conception of Mary

Centuries after Mary lived and died, well-meaning theologians began to exaggerate the circumstances of her own birth and life. Some insisted that she was conceived sinless; others argued that she somehow attained sinlessness while yet in the womb. And, of course, if she were sinless, it was assumed by most medieval theologians that she also remained a virgin throughout her life. Saints even joined in the debate. St. Brigitta of Sweden claimed that she had a vision that confirmed that Mary was conceived without sin.

St. Catherine of Siena, however, received a conflicting message—that Mary did not become sinless until three hours after her conception. Pope Pius IX settled the issue in 1854, when Mary's immaculate conception was made a dogma of the Catholic Church.[5]

Mary Was Her Name

Mary was one of the most common names given to baby girls in the first century—seven in the New Testament (the mother of Jesus, Mary Magdalene, the mother of James and Joseph, Mary of Cleophas, the mother of Mark, the sister of Martha, and Mary the coworker of Paul). Like many names, it evoked the memory of a great Old Testament character—in this case, the sister of Moses and Aaron, Miriam. She was remembered, while the name's original meaning—"the beloved of Yahweh"—was often forgotten. Miriam was the proper Jewish name, but "under the influence of the Aramaic word *mary* it was no doubt pronounced Mariam, the Greek and Latin form of which was Maria, and it meant 'the lady'—and curiously enough this turns into Italian as 'madonna,' into French as 'Notre Dame,' and English as 'Our Lady.'"[6]

Jesus' family tree: Mary and Baby Jesus, descendants of David son of Jesse and the kings of Israel

What If... Mary Had Made a Modern-Day Choice?

What if the unwed teenager Mary had made the wrong choice—a very modern choice—when she was confronted with an embarrassing pregnancy? What if she had slipped out one night and gone to the home of that woman in town with a bad reputation and told her she just simply could not go through with the pregnancy? What if she had married Joseph without telling him that she terminated the pregnancy? What if she had gone with him to pay their taxes to the little town of Bethlehem? What if they had been unable to find room in an inn and were forced to spend the night in a stable? Joseph was exhausted from the journey, and quickly fell asleep on the hay.

But Mary couldn't sleep. She tossed and turned. Finally she arose and walked over to the open door. There were stars in the night sky—ordinary stars, nothing unusual. And there were shepherds out in the field some distance away, barely visible in the moonlight. They were watching their sheep as they normally did.

Mary reflected on the months that had passed. This was just about the time when her little one would have been born. She stroked her abdomen and thought of what might have been. She looked back at Joseph sleeping in the hay. He was a good man. She began to weep softly, pondering in her heart what she had done. Her muffled sobs broke the stillness. Otherwise, it was a silent night in Bethlehem.[7]

Mary's Childhood Prayer

While I was yet a little one
I pleased the Lord of Grace;
And in His holy sanctuary
He granted me a place.
There, sheltered by His tender care,
And by His love inspired,
I strove in all things to fulfill
Whatever He desired....
And oft at my embroidery
Musing upon the Maid
Of whom Messiah should be born—
Thus in my heart I prayed:
"Permit me, Lord, one day to see
That Virgin ever dear,
Predestined in the Courts
Of Zion to appear.
Oh, blest estate, if but I might
Among her handmaids be
But such a favor, O my God,

47

Is far too high for me."
Thus unto God I poured my
prayer,
* And He that prayer*
fulfilled,
Not as my poverty had
hoped,
* But as His bounty*
* willed.*
Erewhile, a trembling child of
dust,
* Now robed in heavenly*
* rays,*
I reign the Mother of my God
* Through sempiternal*
* days...* [8]

Edward Caswall (1814–1878)

Jewish Weddings

The Bible tells us nothing about the marriage of Mary and Joseph, but if it did, it might describe a typical Jewish wedding in first-century Palestine.

The marriage of Mary and Joseph

Jewish weddings were preceded some time before by the payment of a dowry by the intending bridegroom, and by the betrothal. The latter had to take place before two witnesses, and involved the giving and receiving of a ring, together with a certain formula of question and answer, followed by a benediction. After this the two persons were regarded as being as much bound to one another as if they were already married. The marriage proper followed after an interval of varying length, and consisted chiefly of two items: (1) The wedding procession, in which the man fetched his bride to the future home. This procession would be accompanied with shouting, singing and dancing.... (2) The marriage supper. This took place in the house of the husband's family, and was a tremendous affair. Originally the happy pair may have sat under a small tent, but this later on became simply a canopy, under which the bridal couple were enthroned in fine clothing. The meal was lavish to the limit of extravagance, and it was a serious breach of hospitality to run short of anything like wine.[9]

Joseph the Old Man

The New Testament gives very few details about Joseph, the carpenter who married Mary. But what the Bible leaves out, apocryphal writers have eagerly provided. Most of these sources present him as an old man—too old to have possibly been the actual father of Jesus. The *Protoevangelium* gives one such story:

> *And the priest said to Joseph: Thou has been chosen by lot to take into thy keeping the Virgin of the Lord. But Joseph refused, saying: I have children, and I am an old man, and she is a young girl. I am afraid lest I become a laughingstock to the sons of Israel.*

Another source gives the actual age of Joseph—in the words of Jesus:

> *He lived for forty years unmarried; thereafter his wife remained under his care forty-nine years, and then died. And a year after her death, My Mother, the Blessed Mary, was entrusted to him by the priests, that he should keep her until the time of her marriage. She spent two years in his house; and in the third year of her stay with Joseph, in the fifteenth year of her age, she brought Me forth…. The whole age of My father, therefore, that righteous old man, was one hundred and eleven years.*[10]

The Nuptial Blessing

The marriage blessing that was typically used in ancient times was more of a prayer of thanksgiving to God than an actual blessing on the bride and groom. Mary and Joseph probably received the traditional nuptial blessing:

> *Blessed be Thou, O Lord our God, the Creator of man! The barren shall rejoice and cry for joy as she gathers her children with joyfulness to her bosom. Blessed art Thou who makest Zion to rejoice in her children! Make this couple to rejoice with joy according to the joyousness which Thou gavest to the work of Thy hands in the Garden of Eden of old! Blessed art Thou who makest the bride and the bridegroom to rejoice! Blessed art Thou who hast created for the bridegroom and bride joy and gladness, exultation, singing, cheerfulness, mirth, love, brotherly kindness, peace, and friendship! O Lord our God, may there be heard in the cities of Judea and in the streets of Jerusalem the voice of mirth and gladness, the voice of the bridegroom and bride, the voice of the bridegroom's and bride's mutual affection out of their chamber, and the young men's festive song! Blessed art Thou who makest the bridegroom to rejoice with the bride!*[11]

The Nativity

Probably no story in all the world is better known and more often repeated than the story of Jesus' birth. We read it in Luke's Gospel; we sing it in carols; we act it out in dramas; we display it on our mantels; and we mail it out in holiday greeting cards. It is an immortal story told in infinite ways—perhaps no better than in a beautiful cradle hymn penned by Isaac Watts, the father of English hymnody.

Mary, Joseph, and the
shepherds adoring
Baby Jesus

Hush, my dear, lie still and slumber,
  Holy angels guard thy bed;
Heavenly blessings without number
  Gently fall upon thy head.

Sleep, my babe, thy food and raiment,
  House and home thy friends provide,
All without thy care or payment,
  All thy wants are well supplied.

How much better thou'rt attended
  Than the Son of God could be,
When from heaven He descended,
  And became a child like thee.

Soft and easy is thy cradle,
  Coarse and hard the Savior lay,
When His birthplace was a stable
  And His softest bed was hay.

See the kindred shepherds 'round Him,
  Telling wonders from the sky;
When He wept, the mother's blessing
  Soothed and hushed the Holy Child.

  Lo! He slumbers in His manger,
  Where the hornéd oxen fed;
Peace, my darling, here's no danger,
  Here's no ox a-near thy bed.

May'st thou live to know and fear Him,
  Trust and love Him all thy days;
Then go dwell forever near Him,
  See His face and sing His praise.

I could give thee thousand kisses,
  Hoping what I most desire;
Not a mother's fondest wishes
  Can to greater joys aspire.[12]

Isaac Watts

Born in a Manger

There were no Dr. Spock "baby books" for the first-century Palestinian mother, but there were customs passed down from generation to generation, and Jesus was no doubt cared for as most babies were in that era.

> *To place a newborn infant in a manger or trough was not an out-of-the-way proceeding, since the Hebrew word means both trough and cradle, and to this day troughs or mangers are used in the Near East for cradling infants.... The newly born Jewish infant was bathed in water, rubbed with salt—to harden it off—and wrapped in swaddling clothes, from the mistaken idea that movement was bad for its limbs, which would not grow straight and strong unless kept as if it were in splints. If a boy, it was circumcised on the eighth day and received its name. It was usually breast-fed by the mother, and was not weaned fully for two or three years.[13]*

Mary and Jesus and Another Nativity Scene

> *He said: "I am only a messenger of thy Lord, that I may bestow on thee a holy son."*
>
> *[Mary] said: "How shall I have a son, when man hath never touched me? and I am not unchaste."*
>
> *He said: "So shall it be. Thy Lord hath said: 'Easy is this with me'; and we will make him a sign to mankind, and a mercy from us. For it is a thing decreed."*
>
> *And she conceived him, and retired with him to a far-off place.*
>
> *And the throes came upon her by the trunk of a palm. She said: "Oh, would that I had died ere this, and been a thing forgotten!"*
>
> *Then came she with the babe to her people, bearing him. They*

The Sistine Madonna and Jesus (Raphael)

said, "O Mary! now hast thou done a strange thing!

"O sister of Aaron! Thy father was not a man of wickedness, nor unchaste thy mother."

And she made a sign to them, pointing towards the babe. They said, "How shall we speak with him who is in the cradle, an infant?"

It said, "Verily, I am the servant of God; He hath given me the Book, and He hath made me a prophet."

The Koran, Sura XIX—Mary

The Supernatural Childbirth

The Bible confirms the supernatural conception of Jesus, but there is no indication that His birth was anything but normal. But during the Middle Ages, the very process of Jesus' birth became an issue of conflict among the theologians. The "closed uterus" theory arose to discredit any notion that Jesus might have been born "unclean." Rather, it was argued that He sprang forth from the womb supernaturally and entirely clean.[14]

Miracle Tales of Jesus' Childhood

Who was the boy Jesus? The Bible tells us virtually nothing, except for a reference to the flight to Egypt with His parents, and His interaction with the priests at the temple when He was twelve. There have been many efforts to fill the gap of the Bible's silence on His childhood and youth. The apocryphal *Book of James* contains many miraculous stories about the boy Jesus.

§ *The story of the flight into Egypt is like a Grimm fairytale, though not as magical or sinister; dragons and lions and leopards adore the child Jesus, fulfilling Isaiah's prophecy; the two thieves who will hang beside Christ at the Crucifixion rob the holy family, but one of them repents and Jesus promises him salvation. When they are thirsty, a spring gushes forth at their feet; when they are hungry, a palm tree bends its lofty branches to offer them its fruit. In Egypt, the idols of the gods of Hermopolis fall off their pedestals*

A depiction of the apocryphal story of Baby Jesus bidding the palm tree to bend down and give up its fruit

and are shattered, again in fulfillment of a prophecy of Isaiah (Isaiah 19:1), and the governor is converted. Back in Nazareth, the story becomes alarming….The child Jesus performs wonder after wonder: when the son of a scribe destroys a series of pools and dikes Jesus is building in the mud, Jesus strikes him down dead; when another boy hits Jesus, he also is struck down…. At school he knows everything and leaves his teachers dumbfounded. he works more miracles: he raises a boy from the dead, picks up water he has spilled, and stretches the planks Joseph has sawn too short.[15]

Jesus and the Sparrows

Matthew's Gospel records the familiar words of Jesus: "Are not two sparrows sold for a penny? Yet not one of them will fall to the ground apart from the will of your Father." But there is another story about Jesus and sparrows— this one from the apocryphal *Gospel of Thomas:*

When this boy Jesus was five years old he was playing at the ford of a brook, and he gathered together into pools the water that flowed by, and made it at once clean, and commanded it by his word alone. He made soft clay and fashioned from it twelve sparrows. And it was the Sabbath when he did this. And there were also many other children playing with him. Now when a certain Jew saw what Jesus was doing in his play on the Sabbath, he at once went and told his father Joseph: "See, your child is at the brook, and he has taken clay and fashioned twelve birds and has profaned the Sabbath." And when Joseph came to the place and saw it, he cried out to him, saying: "Why do You do on the Sabbath what ought not to be done?" But Jesus clapped his hands and cried to the sparrows: "Off with you!" And the sparrows took flight and went away chirping. The Jews were amazed when they saw this, and went away and told their elders what they had seen Jesus do.[16]

The Carpenter

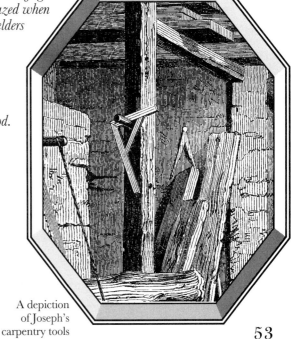

A depiction of Joseph's carpentry tools

Silent at Joseph's side He stood,
And smoothed and trimmed the shapeless wood.
And with firm hand, assured and slow,
Drove in each nail with measured blow.

Absorbed, He planned a wooden cask,
Nor asked for any greater task.
Content to make with humble tools,
Tables and little children's stools.

Lord, give me careful hands to make
Such simple things as for Thy sake.
Happy within Thine house to dwell
If I may make one table well.[17]

Phyllis Hartnoll

The return from Egypt

Young Jesus at Home

Jesus grew up in a strict religious atmosphere, learning the Torah and the Jewish traditions at home in an atmosphere of warmth and security.

At meal times Jesus followed Mary's glance and looked toward Joseph at the head of the family table. He listened attentively while Joseph offered the prayer of blessing. When that greatest of evenings arrived each year, the night of the Passover, Jesus with a youngster's pride in his role spoke his part and addressed Joseph: "Father, why is this night different from every other night?" Then each year of his youth Jesus heard Joseph repeat the already ancient story of the magnificent events of the Exodus and explain the meaning of the paschal lamb. He grew in this understanding until as an adult he heard the Baptist declare that he, Jesus, son of Joseph and Mary, was the Lamb of God who would take away the sins of the world.[18]

Jesus, the Boy Next Door

Jesus did not match their image of what God should look like. He was a man, for goodness' sake, one who hailed from the jerkwater town of Nazareth at that— Mary's boy, a common carpenter. Jesus' neighbors, who had watched him play in the streets with their own children, never could accept him as the Messiah. And Mark notes in a remarkable aside that even Jesus' own family once concluded, "He is out of his mind." His mother and brothers! Mary, who on seeing the angel Gabriel had spontaneously let loose with the annunciation hymn; his brothers, who had spent more time with him than anyone else—these, too, could not reconcile the strange combination of wondrous and ordinary. Jesus' skin got in the way.[19]

Philip Yancey

Young Jesus at Work

We know Jesus in the New Testament as a brilliant rabbi who challenged His followers with radical new ideas. But Jesus was also an artisan and manual laborer.

> *He certainly must have learned his father's trade, that of a carpenter, and when he was grown up, Jesus, like most of the Jews of his time, worked with his hands, making ploughs and yokes for oxen: there is a tradition, which Justin Martyr recorded in the second century, that preserves the memory of his labors. His contemporaries saw him, then, wearing a wood shaving behind the ear, that being the particular mark of the wood workers; and they saw him smoothing wood with a plane and striking it with a mallet.[20]*

A Single Mom and a House Full of Kids

Mary is always named first whenever the couple is referred to, and she is unquestionably the prominent member of the duo. Joseph disappears from the record after Jesus' twelfth year, and it is entirely possible that Mary had the burden of raising her children in their teenage years as a single parent. That Mary had other children has been sharply rejected by Roman Catholics, who argue that the biblical account of his brothers and sisters refers to Joseph's children by a prior marriage. It is reasonable to assume, though, that these children were younger than Jesus because they were still with their mother during the time of Jesus' ministry. The boys are named—five of them, counting Jesus. But the girls will forever remain unnumbered and unnamed.

> *Isn't this the carpenter's son? Isn't His mother's name Mary, and aren't His brothers James, Joseph, Simon and Judas? Aren't all His sisters with us?*
>
> Matthew 13:55-56,
> New International Version

Jesus and Mary studying the Torah

Young Man Jesus

Was Jesus a normal young man physically and emotionally—a man who desired romantic love and marriage and sexual relations? Marjorie Holmes, in a fictional account, suggests He was.

> *Jesus was not sure how much he slept that night. He could hear the sheep stirring, and the sounds of the*

fire, and the nighthawks making their curious cry. And it seemed to him he heard the voice of his father speaking to him gently and firmly about taking a wife. The love of his parents for each other was a part of his semiconscious state. He saw the star that seemed to fall on his mother's breast, and it became a baby, for he could see his father bending over her tenderly, the way he always did whenever a child was born. To love like that, to find a woman whom he could love like that, his own wife who would bear him children to nurse at her breast!… Restless and stirred, yet lying remotely apart, Jesus dreamed.…

What was it, what was it? Jesus sat up in a cold sweat. Then to his relief it came to him: Temptation. He had been wrestling with temptation.… He lay a few moments longer, thinking. What was temptation? Had he not been tempted many times? The girls at the grape treadings, young and lovely, sometimes unsteady from the very smell of the wine. The girls who came into the shop on pretext of some tool to be mended for their fathers—their flirting eyes and sometimes casually touching hands. The matrons who walked the streets of Nazareth, hips swinging seductively, no matter how many little ones be clinging to their skirts.… Was the yearning in his loins evil, or merely nature's response to the vital instinct God himself had planted in males that the race might survive? [21]

The Holy Family (Grosso)

Life's Pattern for a Jewish Man

The life expectancy in the first century was considerably shorter than today (in part because of the high infant mortality rate), but many people did live on to old age. The Talmud offered a full-length life plan for the male Jew—a plan that surely did not correspond with Jesus' life.

> *At five years, the Scriptures; at ten, the Mishnah; at thirteen, the Commandments; at fifteen, the Talmud; at eighteen, marriage; at twenty, the seeking (of sustenance for wife and child); at thirty, strength; at forty, discernment; at fifty, counsel; at sixty, mature age; at seventy, old age; at eighty, hoary age; at ninety, bending; at a hundred, like one that is dead, and has passed and disappeared from the world.[22]*

Is It Possible That Jesus Might Have Been Married?

In a book entitled *Was Jesus Married?* William E. Phipps argues that celibacy was "completely foreign to a biblical outlook," and that Jesus being a good Jew would have naturally gotten married. The belief that He remained unmarried, he insists, was perpetrated by early Christians who extolled celibacy. From a human perspective, Phipps' reasoning might appear well-founded, but not from a divine perspective.

> *If Jesus was only and essentially a first-century Palestinian Jew, then in all likelihood he was married. But if he was the Word made flesh who dwelt among us (John 1:14), then in his person the kingdom of heaven is present, the kingdom in which "they neither marry nor are given in marriage" (Luke 20:34-36).... To believe that he was unmarried is not to deny his humanity, but to affirm that the sexual congress of husband and wife is not an essential part of our humanity.[23]*

Jesus and His Mother

The mother-son relationship has been a very significant one in the history of Christianity: Constantine and Helena, Chrysostom and Anthusa, Augustine and Monica, Gregory the Great and Sylvia, Dominic and Juana, John Wesley and Susanna, the list goes on and on. But the most celebrated mother-son relationship of all is Jesus and Mary.

Some people are troubled by Jesus' treatment of His mother. At times He seemed almost disrespectful, and there is no indication that He accorded her the great honor that has been given her in the generations since.

Although Mary herself recognized that she was blessed—"Surely, from now on all generations will call me blessed"—Jesus did not speak of her in those terms. In fact, He downplayed Mary's blessedness.

When a woman called out from the crowd: "Blessed is the womb that bore You and the breasts that nursed You!" He responded, "Blessed rather are those who hear the word of God and obey it"

(Luke 11:27-28). His reaction was similar on an earlier occasion when He was told His mother and brothers were waiting on the outskirts of the crowd to see Him.

My mother and My brothers are these who hear the word of God and do it.

Luke 8:21, New American Standard Bible

For Jesus, motherhood was secondary to discipleship. There are hints of this outlook when Jesus was only twelve years old. After finding Him in the temple, Mary asked, "Child, why have You treated us like this?" His response was "Did you not know that I must be in My Father's house?" (Luke 2:48-49)

At the wedding of Cana, Jesus responded in a similar manner when Mary showed concern that the guests had run out of wine: "Woman, what concern is that to you and Me? My hour has not yet come" (John 2:4).

Jesus was not being rude to His mother, but He was demonstrating that He was above human relationships—above blood ties—and that both men and women, unrelated or kin, should see themselves as disciples.

Was Mary a Homebody?

Some biblical scholars focus on Mary's domestic duties rather than her discipleship. Charles Ryrie emphasizes that she is a model of womanhood who offers lessons "mostly related to the home." James Hastings offers a similar picture: "Mary was of a retiring nature, unobtrusive, reticent, perhaps even shrinking from observation, so that the impress of her personality was confined to the sweet sanctities of the home circle.... We see in the little that is told of her what a true woman ought to be." Responding to these male appraisals, Dorothy Pape writes:

The interior of a first-century Palestinian home

> *Mary may well have been retiring and home-loving, but with the possible exception of the angel's announcement of the coming conception, the scriptural record never shows us Mary at home. She is hurrying off to Elizabeth, then going to Bethlehem for the census, then to Jerusalem for purification rites, down to Egypt, back to Nazareth, then to Jerusalem again for the Passover, to Cana for the wedding, to Capernaum, to a city near the Sea of Galilee with her other sons to persuade Jesus to come home, and finally to Jerusalem again. It therefore requires an exercise of imagination to learn from her lessons "mostly related to the home."* [24]

Jesus at Joseph's Funeral

A story from the apocryphal writing known as *The History of Joseph the Carpenter* quotes a prayer that Jesus offered at His father's funeral:

> *Oh Lord of all mercy, seeing eyes and hearing ear, hear my cry and my plea for Joseph, the old man, and send Michael, the chief of Your angels, and Gabriel, the messenger of light, and all the armies of Your angels and Your choirs, so that they may march with the soul of my father Joseph, until they bring him to You.* [25]

Dying Words to a Mother

While Jesus was suffering the excruciating pain of crucifixion, His thoughts and concerns were for His mother. Who would look after her when He was gone? In that moment of utter anguish, the privilege—and burden—fell on John, His beloved disciple. They were both agonizing with Him at the foot of the cross. To His mother, He said, "Woman, behold thy son." To John, "Behold thy mother." St. Ambrose referred to these words as:

Christ's "family testament." [26]

Take Up Your Cross: Mixed Messages for New Testament Families

When viewed in the light of other ancient records, the New Testament presents some very unconventional teachings about parents, children, and family life in general. Jesus and the apostles—particularly Paul and Peter—had a radically different standard for family life than was known in Judaism or in other cultures in the ancient world. No one could doubt the New Testament focus on the family, but there are mixed messages that can seem confusing to the modern Christian. On the one hand, we see a heightened focus and concern for women and children and the home that is not evident elsewhere, and on the other hand, we see a new definition of family with the emphasis on brothers and sisters in Christ and a call for sacrifice and self-denial—to leave behind one's family, if necessary, for the sake of the Gospel.

The New Testament deals with many facets of family life. As Jesus' ministry begins, we see Him as a single adult calling disciples to follow Him—to leave behind their families and give themselves wholly to the Gospel. The situation is similar with Paul's ministry. In both cases we have a powerful reminder that singles are as much a part of the Christian community as married couples are. Children are another theme in the Gospels. Jesus was known for His revolutionary rhetoric—for making statements that stunned His hearers. So it was with His remarks concerning children. Jesus and Paul were also revolutionary in their attitude regarding women and home life. Issues relating to marriage and divorce and male and female relationships were an essential aspect of the Gospel.

Child Abuse in the Ancient World

The New Testament perspective on the family and children was very different than that which was common among the Greeks and Romans.

> *There is evidence enough in the sources so far available to us to indicate that the sexual abuse of children was far more common in the past than today…. The child in antiquity lived his earliest years in an atmosphere of sexual abuse. Growing up in Greece and Rome often*

included being used sexually by older men. Boy brothels flourished in every city, and one could even contract for the use of a rent-a-boy service in Athens. Aristotle's main objection to Plato's idea that children should be held in common was that when men had sex with boys they wouldn't know if they were their own sons, which Aristotle says would be "most unseemly." [1]

Jewish Family Life

Jewish family life stood out in stark contrast to the surrounding pagan world. An important source on Jewish social life and family relationships in the first century is the well-known Jewish writer and historian Josephus. He was a staunch defender of the uncompromising Jewish moral code.

The exterior of a first-century Palestinian dwelling

The Law recognizes no sexual connections, except the natural union of man and wife, and that only for the procreation of children. Sodomy it abhors, and punishes any guilty of such assault with death. It commands us, in taking a wife, not to be influenced by dowry, not to carry off a woman by force, nor yet to win her by guile and deceit, but to sue from him who is authorized to give her away the hand of one who is not ineligible on account of nearness of kin.

The rabbinical tradition known as the Mishnah is another source that gives insight on Jewish family life—though it applies more to the period after A.D. 70 than the period before. It gives many different perspectives on family relationships, including the authority of a father over his daughter.

> *The father has control over his daughter as touching her betrothal whether it is effected by money, by writ, or by intercourse; and he has the right...to the work of her hands, and [the right] to set her vows, and he receives her bill of divorce.*[2]

Social Outcasts and Jewish Festivals

According to the Mishnah, only heterosexual, healthy, "whole" men were required to participate in the religious festivals.

> *All are subject to the command to appear excepting a deaf mute, an imbecile, a child, one of doubtful sex, one of double sex, women, slaves that have not been freed, a man that is lame or blind or sick or aged, and one that cannot go up [to Jerusalem] on his feet.*[3]

Putting Jesus Above Family

> *Do not suppose that I have come to bring peace to the earth. I did not come to bring peace, but a sword. For I have come to turn "a man against his father, a daughter against her mother, a daughter-in-law against her mother-in-law—a man's enemies will be the members of his own household." Anyone who loves his father or mother more than Me is not worthy of Me; anyone who loves his son or daughter more than Me is not worthy of Me.*

> Matthew 10:34-37, New International Version

Are the Gospels Pro-Family?

Today it is difficult to know exactly what the term "pro-family" means. Politicians of all stripes call for pro-family policies, and no one would want to admit they are anti-family. But the relative meaning of the term is confusing not only for the modern era but for ancient times as well.

> *There is good reason to doubt the Gospels are as pro-family as we often pretend they are. After all, in their accounts Jesus is unmarried, and his twelve disciples are either single or leave families as decisively as they drop their fishing nets. Even as a boy, Jesus exhibits a startling detachment from his biological family. Luke records anxious parents returning to the Jerusalem temple, asking their son why he has been so inconsiderate of their feelings. His bemused reply signaled his own priority: "Did you not know I was bound to be in my Father's house?" (Luke 2:49)*

That's all he said? Just "follow me"?
Nothing about travel expenses, health insurance,
pension plan…?

Later in the Gospels, the adult Jesus forthrightly proclaims a kingdom that will—he makes no bones about it—divide and destroy families. Brother will betray brother to death; parents and children will turn on one another (Matthew 10:21).[4]

Roughing It for Jesus

On the road someone asked if he could go along. "I'll go with you, wherever," he said.

Jesus was curt, "Are you ready to rough it? We're not staying in the best inns, you know." [5]

Despised and Rejected

Homeless!
The Living Bread
Hungered
While all beside were fed.
To their warm holes the foxes ran,
Birds flew to nest when the west was red,
But the Son of Man
Had not where to lay His head,

Open door
Henceforth for all
Hungers,
Hearth and Banquet Hall
For hurt and loneliness is He
Thrust from Nazareth to roam,
Vagabond of Galilee,
Who is every outcast's Home.[6]

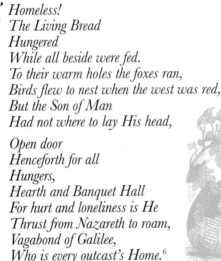

Katherine Lee Bates

Jesus and the Ideal of Family

Although Jesus called His followers to a relationship that was beyond that of family ties, He Himself recognized the family as the ultimate ideal of relational bonding. There was nothing else—no

Jesus blessing the little children

other concept—that had the verbal force to illustrate the loyalty, the love, the close connectedness, as that of the family.

His entire theology may be described as a transfiguration of the family. God is a father, man is his child; and from the father to the child there is conveyed the precious and patient message of paternal love. When the prodigal boy, in that parable which most perfectly tells the story of the sinning and repentant life, "came to himself," his first words were, "I will arise and go to my father," and while he is yet afar off the waiting father sees him coming and is moved with compassion. Repentance, that is to say, is but the homesickness of the soul, and the uninterrupted and watching care of the parent is the fairest earthly type of the unfailing forgiveness of God. The family is, to the mind of Jesus, the nearest of human analogies to the divine order which it was his mission to reveal.

To all these aspects of his teaching, which indicated the thought of Jesus concerning the family, may be further added his habitual sympathy for domestic life itself and his habitual reverence for women. Jesus, though having "not where to lay his head," was as far as possible from the habits of celibate asceticism. He shared the gaiety of the wedding feast; he lived until manhood in the tranquil simplicity of a village home; he was subject unto his parents; he found respite from the strain of his last days in the family circle at Bethany.[7]

New Teachings on Divorce

At the time of Christ there were two rival schools of Jewish thought led by rabbis Schammai and Hillel. Controversy raged between them over many issues, including divorce. Hillel argued that men could divorce their wives for any cause, whereas Schammai insisted that divorce was permitted only when the wife was unfaithful or guilty of some other serious sin against her husband.

This question of divorce having divided the rabbis, some of them thought to confound Jesus by asking him to interpret the law, for however he might decide, one of the schools must become offended and he might thus be drawn into a bitter dispute; therefore, they asked, "Is it lawful for a man to put away his wife for any cause?" The custom of divorcing wives for any cause had become so general that the whole Jewish nation had degenerated into the grossest sensualism…. However serious the question, Jesus answered it with his usual wisdom and fearlessness, and by so doing raised woman from her servile condition of the time…. Said he, "Have you not read that God created man and woman to be husband and wife, and to be helpmeets to each other; and are you ignorant of the blessings which God placed on marriage, and that in instituting that sacred bond he ordained that there should be no relationship on earth so dear, so binding, so holy as that of man and wife…."

"But," asked they who questioned him, "did not Moses permit divorcements, and for no better excuse than the wish of the husband?" "Yes," answered Jesus, "Moses gave laws permitting divorce, but it was not because he approved the dissolution of marriage, but rather to prevent greater evils." [8]

Mary, Martha, and Jesus

New Priorities for Homemakers and Mothers

The woman as wife, mother, and homemaker is often presumed to focus her priorities on the home and family, but Jesus had a different outlook. While never suggesting that homemaking was unimportant, He made it very clear that Christian discipleship was paramount.

> *Jesus tells Martha of Bethany that being busy in the kitchen over food is not as good a choice as sitting at the Master's feet learning. He chides his mother for trying to make him place blood ties before kingdom ties. To the woman in the crowd who cries out to him, "Blessed is the womb which bore you, and the breasts which nursed you!" he quickly replies, "Blessed rather are those who hear the word of God and keep it" (Luke 11:27-28). Jesus does not disparage relationships; he affirms the created sociability of persons, and he uses homey illustrations from family and village life in his parables. He also affirms parenthood as an important calling for both men and women and a role that deserves respect from children. But he does not allow them to be idolized.* [9]

Women and Home Life in Jesus' Parables

Jesus often reflected on family life and the home in His parables. In this sense His teaching was unique. Other teachers in ancient times spoke in parables, but rarely did they refer to women and their duties in the home. For Jesus, this subject matter was simply part of life.

> *The parables portray women in natural activities which illustrate various points which Jesus wished to make. Thus, a woman kneading yeast into flour illustrates the hidden but pervasive work of the kingdom (Matthew 13:33). A woman looking for a lost coin (from her dowry?) illustrates the concern of God for lost sinners (Luke 15:8-10). Prepared and unprepared bridesmaids are examples of readiness for the Lord's return (Matthew 25:1-13). A persistent woman confronting a lazy judge teaches about the need for faithful prayer and not losing heart (Luke 18:1-8). And a poor widow who gives the little that she has shows that devotion is not measured by the magnitude of our gifts but the commitment of our hearts (Mark 12:38-44).[10]*

"Let the one who is without sin cast the first stone."

Jesus Challenges the Double Standard?

In the ancient world, as in the centuries since, there has been a double standard for men and women, particularly on issues relating to marital infidelity. Then, even more than today in Western society, it was taken for granted that men were not expected to abide by the same standards of morality that women were. But Jesus insisted that standards of purity were the same for men as they were for women. When He was asked to pronounce condemnation on a woman guilty of adultery, He overturned custom by making the men equally accountable for their sin. The scribes and Pharisees reminded Jesus that the penalty for adultery was stoning—a penalty more rigorously upheld against women than men. Jesus' response was, "Let anyone among you who is without sin be the first to throw a stone at her." In renouncing this double standard, Jesus did not presume there were no gender distinctions in the tendency toward sexual sins. In the Sermon on the Mount, He spoke directly to men in condemning the sin of lust: "You have heard that it was said, 'You shall not commit adultery.' But I say to you that everyone who looks at a woman with lust has already committed adultery with her in his heart" (Matthew 5:27-28). Unlike the other Jewish rabbis of the day, Jesus did not demand that women and men be separated in order to avoid sexual sins. Rather, they should live on a higher standard than had previously been taught. "It is not the presence of a woman, but the sinful thoughts of a man, which makes the situation dangerous. Jesus, therefore, called upon His [male] disciples to discipline their thoughts rather than to avoid women." [11]

Jesus and Children

That a child should be held up as a living example for true religious faith was one of Jesus' most remarkable teachings, and it placed an infinite value on children for all generations that would follow.

In making the child the model of the life of faith, he exactly reversed the expectations of his listeners. For that reason alone the accounts of his teaching on children have the ring of truth. The attitudes expressed were so exceptional for that time that no one would have thought of inventing the stories. They were remembered, apparently, because they had been a surprise, not because he had touched upon a familiar, sentimental theme. [12]

"I know he said to let the little kids come to him, but I really think he'd want Andrew or somebody to handle the junior highs."

Kissing Cousins and More

In New Testament times, kissing carried many more messages than today. Kissing was a routine custom of life, but it was practiced strictly within specified cultural norms.

Friends kissed one another, as did parents and children, brothers and sisters, cousins, and, naturally enough, husbands and wives who were on good terms. Kissing is very often spoken of in the Bible, and one could easily use it to draw up a list of all the kinds of kisses: love-kisses, kisses of affection, and those kisses which were called for by civility. One was required, for example, to kiss any guest coming into one's house; a superior would show his benevolence by kissing his inferior; the inferior, on the other hand, would kiss the superior's hand or his knees, or even, if he wished to show limitless respect, his feet. A rabbi's disciples would greet him by kissing his hand: the only too-well-known kiss of Judas was no doubt a gesture of this kind rather than the kiss on the cheek that so many painters have represented. Those who belonged to the same religious group would exchanged the "kiss of peace;" this was the practice of the Essenes, and among the early Christians it was the mark of brotherly love.[13]

Accommodations in Palestine

During His adult ministry, Jesus had no home He could call His own. He spent much of His time traveling from place to place in Palestine, probably staying with ordinary people in very ordinary homes—not so different looking than many Palestinian homes today.

A two-story first-century Palestinian dwelling

❧ The houses of the poor in villages were, as they often still are, just one big square box-like apartment, of ground-floor only, and divided into two parts, not by a wall, but by one part being on a higher level than the other. The upper part had on it the beds, chests for clothes, and cooking utensils, and was used by the family. The lower part, when necessary, could house the livestock, but when these were outside, it could be used for other purposes, such as the children's play, or any necessary handicrafts. The roof would be flat, and not made of very thick material, perhaps rough rafters with branches laid across, and the whole plastered with mud, so that to "take off the roof" and let someone down through it, as was done at Capernaum, would be quite easy.[14]

Paul's Family Heritage

Paul was born in a city between the mountains and the sea. The year was probably A.D. 1, but all early details are shadowy except his clear claim: "I am a Jew of Tarsus, a citizen of no mean city...of the people of Israel, of the tribe of Benjamin, a Hebrew born of Hebrews."... His father most likely was a master tentmaker, whose craftsmen worked in leather and in cilicium, the cloth woven from the hair of the large long-haired black goats which grazed, as they still do, on the slopes of the Taurus. The black tents of Tarsus were used by caravans, nomads and armies all over Asia Minor and Syria. Of the mother, nothing is known; Paul never mentions her, either because she died in his infancy or because of some alienation or because he simply had no particular occasion to do so. He had at least one sister, and they were born to wealth; his father was a citizen or burgess of Tarsus and in a reform fifteen years earlier the rank of citizen had been removed from all householders without considerable fortune or property.... He was given a Jewish name at the rite of circumcision on the eighth day after birth: "Saul," chosen either for its meaning, "asked for," or in honor of the most famous Benjaminite in history, King Saul.[15]

John Pollock

Paul's "Mother"

Greet Rufus, chosen in the Lord, and his mother, who has been a mother to me, too.

Romans 16:13,
New International Version

Through an overflowing of "motherly" love and care for the Apostle, a tender relationship had been established. The most sturdy, self-reliant, and ruggedly resourceful still need occasional "mothering," and in this gracious tribute, Paul pays the mother of Rufus the highest compliment which even an apostle could confer.[16]

Herbert F. Stevenson

A tenth-century depiction of Paul being mocked by listeners

Paul's Next of Kin

Most scholars believe that Paul was unmarried, but we do read about his close kin in Acts 23:16-22. As is often true, however, the biblical account leaves us wishing we had more details.

> *Paul had one passion, namely, Christ, and thus the passage before us is the only reference we have to any of the Apostle's natural relatives—his sister and her son—both of whom are unnamed. Whether his sister and his nephew were Christians, we are not told. The latter's eagerness to save his uncle from imminent danger suggests he had a deep regard for him. How could mother and son be so closely related to the mighty Apostle, and not share his devotion for Christ! If mother and son were among his kinsmen at Rome whom Paul mentions (Romans 16:7, 11), then they might have come up to Jerusalem to keep the Feast. While there the son heard of the plot to kill his notable uncle, and thus became the means of his escape from death. Ever grateful for the assistance of those who loved him in the Lord, Paul must have been thankful for the nephew who came to him as soon as he heard of the intention of the Apostle's foes to get rid of him. Here again, we wonder at the silence of Scripture as to the identity of many it mentions! Why does Paul give us the names of other women and their sons, yet withhold the names of his own dear sister to whom he must have been attached in childhood, now, probably a widow, and her son?* [17]

Timothy instructed by his mother and grandmother

Timothy's Family Heritage

The New Testament gives very few glimpses of Christian families, and those that are presented do not match the "traditional" ideal of father, mother, and children living together in a well-ordered household. Timothy's family is an example. He was the product of a mixed marriage, the son of a Greek father and a Jewish mother who made their home in Lystra.

> *The fact that his mother married a Greek is not surprising. The farther from Jerusalem, the less rigid were the Jews in following the ban on intermarriage…. Where Timothy's father*

stood is unknown. He certainly didn't prevent his wife from instructing their son in the Scriptures. Nor did he interfere with his son being named Timotheus, which literally means "honoring God" or "dear to God." The name itself was Greek, and this must have satisfied the father; the meaning of the name must have satisfied the mother.

The father, however, hadn't allowed Timothy to be circumcised, so he obviously wasn't a proselyte or even a secret admirer of his wife's faith.... It is also possible that he had recently died, leaving the teenaged boy, his mother, and grandmother to fend for themselves in the Gentile city of Lystra....

In Lystra, Timothy may never have seen a Scripture scroll, but his mother Eunice was a walking, talking scroll, his living Scripture.... Years later Paul could remind Timothy not only to remember the instruction, but also to remember the godly example of the one from whom he had learned it.[18]

Paul's Counsel to Married Couples

Although there is no evidence that Paul himself was married, he did not hesitate giving counsel to those who were. His words on submission and headship are often quoted today to support a "traditional" perspective on marriage, but in the first century his admonitions were nothing short of revolutionary. It was a given that the man was the "head" of the home in ancient times—in the Roman world and in Judaism. But that a man would love and care for his wife as he loved and cared for "his own body" and "just as Christ loved the church and gave Himself for it" was unthinkable. How could any man possibly do that? The standard for the husband was impossible and the standard for the wife was redundant. So why did Paul write it?

If a wife was already subject, why say it to her at all? The answer is in "as to the Lord" and "as the church is subject to Christ, so also the wives ought to be to their husbands in everything." The extent of their subjection was already legally established; it was their manner Paul was talking about. Wives could, and undoubtedly did, use the timeless methods of the underdog to get back at those who had absolute power over them. Just as slaves used sullenness, deceit, sabotage, and wastefulness to make life miserable for their masters, so wives also had their ways to deal with their husbands.

But this was not the Christian way. If the wife imitated the manner of the church in serving Christ, it would be a loving, respectful service without evil motive or hidden barb. And it would not be just sometime, or when he might find out what she had done, but in everything.

The husband also was to work out his mutual submission to his wife by using his absolute legal power over her not to his own advantage but as Christ exercises his power over the church, as Savior of the body. Again, it was his manner that would turn his advantage into service and loving protection, not dictatorship or authoritarianism. The "headship" concept expressed here is one of loving service and care, not one of domination.[19]

Mothers and Babies Kept Safe in Childbirth

In his first letter to Timothy, Paul writes that "women will be saved through childbearing—if they continue in faith, love, and holiness with propriety." It is a confusing passage to Bible scholars. Women are obviously not saved spiritually by bearing children. They are saved by grace, through faith. Nor are faithful women saved physically. Many godly women have died in childbirth—and so have their babies. Because of the dangers involved in childbirth, religious rituals and superstitions were prevalent in the ancient world.

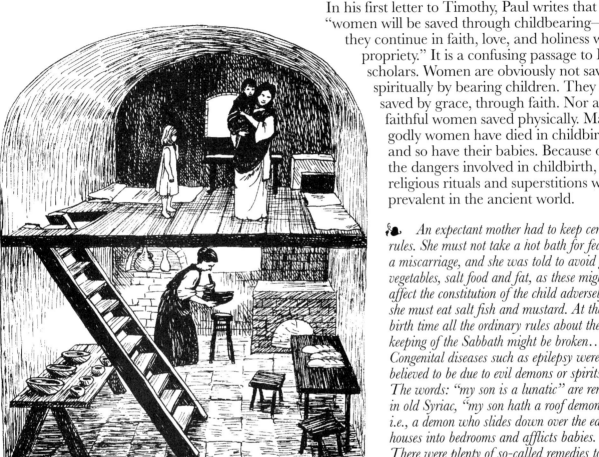

A dwelling similar to what Priscilla and Aquila may have used for their house church

An expectant mother had to keep certain rules. She must not take a hot bath for fear of a miscarriage, and she was told to avoid green vegetables, salt food and fat, as these might affect the constitution of the child adversely, but she must eat salt fish and mustard. At the birth time all the ordinary rules about the keeping of the Sabbath might be broken.... Congenital diseases such as epilepsy were believed to be due to evil demons or spirits. The words: "my son is a lunatic" are rendered in old Syriac, "my son hath a roof demon," i.e., a demon who slides down over the eaves of houses into bedrooms and afflicts babies. There were plenty of so-called remedies to ease confinements and prevent miscarriage, barrenness, or too many children. Some of these must have been purely magical.... Powdered ivory drunk in wine or water was believed to help on an easy birth. On the whole, the Christians abandoned most of these beliefs and practices, though as the movement spread, it was difficult to stamp them out among people who had long pagan tradition behind them.[20]

Paul and Child Discipline

Neither Jesus nor Paul quoted the Old Testament proverbs that spoke of corporal punishment. What were their views on spanking? Only Paul touches on the issue of child discipline, and he focuses

73

as much on the parent as the child. In Colossians, he admonishes children to obey their parents and fathers not to embitter their children. He repeats this in Ephesians 6:1-4:

Children, obey your parents in the Lord, for this is right. "Honor your father and mother"—which is the first commandment with a promise that it may go well with you and that you may enjoy long life on the earth.

Fathers, do not exasperate your children; instead, bring them up in the training and instruction of the Lord.

Taken together, these are Paul's only admonitions concerning discipline and the obedience of children. In neither epistle, however, does Paul explicitly advocate corporal punishment or the use of the rod. Instead, he emphasizes the necessity for paternal restraint and care of children to prevent "anger" and "wrath" from arising. Surely this indicates his compassion for children and his desire to have them nurtured rather than punished, knowing, as he did from his own experience, that punishments, especially beatings with rods, produce wrath, not love. Corporal punishment is not and cannot be grounded in words ascribed either to Jesus or to Paul. [21]

Paul and Thecla

One of the most enduring apocryphal stories about the Apostle Paul is the account of him and his most faithful female disciple, Thecla. According to legend, she became a follower of Paul and went from place to place, disguised as a man, preaching the Gospel and baptizing those she converted. She later went to a mountain cave in Seleucia, where she founded a spiritual retreat and ministered until she was ninety years old. The apocryphal writing *The Acts of Paul and Thecla* tells how Paul first met her when he was preaching in the home of Onesiphorus at Iconium. Thecla was a next-door neighbor and she sat in the window of her house, clinging to every word he said—so much so that her now distraught mother summoned her daughter's fiancé, Thamyris, to rescue her from falling under the sway of Paul's persuasive personality. To Thamyris, the mother lamented:

"My daughter, tied to the window like a spider, lays hold of what is said by Paul with a strange eagerness."

Going to Thecla and kissing her, Thamyris asked: "Thecla, my betrothed, why dost thou sit thus? Turn 'round to thy Thamyris and be ashamed." But neither he nor her mother could persuade her to change her mind. Thamyris took his case to the proconsul, who demanded that Paul come before him. A crowd of men cried: "Away with the magician, for he has corrupted all our wives and sweethearts!" Thecla came to the defense of Paul when he was arrested. [22]

O Death, Where Is Thy Sting?

"O Death, where is thy sting? O grave, where is thy victory?" These words of Paul in his first letter to the Corinthians (15:55) must have rang in his ears as he was led away for execution. Today when we speak of dying with dignity, we cannot comprehend the humiliation of execution in ancient times.

This was the ultimate sting of death, and Paul could not have known when he wrote to the Christians of Corinth that Peter, like Jesus, would suffer such an awful death, and that he himself would be executed at the hands of the Romans.

The date honored in the city of their martyrdom is June 29, 67, Peter nailed to a cross as a public spectacle at Nero's Circus on the Vatican, head downward at his own request, and Paul, as a Roman citizen, beheaded in a less public place....

They marched him out through the walls past the pyramid of Cestius which still stands, on to the Ostian Way toward the sea. Crowds journeying to or from Ostia would recognize an execution squad by the lictors with their fasces of rods and axe, and the executioner carrying a sword, which in Nero's reign had replaced the axe; by the escort, and by the manacled criminal, walking stiffly and bandy-legged, ragged and filthy from his prison: but not ashamed or degraded. He was going to a feast, to a triumph, to the crowning day to which he had pressed forward....

They marched Paul to the third milestone on the Ostian Way, to a little pinewood in the glade, probably a place of tombs, known then as the Aquae Salviae or Healing Waters, and now as Tre Fontane where an abbey stands in his honor. He is believed to have been put overnight in a tiny cell, for his was a common place of execution. If Luke was allowed to stay by his window, if Timothy or Mark had reached Rome in time, the sounds of the night vigil would not be weeping but singing: "as sorrowful yet always rejoicing; as dying and behold, we live." [23]

Blest Be the Tie that Binds: Family Life in the Early Centuries

CHAPTER

5 The post-Apostolic period was a time that often witnessed a strain on Christian family life—especially during times of religious persecution and oppression. State-sponsored tyranny under pagan emperors was not a constant menace, but it served as a powerful psychological threat to Christians and those who contemplated converting to the faith. Families were separated by dislocation, death, and desertions of the faith. But the very oppression that separated loved ones sometimes served to bring them closer together spiritually. This era in the Christian Church offers lessons for today—especially lessons on how times of difficulty can strengthen family ties.

So it was in the life of the young Origenes Adamantius, known to historians as Origen, who would become one of the great systematic theologians of the Early Church. He was born into a Christian home in Alexandria in A.D. 185. As a youth he memorized lengthy passages of the Bible and often perplexed his father Leonides with difficult theological questions. The happy home life, however, was suddenly disrupted in 202, when his father was imprisoned under the reign of Septimius Severus. The sixteen-year-old boy might have been utterly distraught, but instead, the awful ordeal strengthened his faith:

> *He wrote to his father in prison, beseeching him not to deny Christ for the sake of his family, and strongly desired to give himself up to the heathen authorities, but was prevented by his mother, who hid his clothes. Leonides died a martyr, and, as his property was confiscated, he left a helpless widow with seven children.[1]*

Nurtured in the Faith

The post-Apostolic period was one of intense evangelism, and many pagans were converted to Christianity through the witness of their neighbors and coworkers. But the greatest focus of evangelism was in the home. Children were brought up in the faith at home and expected to make a personal commitment to Christ and carry on with the faith in the next generation.

Early Christians gathered at an agape meal

We know all too little of the effect of this sort of home on the children. But there is at any rate some evidence that Christian homes were making their mark very early upon the children brought up in them. Bishop Polycarp was brought up in a Christian home, so was Marcion. Two of the Christians martyred with Justin c. A.D. 165 were Paeon and Euelpistus. The former, replying to the prefect's enquiry as to where he learnt his Christianity, replied, "From our parents we received this good confession." And Euelpistus answered, "I willingly heard the words of Justin. But from my parents too I learned to be a Christian." Justin Martyr himself, though born of pagan stock, informs us that "many men and women of the age of sixty and seventy years have been disciples of Christ from childhood," and this agrees with the statement of Pliny that in Bithynia in A.D. 112 he had found among the Christians not only adults but little children.[2]

The Extended Christian Family

For early Christians, family meant more than blood ties. The family was the Christian community, and believers cared for one another—especially during difficult times of persecution. An illustration of this concern is presented by a second-century pagan satirist named Lucian, who attempted to ridicule Christians by telling the story of a Proteus Peregrinus, a charlatan who joined with the Christians. He was imprisoned, and during that time, according to Lucian:

> [The Christians] left no stone unturned in their endeavor to procure his release. When this proved impossible, they looked after his wants in all other matters with untiring solicitude and devotion. From earliest dawn old women ("widows," they are called) and orphan children might be seen waiting about the prison doors; while the officers of the church, by bribing the jailers, were able to spend the night inside with him. Meals were brought in, and they went through their sacred formulas.[3]

Christian Emperors and Family Life

Christianity brought about changes in family life from the earliest days, but it was not until the reign of Constantine that persecution of Christians was officially banned and that the Christian faith began to have a significant influence on the laws of the Roman Empire. In 321, Emperor Constantine gave women property rights, except in some cases when landed estates were sold. He also instituted the death penalty for rape of consecrated virgins and of widows, and he abolished the penalties in Roman law for celibacy and childlessness. In 390, Emperor Theodosius I gave mothers rights of guardianship, which had previously been granted only to men. Theodosius II, a generation later, sought to curb prostitution—though with little success.[4]

Asceticism and Family Life

There was a negative slant to family life in the early centuries—one that related to the ideal of celibacy and asceticism. Here again, Origen is an example. After the death of his father, when he was only eighteen, he became the head of the catechetical school of Alexandria, and he became one of the most renowned scholars of his day. But his personal life was not one that allowed any room for marriage and family.

✦ *His mode of life during the whole period was strictly ascetic. He made it a matter of principle to renounce every earthly thing not indispensably necessary. He refused the gifts of his pupils, and in literal obedience to his Savior's injunction he had but one coat, no shoes, and took no thought of the morrow. He rarely ate flesh, never drank wine; devoted the great part of the night to prayer and study, and slept on the bare floor. Nay, in his youthful zeal for ascetic holiness, he even committed the act of self-emasculation, partly to fulfill literally the mysterious words of Christ, in Matthew 19:12 [there are eunuchs who have made themselves eunuchs] for the sake of the kingdom of God, partly to secure himself against all temptation and calumny which might arise from his intercourse with many female catechumens.[5]*

79

Low Ratings for Marriage

> *When Jerome, writing in the fourth century, compared virginity, widowhood, and marriage, he gave virginity a numerical value of 100, widowhood 60, and marriage 30.* [6]

Adultery in Marriage

Is it possible for married love life to be too good—so good that it is sinful? St. Jerome thought so.

> *Anyone who is too passionate a love with his own wife is himself an adulterer.* [7]

Be Fruitful and Multiply

Despite his focus on celibacy, Jerome did not entirely dismiss the importance of marriage. In a letter to a friend, he upholds marriage—but only for its potential to increase asceticism:

> *To prefer chastity is not to disparage matrimony.... Married ladies can be proud to come after nuns, for God Himself told them to be fruitful, multiply and replenish the earth.... A child born from marriage is virgin flesh.... I praise matrimony. But only because it produces virgins.* [8]

Jerome with Marcella and his mother and sister

Marital Intimacy in the Garden of Eden

The Church Fathers, who stressed the spiritual benefits of celibacy, argued that sexual desire was not part of God's creative design but rather it was a result of the Fall. "According to St. Augustine, before the Fall sexual intercourse occurred without lust, the organs of reproduction being activated by calm rational volition, not by uncontrollable passion, as a man's will and reason were then in perfect harmony with God." [9]

An Ideal Marriage Relationship

Tertullian, who is well known for his strong words to women ("You are the devil's gateway.... You destroyed God's image, man") was capable of saying very positive things regarding marriage:

Whence are we to find words enough fully to tell the happiness of that marriage which the Church cements… which angels carry back the news of (to heaven), which the Father holds for ratified? For even on the earth children do not rightly and lawfully wed without their father's consent. What kind of yoke is that of two believers, partakers of one hope, one desire, one discipline, one and the same service? Both are brethren, both fellow servants, no difference of spirit or flesh; nay they are truly two in one flesh. Where the flesh is one, one is the spirit too. Together they pray, together prostrate themselves, together perform their fasts; mutually teaching, mutually exhorting, mutually sustaining. Equally are they both found in the Church of God; equally at the banquet of God; equally in straits, in persecution, in refreshments. Neither hides ought from the other; neither shuns the other; neither is troublesome to the other…. Between the two echo psalms and hymns; and they mutually challenge each other. [10]

A meeting of early Christians in Rome

The Model Wife and Husband

Clement, an early Church Father, clearly differentiated the roles of husband and wife:

 The ideal wife "loves her husband from the heart, embraces, soothes, and pleases him, acts the slave to him, and is obedient to him in all things except when she would be disobedient to God." Though revering him, she submitted to sex only out of marital duty to help fulfill her function as a woman.

The ideal husband as a superior creation of God, did not take advantage of his wife. He never made her submit to sex except when, in a calm mind, he could focus on the lofty procreative result of his mating, and not on the base means by which it was attained. Consequently, there was no justification for sex with a menopausal woman. The husband who could restrain himself from stealing the pearl of virginity from his wife, however, was much honored. [11]

84

The Wife's Domain

Women had very few opportunities to serve in public roles in the ancient world; the home was their domain. Christians typically followed the same pattern of life, but that does not mean that women did not wield power and influence, as John Chrysostom specified:

> *To woman is assigned the presidency of the household…. A woman is not able to hurl a spear or shoot an arrow, but she can grasp the distaff, weave at the loom…. She cannot express her opinion in a legislative assembly, but she can express it at home, and often she is more shrewd about household matters than her husband. She cannot handle state business well, but she can raise children correctly, and children are our principal wealth…. She provides complete security for her husband and frees him from all such household concerns, concerns about money, woolworking, the preparation of food and decent clothing.* [12]

Be Not Unequally Yoked

> *Mixed marriage with heathens, and also with heretics were unanimously condemned by the voice of the church in agreement with the Mosaic legislation, unless formed before conversion, in which case they were considered valid. Tertullian even classes such marriages with adultery. What heathen, he asks, will let his wife attend the nightly meetings of the church…rise in the night for prayer, and show hospitality to strange brethren? Cyprian calls marriage with an unbeliever a prostitution of the members of Christ.* [13]

The Church Fathers and Childhood

It was natural that the Church Fathers would part company from pagan philosophers and others who demeaned childhood. Jesus had set a new standard.

Baptism of a child in the third century in Rome

> *[The Fathers manifested] compassion for children by asserting that children had souls, were important to God, could be taught, should not be killed, maimed, or abandoned, and that they were useful to the self-image of the parents. This is not to assert that children's conditions improved automatically. However, the Church began to bring serious pressure on the State in the fourth century to legislate an end to the life-endangering practices. The barbarian tribes, both as a result of their own customs and under the influence of Christian teachings, legislated against infanticide. Yet no one could claim that the life of a newborn child was very secure by A.D. 500, or that empathy was yet part of the psychological equipment of parents.* [14]

Abortion and Infanticide

A mosaic depicting early Christians in Lyon, including a child, victorious in the face of martyrdom

The Early Church taught that abortion was murder—a serious sin against God and a fellow human being. Pagans routinely aborted the unborn child, but the church and individual Christians demanded a standard that did not conform to the pattern of the world. They also condemned the common practice of infanticide and the exposure of babies—especially little girls. In many cases they rescued these children and placed them in Christian homes to be reared in the faith. Tertullian is representative of the Church Fathers in his strong stance against abortion.

> *In our case, murder being once for all forbidden, we may not destroy even the fetus in the womb, while as yet the human being derives blood from other parts of the body for its sustenance. To hinder a birth is merely a speedier man-killing; nor does it matter whether you take away a life that is born, or destroy one that is coming to birth. That is a man which is going to be one; you have the fruit already in the seed.*

In another work, Tertullian made a personal plea against abortion by appealing to mothers and their maternal instincts.

> *I call on you, mothers, whether you are not pregnant or have already borne children; let women who are barren and men keep silence! We are looking for the truth about the nature of woman; we are examining the reality of your pains. Tell us: Do you feel any stirring of life within you in the fetus? Does your groin tremble, your sides shake, your whole stomach throb as the burden you carry changes its position? Are not these moments a source of joy and assurance that the child within you is alive and playful? Should his restlessness subside, would you not be immediately concerned for him?* [15]

83

Grandparents' Rights

It is normal for parents of married children to want grandchildren, but taking their married children to court to force the issue might seem to be taking the matter to an extreme. Yet this is what happened in Rome in the late fourth century when Melania the Younger, the daughter of wealthy Christian aristocrats, decided to follow her grandmother Melania the Elder into the ascetic celibate life of a holy woman.

> *She was anxious to embrace the life of her grandmother, but her parents expected her to produce children to whom the wealth of the family would be transmitted and in whom the lineage would continue. After her marriage she produced first a daughter, who was dedicated to God as a virgin at the time of her birth. Subsequently she gave birth to a son, on whose shoulders the continuation of the line would presumably fall. Both children died in infancy; after their deaths, Melania prevailed upon her husband to live chastely with her. They both began to sell all their property so that they might undertake the ascetic life. Their action met with fierce opposition from Melania's parents, who attempted to bring legal action against the two on grounds that they were still minors.*

In the end, Emperor Honorious intervened in behalf of Melania and her husband. They later established monasteries—one for men and one for women—on the Mount of Olives, and Melania was recognized as a Bible teacher and theologian.[16]

A Father's Plea for His Daughter

Around A.D. 200, when Emperor Septimius Severus decreed that Christians in North Africa be put to death, it wreaked havoc on families and brought anguish to Christians and non-Christians alike. Among the martyrs was a young mother named Perpetua, who gave the following testimony prior to her death:

> *My father arrived from the city, worn with worry, and he came to see me with the idea of persuading me.*
>
> *"Daughter," he said, "have pity on my gray head—have pity on me your father, if I deserve to be called your father, if I have*

"The Martyr's Daughter," a nineteenth-century artist's depiction of early Christian family life

favored you above all your brothers, if I have raised you to reach this prime of your life. Do not abandon me to be the reproach of me. Think of your brothers, think of your mother and your aunt, think of your child, who will not be able to live once you are gone. Give up your pride! You will destroy all of us! None of us will ever be able to speak freely again if anything happens to you."

This was the way my father spoke out of love for me, kissing my hands and throwing himself down before me.... I tried to comfort him, saying, "It will all happen in the prisoner's dock as God wills; for you may be sure that we are not left to ourselves but are all in His power." [17]

Mother and Baby

Maternal instincts are much the same in all cultures and throughout all generations, but they are often described in different ways. Here is the perspective of a Church Father.

Because the mother loves to nourish her little one, she does not on that account want him to remain little. She holds him in her lap, fondles him with her hands, soothes him with caresses, feeds him with her milk, does everything for the little one; but she wants him to grow, so that she may not always have to do these things. [18]

St. Augustine

The Importance of Parenting

Higher than every painter, higher than every sculptor and than all artists do I regard the one who is skilled in the art of forming the soul of children. [19]

John Chrysostom

Good Advice for Parents

John Chrysostom was considered the greatest preacher of the Early Church—referred to as "golden-mouthed." One of his sermons, delivered in A.D. 388, was titled, "An Address on Vainglory and the Right Way for Parents to Bring Up Their Children." Here he focuses primarily on moral development and admonishes parents not to dress their little boys in "fine raiment and golden ornaments," rather he should spend his time with a

Antichristian graffiti mocking a boy's faith in Christ. The inscription reads "Alexamenos worships his god."

"strict tutor" who will make sure he does not grow long hair. He also insisted that child discipline begin early:

> *If good precepts are impressed on the soul while it is yet tender, no man will be able to destroy them when they have set firm, even as does a waxen seal. The child is still trembling and fearful and afraid in look and speech and in all else. Make use of the beginning of his life as thou shouldst. Thou wilt be the first to benefit, if thou has a good son, and then God. Thou dost labor for thyself.*

In some respects Chrysostom was ahead of his time when it came to the matter of corporal punishment:

> *Punish him, now with a stern look, now with incisive, now with reproachful, words; at other times win him with gentleness and promises.... Let him rather at all times fear blows but not receive them.... Our human nature has some need for forbearance.* [20]

A Mother's Answered Prayers for a Wayward Son

St. Augustine gives a fascinating account of his mother's concern for him when he was a young man "sowing his wild oats." His gratitude for his mother is offered in a prayer to God:

St. Augustine with his mother at her deathbed

> *That faithful servant of Yours, my mother, came to You in my behalf with more tears than most mothers shed at a child's funeral. Her faith in You had made plain to her that I was spiritually dead. And You heard her, Lord, You heard her. You didn't ignore the tears that fell from her eyes and watered the earth everywhere she prayed. You heard her and sent her a dream that so relieved her mind that she allowed me to live with her and to eat at the same table in*

the house. That was something she had refused to permit for some time because she so loathed the blasphemy and error in which I was swimming. In her dream she saw herself standing on a kind of measuring rule or wooden yardstick, wailing and overcome with grief. A radiant young man approached her in a happy and laughing mood and asked her the reasons for all this protracted weeping.... She replied that she was mourning the ruin of my soul. He then admonished her and, in a reassuring way, ordered her to look more carefully and she would see that I was standing next to her on the same measuring rule.... When Mother told me about her dream, I tried to disparage it, saying I interpreted it to mean she shouldn't give up hope, because one day she would be as I was. She, however, came back at me immediately, saying, "No, it was not told me 'Where he is, there you will be,' but rather, 'Where you are, there he will be....' " Nearly nine years were to pass during which I sank deeper into the mire and false darkness. I tried to climb out, but each time I fell backward and sprawled in the muck. And all the while this devout, gentle, modest widow...was heartened by this hope. She never stopped her sighing and weeping; she never stopped beseeching You at all hours of the day and night, pounding away on my behalf before Your presence. [21]

Christians Living the Good Life

Gregory Nazianzen was no doubt exaggerating the good life that some Christians were living in the generation following Constantine, but his description gives a picture of home life among wealthy and worldly "saints."

We repose in splendor on high and sumptuous cushions, upon the most exquisite covers, which one is almost afraid to touch, and are vexed if we but hear the voice of a moaning pauper; our chamber must breathe the odor of flowers, even rare flowers; our table must flow with the most fragrant and costly ointment, so that we become perfectly effeminate. Slaves must stand ready, richly adorned and in order, with waving maidenlike hair, and faces shorn perfectly smooth, more adorned throughout than is good for lascivious eyes; some to hold cups both delicately and firmly with the tips of their fingers, others to fan fresh air upon the head. Our tables must bend under the load of dishes, while all the kingdoms of nature, air, water, and earth, furnish copious contributions, and there must be almost no room for the artificial products of cook and baker. [22]

Tough Times for Children

After the fall of the Roman Empire, marauding bands of barbarians pillaged towns and villages; there was an utter breakdown of law and order. In A.D. 413, during this time of uncertainty, Jerome wrote to a friend about the perilous future for his little girl:

A Roman matron going to church with her young child

> *Such are the times, then, into which your Pactula has been born. Slaughter and death are the toys of her childhood. She will know tears before laughter, sorrow before joy. Scarcely arrived on the stage of this world, soon she must exit. That the world was always like this—what else can she believe? Of the past she knows nothing; from the present she flies; she longs for the future.* [23]

Advice for Home Schooling

The fourth-century Church Father Jerome was deeply concerned about the education of children—so much so that he wrote a lengthy letter to the daughter-in-law of his friend and colleague Paula about the home schooling of her baby daughter, also named Paula.

> *Let your child of promise have a training from her parents worthy of her birth…. Let boys with their wanton frolics be kept far from Paula: let even her maids and attendants hold aloof from association with the worldly, lest they render their evil knowledge worse by teaching it to her. Have a set of letters made for her, of boxwood or of ivory, and tell her their names. Let her play with them, making play a road to learning, and let her not only grasp the right order of the letters and remember their names in a simple song, but also frequently upset their order and mix the last letters with the middle ones, the middle with the first. Thus she will know them all by sight as well as by sound. When she begins with uncertain hand to use the pen, either let another hand be put over hers to guide her baby fingers, or else have the letters marked on the tablet so that her writing may follow their outlines and keep their limits without straying away. Offer her prizes for spelling, tempting her with such trifling gifts as please young children. Let her have companions too in her lessons, so that she may seek to rival them and be stimulated by any praise they win. You must not scold her if she is somewhat slow; praise is the best sharpener of wits. Let her be glad when she is first and sorry when she falls behind. Above all, take care not to make her lessons distasteful; a childish dislike often lasts longer than childhood. The very words from which she will get into the way of forming sentences should not be taken at haphazard but be definitely chosen and arranged on purpose. For example, let her have the names of the prophets and the apostles, and the whole list of patriarchs from Adam downwards, as Matthew and Luke give it. She will then be doing two things at the same time and will remember them afterwards.* [24]

Saintly Little Children

The stories of the saints became an important part of Christian literature in the Early Church and the centuries following. Frequently these stories included miraculous tales of infancy and childhood. St. Nicholas allegedly stood to his feet right after he was born and during his first days of infancy began a schedule of fasting by nursing only once a day on Wednesdays and Fridays. The infant St. Ambrose endured a frightful encounter with bees that pointed to his future greatness:

Ambrose, then, was born when his father Ambrose held the office of Prefect of Gaul. When he was a baby, he was sleeping in his cradle with his mouth open, in the courtyard of the governor's palace, when suddenly a swarm of bees came and so covered his face and mouth that they kept on going in and out of his mouth in continuous succession. His father was taking a walk nearby, with his mother and their daughter, and told the girl who was employed to suckle the babe not to drive the bees away, for he was afraid of their injuring him; and with a father's solicitude he waited to see how the marvel would end. And presently the bees flew off and soared to such a height in the air that it was impossible for human eyes to see them. It frightened his father. "If that little one lives," he said, "he will become something very big." [25]

Romanus, a Christian martyr, beaten in front of a woman and child

"A Nursery of Bishops and Saints"

The writings and lives of the Church Fathers are well known. But the lives of the "Mothers" are often forgotten. One of these lesser-known figures of the Early Church was Macrina. Had she not been the sister of Basil and Gregory (two of the influential trio of theologians known as the Cappadocian Fathers), she probably would have been forgotten altogether. She was a Bible teacher who founded a religious community with a hospital, and she had a powerful influence over her brothers' decision to enter the ministry. But Macrina was only one woman in a line of strong and influential women. Her grandmother, Macrina the Elder, and her grandfather suffered severe persecution under the reigns of Emperors Galerius and Maximianus. They hid with some of their servants in a mountainous region near Pontus, where they "endured great privations for seven years."

Macrina's mother Emmelia was a pious Christian who devoted her energy to passing the faith on to her ten children. Three of her sons —Gregory, Peter, and Basil—became bishops, and they along with Macrina were latter canonized as saints. Her household became known as "a nursery of bishops and saints."

Macrina's brother Gregory wrote her biography, where he elaborated on this "nursery"—especially as it pertained to her education as a child:

The education of the child was her mother's task. She taught her not those tragic passions of womanhood which afforded poets their suggestions and plots… but such parts of inspired Scripture as you think were incomprehensible to young children were the subject of the girl's

studies.... When she rose from bed, or engaged in household duties, or rested, or partook of food, or retired from table, when she went to bed or rose in the night for prayer, the Psalter was her constant companion, like a good fellow traveler that never deserted her... Macrina also trained her younger brother Peter: She took him soon after birth from the nurse's breast and reared him herself and educated him on a lofty system of training, practicing him from infancy in holy studies, so as not to give his soul leisure to turn to vain things. Thus having become all things to the lad—father, teacher, tutor, mother, giver of all good advice—he aspired to the high mark of philosophy. [26]

The Fruit of a Good Christian Upbringing

During the persecution of Emperor Diocletian in the early fourth century, a young girl named Agnes was martyred for her strong Christian faith. The following century the poet Prudentius memorialized her as a living and dying saint. It may be doubted that she attained the seeming perfection he ascribed to her, but she stands as a role model to young people today for her love for the Lord and her unflinching faith.

> *So brave a girl, a martyr famed*
> *Was Agnes, who in Romulus' home*
> *Lies buried in a tomb. She sees*
> *In death Rome's towering roofs*
> *And so she keeps her people safe.*
> *She also shields the pilgrims there*
> *Who pray with pure and faithful hearts.*
> *A double crown of martyrdom*
> *Sets this noted girl apart:*
> *Virginity free from any fault,*
> *Then honor from a death she chose.*
>
> *Hardly old enough to wed,*
> *She was a little girl, they say,*
> *By chance a child of tender years,*
> *But aglow for Christ, with manly heart,*
> *She defied the shameless laws.*
> *For pagan idols she would not*
> *Desert her holy, sacred faith.*
> *First lured by many skillful tricks—*
> *Now the lures of fawning judge,*
> *Now the raging butcher's threats—*
> *She stood her ground tenaciously,*
> *Of savage strength she freely gave*
> *Her body to the harsh abuse;*
> *She did not flee impending death....* [27]

More than Celibacy: Medieval Family Life

CHAPTER

6

Most modern-day Christians do not readily identify with the Middle Ages—those one thousand years between roughly A.D. 500 and 1500. It is not so much that this era was too long ago, but rather that we often think it really does not belong to us— particularly if we are Protestants.

The first century of Jesus and Paul and even the Old Testament era belong to us. It is our heritage, depicted in full color in our childhood Sunday School lessons. We are one with those early believers, and so also with those faithful saints (if we know about them) in the centuries that followed. But as the Roman Catholic Church emerges in the fifth and sixth centuries, we begin to tune out, and too often we do not tune in again until the Reformation, when we find Martin Luther nailing his 95 Theses to the church door in 1517.

But whatever our instincts might be, we cannot simply discard one thousand years of Christian history. The church of the Middle Ages is our heritage, and there are many lessons that challenge us in the realm of family life.

Medieval Country Life

It is natural to think that with the passage of time comes progress—that the world in A.D. 700, for example, would be far more advanced than the world of 100 B.C. But that was not necessarily true. Indeed, after the fall of the Roman Empire, the barbarian world of Western Europe was uncivilized in comparison to the Greek and Roman civilizations.

The new Western world which emerged, the world of the first half of the Middle Ages, was to be a world where countrysides were vastly more important than towns—which indeed shrank to vanishing point—and where life was a very primitive thing and a great contrast to life in the centuries-old urban civilization of the Hellenistic East where the Church was born and for four hundred years had its first developments. This world of peasants and country-bred, fighting warrior-lords and barbarian princes was an all but illiterate world, and the language they spoke was moving ever further and further away, not from the tongue of Cicero only, but from anything that resembled grammatical Latin…. Life in this vast Western backwoods—on this vast frontier—was hard and cruel, of course; filled with all the violent crime one cares to imagine.[1]

Diversity in Family Living

Many church history texts give the impression that the medieval period was a time when Christian family life was denigrated—particularly by the priority placed on celibacy. In reality, however, the Christian family continued to play a crucial role in society and in the church.

It is difficult to make generalizations about the medieval Christian family because the era encompasses such a vast span of time and such a wide variety of cultures. Likewise, as is true today, families in the Middle Ages came in all stripes and sizes—and social standing. The wealthy families have left the most detailed records of their lives, but the peasants are those who would most closely parallel average families today.

Medieval Homes

A typical medieval peasant home might have had two separate partitioned areas for the family, with an attached barn to house the animals. Modern standards of privacy and cleanliness were unknown, and there was very little in the physical make-up of the home that would seem to be conducive to building a healthy Christian family.

A medieval country house

A medieval kitchen

 Interiors were lighted by a few windows, shuttered but unglazed, and by doors, often open during the daytime, through which children and animals wandered freely. Floors were of beaten earth covered with straw or rushes. In the center, a fire of wood or of peat…burned on a raised stone hearth, vented through a hole in the roof. Some hearths were crowned by hoods or funnels to channel the smoke to the makeshift chimney, which might be capped by a barrel with its ends knocked out. The atmosphere of the house was perpetually smoky from the fire burning all day as water, milk, or porridge simmered in pots on a trivet or in footed brass or iron kettles. [2]

Living in the Shadow of the Church

 Family life in the Middle Ages developed its own routine—always in the shadow of the Church which spread out over Europe in the centuries following the fall of Rome. It was the church that brought communities and families together, and unlike today, everyone went to the same church, with no competing denominations to tempt family loyalties. Indeed, the church was a powerful institution that influenced every aspect of daily life, providing ritual and transition as people moved from one stage to the next—from courtship to marriage to the birth of children and on through life.

Courtship

 Life in this earlier era was not easy, but life's pleasures and merriment and lovemaking were just as real then as now. Among the nobility, marriages were often arranged when children were young, but peasant youth courted more freely and organized their own village festivities.

 In Crosscombe [England], young men joined the Younglyngs' Guild, young women the Maidens' Guild. On a certain day the maidens blocked the village streets and permitted the young men to pass only by payment of a fine. Next day the Younglyngs blocked the streets and the maidens had to pay the fine, which in both cases went to the parish church. On May Day a king and queen were chosen, with dancing and games. [3]

Courtship

93

Advice on Choosing a Partner

What should a young man look for in a wife? Above all, according to a medieval book on manners, he should not marry simply for money. He should look for a young woman who is "meek, courteous, and wise," rather than simply looking for a good cook. Far better to eat in peace than to be served "a hundred dishes" and eat in strife. What should a young woman look for in a husband? If only one man is interested in her, she should "scorn him not, whatever he be." She should seek her friends' advice, and once married she should manage her home with "fair and meek words." [4]

Spinsters

When peasant families were unable to arrange marriages for their daughters, a common alternative was a "career" in spinning. Five spinners kept one weaver supplied, so there was always a need for more spinners, and single women typically filled those roles—so much so that single women were called "spinsters." [5]

Secret Marriage Ceremony

The marriage ceremony marked the beginning of a new family—one that was very closely tied to a larger extended family. Marriages were typically arranged with a dowry expected for the bride—sometimes as meager as a few small coins or in cases of extreme poverty perhaps nothing at all.

In rural areas, marriages were sometimes sealed with no more than a spontaneous kiss—a custom that often resulted in broken promises and illegitimate children. Indeed, court records show many fines assessed for premarital sex ("legerwite") and for giving birth to a child out of wedlock ("childwite"). A double standard prevailed. The woman was found guilty and penalized, while the man's complicity was typically ignored. And frequently the woman had been tricked into yielding to her new "husband." Robert Manning laments this practice in verse:

> ...*Beguile a woman with words;*
> *To give her troth but lightly*
> *For nothing but to lie by her;*
> *With that guile thou makest her assent*
> *And bringest you both to cumberment.*

In 1215, the Church ruled that weddings must be public in an effort to solidify marriages. Still, many young couples

A woman spinning

continued to say their vows in private—in the woods or in bed—and the Church continued to condemn these "clandestine marriages." [6]

Public Wedding Vows

The public wedding ceremony in medieval times was simple. The couple usually met with the village priest in front of the church door, where relatives and friends gathered around. The first order of business was to establish that there were no reasons why the couple should not be married—specifically to verify they were not close kin. Then the groom specified the amount of dowry for his bride, giving her a ring as a "token" of that gift. The wedding ring was symbolic, as a fourteenth-century preacher explained to the bridal couple:

A medieval wedding ceremony

> It must be "put and set by the husband upon the fourth finger of the woman, to show that a true love and cordial affection be between them, because, as doctors say, there is a vein coming from the heart of a woman to the fourth finger, and therefore the ring is put on the same finger, so that she should keep unity and love with him, and he with her." [7]

❧ ❧ A Medieval Wedding Gift ❧ ❧

A beautiful medieval wedding tradition that has been forgotten in modern times is the custom of the groom presenting a gift of money to the bride at the church door that is then taken and distributed to the poor. A marriage was a community affair, and it was an occasion when the most needy in the village were not forgotten. [8]

Making Light of Marital Discord

Medieval comedians enjoyed making light of marital discord. Indeed, it is through humor that we can perhaps best resonate with medieval family life. Here in an age when divorce was rare, we see the battle of the sexes played out, not in the courts or in the therapist's office, but in street theater. The English *Chester Deluge Play* is an example. Here Noah, who like medieval men is supposed to be the "head" of his family, is trying to get his wife to come into the ark, but she insists that her "gossips" come with her. When he tries to coax her she shouts:

> ℥ *By Christ, no! ere I see more need,*
> *Though thou stand all day and rave.*

Noah's response is characteristic of the rough medieval sense of humor, and most assuredly drew boisterous laughter:

> ℥ *Lord how crabbed are women alway!*
> *They never are meek, that dare I say*
> *And that is well seen of me today*
> *In witness of you, each one.*
> *Good wife, let be all this trouble and stir*
> *That thou makest in this place here*
> *For all men think thou art my master.*
> *(And so thou art, by St. John!)*

Still Mrs. Noah refuses to enter the ark. The animals enter but she lingers, talking and drinking with her "gossips." Finally, her sons forcibly escort her into the ark, but she has the last laugh. She clobbers Noah on the head and says:

> ℥ *And have thou that for thy not! [Nut—referring to his head]*
> *Aha Mary! This is hot.* [9]

Wife Beating

The wife might clobber her husband in a dramatic parody, but in the home itself the couple were to model appropriate male headship and wifely submission. How often the theory was put into practice is impossible to determine, but churchmen were not hesitant to champion the husband's control over his wife. A fifteenth-century Dominican wrote:

> ❧ *A man may chastise his wife and beat her*
> *for correction, for she is of his household,*
> *therefore the lord may chastise his own.*

One husband in Paris instructed his wife to behave like a dog—and accept punishment like a dog—because that was her proper role as a Christian wife:

A medieval depiction of wife beating

Copy the behavior of a dog who always has his heart and his eye upon his master; even if his master whip him and throw stones at him, the dog follows, wagging his tail....Wherefore for a better and stronger reason, women ought to have a perfect and solemn love for their husbands. [10]

Battles of the Sexes

We should not presume that such instructions were automatically accepted by wives. Indeed, there is ample evidence to suggest that women may have had their own means of inflicting misery on their husbands. In *Canterbury Tales*, Chaucer's Wife of Bath recalls with delight the affliction she caused her three previous husbands:

O Lord! the pain I did them and the wo[e].

Her fifth husband took delight in reading to her from the "book of wicked wives," beginning with Eve, but she finally put an end to it:

When I saw that he would never stop
Reading this cursed book, all night no doubt,
I suddenly grabbed and tore three pages out
Where he was reading, at the very place,
And fisted such a buffet in his face
That backwards down into our fire he fell.

His immediate response was to strike her on the head, but eventually they made up and he gave her "the government of the house and land" and burned the book. [11]

Marital Love

It would be a distortion of medieval life to imagine that marriage relationships were always characterized by conflict. To the contrary, men often expressed appreciation for women—especially as they envisioned them in domestic circumstances. Whether wives had the same appreciation for their husbands is less obvious since women's opinions were rarely recorded for posterity.

A woman is a worthy thing,
They do the wash and do the wring.
"Lullay, lullay," she doth sing,
And yet she hath but care and woe.
A woman is a worthy wight,
She serveth man both day and night,
Thereto she putteth all her might
And yet she hath but care and woe. [12]

> ## Last Will and Testament of Stephen Thomas
> ### (1418, English Court of Probate)
>
> The Holy Trinity keep you now, dear and trusty wife…. I pray you, as my trust is wholly in you, over all other creatures, that this last will be fulfilled, and all other that I ordained at home, for all the love that ever was between man and woman. [13]

Sexual Abstinence

In medieval times, celibacy was extolled as an ideal not only for those who forsook marriage for full-time ministry, but also for married couples. Gregory of Tours, a sixth-century bishop, encouraged this practice by telling a story of a young couple who made just such a decision. On their wedding night, after the bride and groom were led off to their bedroom, the bride began to weep. To her new husband, she confessed:

> *I had determined to preserve my poor body for Christ, untouched by intercourse with man…. At the moment when …I should have put on the stole of purity, this wedding gown brings me shame instead of honor.*

The startled husband protested, insisting that it was their duty to carry on the family name, but finally he relented:

> *If you are determined to abstain from intercourse with me, then I will agree to what you want to do.*

They lived happily ever after, as Gregory relates: "Hand in hand they went to sleep, and for many years after this they lay each night in one bed, but they remained chaste in a way which we can only admire." When they died they were buried separately, but the following morning, according to Gregory, their tombs were found together—"a miracle that proved their chastity." [14]

Contraception

Birth control was condemned by the Church as an act that interfered with nature and undermined God's command to be fruitful and multiply. By the fifteenth century, as various forms of contraception became more widely known, preachers minced no words in their graphic denunciations.

❧ *May a person in any case copulate and prevent the fruits of marriage? I say that this is often a sin which deserves the fire. To answer shortly, every way which impedes offspring in the union of man and wife is indecent and must be reproved.*

Jean Gerson

❧ *Listen: each time you come together in a way where you cannot generate, each time is a mortal sin…. Each time that you have joined yourselves in a way that you cannot give birth and generate children, there has always been sin. How big a sin? Oh, a very great sin! Oh, a very great sort of sin!* [15]

Bernadine of Siena

Mother with baby

Pregnancy and Childbirth

The Diseases of Women, a medieval gynecological guide, offered a wide range of treatments and potions to relieve women in labor, including "rubbing the woman's flanks with oil of roses, feeding her vinegar and sugar, powdered ivory, or eagle's dung, placing a magnet in her hand or suspending coral around her neck." But along with these questionable home remedies, it also offered sound medical advice:

    📖 *If the child does not come forth in the order in which it should, that is, if the legs or arms should come out first, let the midwife with her small and gentle hand moistened with a decoction of flaxseed and chick peas, put the child back in its place in the proper position.* [16]

Nursing Mothers

New mothers, whether peasant or upper class, were expected to nurse their own babies. If they did not, it was often presumed that they were either seeking greater sexual pleasure in marriage or a more active social life. Bernadine of Siena, a fifteenth-century preacher, strongly condemned this practice:

> *Is there one who hath borne a child? [he demanded of his congregation]. Didst thou ever give him to a nurse to be suckled? What moved thee to do this? Why? To procure thyself more pleasure!... When thou didst give him to a nurse at once didst thou place pleasure before God, and thus didst thou fall into sin.... Thou has done worse than the she-ass, for the she-ass when she hath brought forth her foal doth rear it and nurture it.... If thou shouldst give thy child to a nurse because thou art weak in health or if thou has not milk to suffice it, or for other such lawful reasons, thou sinnest not; but if thou do so in order better to disport thyself, I say that then thou sinnest.* [17]

Popular Children's Names

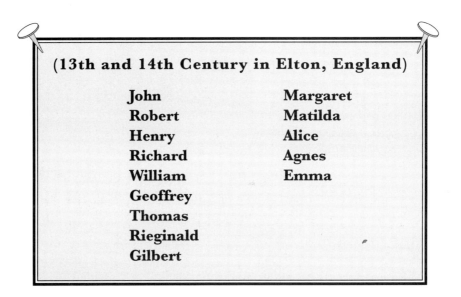

(13th and 14th Century in Elton, England)

John	**Margaret**
Robert	**Matilda**
Henry	**Alice**
Richard	**Agnes**
William	**Emma**
Geoffrey	
Thomas	
Rieginald	
Gilbert	

Abortion and Infanticide

There was a dark side of Christian family life in medieval times that sometimes manifested itself in abortion and infanticide. The Church condemned these crimes and placed harsh penalties on those found guilty.

> *Penalties were progressively more severe for three stages: killing an embryo before it showed signs of life (before "the soul entered the body"); after "animation"; and after actual birth. The Penitential of Theodore assessed a year's penance if a woman committed abortion before the fetus showed life; three years if more than forty days had passed since conception; and ten years if she killed the child after it was born. Allowance was made for economic motivation: "If a poor woman slays her child, she shall do penance for seven years" rather*

than ten. The Penitential of Columban (c. 600) punished a "layman or woman" with a year on bread and water and two years' abstinence from wine and meat for "overlaying" a child, that is, killing him by inadvertently rolling over on him in bed, an accident frequently mentioned in later penitentials and in legal records up to modern times. [18]

Life Without Children

What place did children have in the medieval family? This is an issue that has been debated by historians. In his classic *Centuries of Childhood*, Philippe Aries writes:

> *Medieval art until about the twelfth century did not know childhood or did not attempt to portray it. It is hard to believe that this neglect was due to incompetence or incapacity; it seems more probably that there was no place for childhood in the medieval world.* [19]

Little Adults

This does not mean that children were not valued, but rather that they were often perceived as little adults. As such they were expected to make adult decisions—ones that would affect their entire lives. The prayer of Orderic Vitalis, a twelfth-century chronicler, illustrates this. He recounts the pain he suffered when separated from his family as a young child:

> *When five years old I became a scholar at Shrewsbury and dedicated my first lessons to You, O God, in the church of St. Peter and St. Paul. The well-known priest, Sigward, taught me my letters, psalms, hymns and other learning.... Then, fearing that affection for my parents might deflect me from Your worship, You led my father Odeler to give me entirely to You. Weeping, he gave me, a weeping child to Rainald the monk, sent me into exile for Your love and never saw me again. A small boy did not presume to withstand his father, so I left my country, my parents, my kindred and friends who wept bitterly at the parting.* [20]

St. Dominic receiving the rosary

103

A Toddler Chooses God

Edburga, the daughter of a tenth-century English royal family, was hardly more than a toddler when she made a very adult decision to enter the convent. When she was just three years old, her father took her apart and placed before her religious and worldly objects and told her to select what she wanted. She reached out for the Bible and chalice and disregarded the jewels and gold ornaments. With that sign of God's will, her father placed her in a convent. [21]

What Is a Child?

One of the most telling glimpses of children and attitudes toward children in medieval times comes from Bartholomaeus Anglicus, a thirteenth-century Franciscan monk, who gave a definition of a child in his encyclopedia, *On the Properties of Things.* His description shows us that children have changed very little through the centuries.

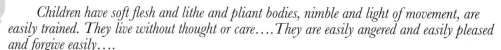

Children have soft flesh and lithe and pliant bodies, nimble and light of movement, are easily trained. They live without thought or care....They are easily angered and easily pleased and forgive easily....

Children often have bad habits, and think only of the present, ignoring the future. They love games and vain pursuits, disregarding what is profitable and useful....They cry and weep more over the loss of an apple than over the loss of an inheritance. They forget favors done for them. They desire everything they see, and call and reach for it.

They love talking to other children and avoid the company of old men. They keep no secrets but repeat all that they see and hear. Suddenly they laugh, suddenly they weep, and are continuously yelling, chattering, and laughing. They are scarcely silent when they are asleep. When they have been washed, they dirty themselves again. While they are being bathed or combed by their mothers they kick and sprawl and move their feet and hands and resist with all their might. They think only about their stomachs, always wanting to eat and drink. [22]

Adult Children Away from Home

Adult children in medieval times, like adult children today, often felt obligated to explain to their parents why they did not visit home more often. So it was with St. Catherine of Siena.

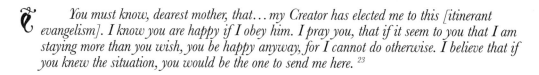

You must know, dearest mother, that... my Creator has elected me to this [itinerant evangelism]. I know you are happy if I obey him. I pray you, that if it seem to you that I am staying more than you wish, you be happy anyway, for I cannot do otherwise. I believe that if you knew the situation, you would be the one to send me here. [23]

Children's Crusades

A German boy named Nicholas and a French shepherd boy named Stephen were the ringleaders in what became known as the Children's Crusades. "Parents struggled to deter their children, but thousands of boys (and some girls in boys' clothing), averaging twelve years, slipped away." It was a fiasco, and many died of starvation or at sea, and others were taken into slavery. [24]

The Children's Crusade of 1212 A.D. faltered when 98% of the volunteers showed up without signed permission slips.

Busy Dads with No Time for Kids

Fathers in the Middle Ages, like fathers in every era, often found that life was too filled with important things to bother with children. Such was the case with the middle-aged Abelard, an eleventh-century philosopher, who fathered a child by his young student Heloise. In his autobiography he writes:

 [What accord] has study with nurses, writing materials with cradles, books and desks with spinning wheels, reeds and ink with spindles! Who intent upon sacred and philosophical reflections could endure the squalling of children, the lullabies of nurses and the noisy crowd of men and women! Who would stand for the disagreeable and constant dirt of little children! [25]

Mourning the Death of Children

The loss of a child is the most painful sorrow a parent can endure. When the loss is more than one child, the grief is overwhelming. Many families suffered such trials in the 1340s during the Black Death when a generation of hopes and dreams perished with the plague. So writes Ser Lapo Mazzei:

 [My sons] Amerigo and Martino died the same day, in my arms, within a few hours. God knows what hopes I had for the eldest, already a companion to me . . . and God knows how for many years he never failed, night and morning, to say his prayers on his knees in his room. . . . And at the same time [my daughter] Antonia was in bed, sick to death, and the middle boy with her, and he died there. How my heart broke when the little ones cried, and their mother not well herself or strong, hearing the words of the elder boy. And now all three of them dead! [26]

Proper Family Table Manners

It is also an unmannerly part for a man to lay his nose upon the cup where another must drink; or upon the meat that another must eat, to the end to smell unto it; but rather I would wish he should not smell at all, no not to that which he himself should eat and drink because it might chance there might fall some drop from his nose…. Neither, by my advice, shalt thou reach to any man that cup of wine whereof thyself has drunk and tasted without he be more than a familiar friend unto thee. And much less must thou give any part of the pear or the fruit which thou has bitten in thy mouth before. [27]

Proper Social Graces

When a man talketh with one, it is no good manner to come so near that he must needs breathe in his face, for there be many that cannot abide to feel that air of another man's breath albeit there come no ill savour from him. These and like fashions be very unseemly and would be eschewed because their senses with whom we acquaint ourselves, cannot brook nor bear them. [28]

Proper Manners for Children

Whenever you come unto a door, say, "God be here," ere you go further, and speak courteously, wherever you are, to sire or dame or their household…. Whether you spit near or far, hold your hand before your mouth to hide it…. Do not scratch yourself at the table so that men call you a daw, nor wipe your nose or nostrils, else men will say you are come of churls. Make neither the cat nor the dog your fellow at the table. And do not play with the spoon, or your trencher, or your knife; but lead your life in cleanliness and honest manners. This book is made for young children that bide not long at the school. It may soon be conned and learned, and will make them good if they be bad. God give them grace to be virtuous, for so they may thrive, Amen! [29]

Mother and children in the kitchen

Medieval Devotional Manuals for the Family

In fifteenth-century Germany, with the invention of the printing press, a wide variety of devotional manuals were published for family education and spiritual renewal. The manuals admonished "parents to teach their children the Creed, the Ten Commandments, the Lord's Prayer, to have them pray morning and evening and to take them to church to hear the mass and preaching." *The Soul's Guide* describes the Christian home as the first school young children attend and their first church.

The Path to Heaven depicts the Christian household led by the father who goes to church every Sunday with his wife, children and servants, and then returns home to review "the subject of the sermon and hears them recite the Commandments, Lord's Prayer and Creed and the seven mortal sins."

Another spiritual manual, *The Soul's Comfort*, encouraged family devotions and offered allegorical warnings to those who strayed from God. "It tells of a man whose soul after death was found, not in his body but in his money-chest and of a girl who, while dancing on Friday, was violently struck by the devil but recovered on giving her promise to amend her ways." [30]

Parents and children in the home

A Father's Grief for a Daughter

The unknown author of this fourteenth-century allegorical poem laments the death of his daughter Marguerite. She is buried in a churchyard, where one summer day while visiting her grave he has a heavenly vision. The poem illustrates not only a parent's love for a child, but also how Christian faith served to assuage sorrow.

> *...I saw beyond that merry mere*
> *a crystal cliff that shone full bright,*
> *many a noble ray stood forth;*
> *at the foot thereof there sat a child,—*
> *so debonair, a maid of grace;*
> *glistening white was her rich robe;*
> *I knew her well, I had seen her ere.*
>
> *As gleaming gold, refin'd and pure,*
> *so shone that glory 'neath the cliff;*
> *long toward her there I look'd,—*
> *the longer, I knew her more and more....*

"Immaculate," said that merry queen,
"Unblemish'd I am, without a stain;
and this may I with grace avow;
but 'matchless queen'—that said I ne'er.
We all in bliss are Brides of the Lamb,
a hundred and forty-thousand in all,
as in the Apocalypse it is clear;
Saint John beheld them in a throng,
On the hill of Zion that beauteous spot,
the Apostle beheld them in dream divine,
array'd for the Bridal on the hill-top—
the City New Jerusalem." [31]

Chess players

The Games People Played

Preachers in the Middle Ages often denounced worldly pastimes: "Idle plays and japes, carolings, making of fool countenances…[giving] gifts to jongleurs to hear idle tales…smiting…wrestling, [and] doing deeds of strength." Much of the leisure time activities, however, were not so different than today.

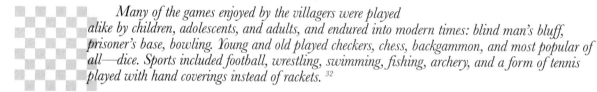

Many of the games enjoyed by the villagers were played alike by children, adolescents, and adults, and endured into modern times: blind man's bluff, prisoner's base, bowling. Young and old played checkers, chess, backgammon, and most popular of all—dice. Sports included football, wrestling, swimming, fishing, archery, and a form of tennis played with hand coverings instead of rackets. [32]

A Man's Responsibility for His Family

Erasmus, the great Renaissance humanist, ridiculed relics and the cult of the saints and pilgrimages. Far better to care for one's family than to go on a pilgrimage, so says Erasmus through the character Menedemus in his "The Religious Pilgrimage."

OGYGIUS: *But hark ye, haven't I set you agog to go on pilgrimages?*

MENEDEMUS: *Perhaps you may…but as I find myself at present, I have enough to do to travel my Roman stations.*

OGYGIUS: *Roman ones, you who never saw Rome?*

MENEDEMUS: *I'll tell you! After that manner I walk about my house, I go to my study, and take care of my daughter's safety; thence I go into my shop and see what my servants are doing; then into the kitchen, and see if anything be amiss there; and so from one place to another, to observe what my wife, and what my children are doing, taking care that every one be at his business. These are my Roman stations.*

OGYGIUS: But St. James would take care of those things for you.

MENEDEMUS: Holy Scripture enjoins me to look after them myself, but I do not find any text to leave them to the saints. [33]

Death in a Medieval Village

Village funerals were not elaborate affairs, but they did offer an occasion for the local priest to admonish people to examine their own souls:

Good men, as ye all see, here is a mirror to us all: a corpse brought to the church. God have mercy on him, and bring him into his bliss that shall last forever. . . . Wherefore each man and woman that is wise, make him ready thereto; for we all shall die, and we know not how soon. [34]

Disputations and Dirty Diapers: Reformers and Their Families

7

Martin Luther, the great sixteenth-century Reformer, "placed the home at the center of the universe." He was a family man and so also were his fellow Reformers. Many of them were monks or priests who had forsaken their vows and married. As such, they are the first generation of churchmen since the Early Church to view the issues of marriage and family from a personal perspective. To them matters relating to the family were of supreme importance—not to be controlled by the Church, but to be lived out in daily life. The Reformers were men and women of their times, and in many respects, they were much more closely tied to the Middle Ages than to modern times. The period of the Renaissance and Reformation was nothing short of a revolution in learning and in the exchange of ideas, but many old habits and customs died hard, as is seen in the lives of the Reformers.

Martin Luther, A Child of the Middle Ages

The early Reformers were themselves medieval men and women born and nurtured in the cradle of the Middle Ages. Martin Luther grew up in an atmosphere of fear and superstition:

> *The woods and winds and water were peopled by elves, gnomes, fairies, mermen and mermaids, sprites and witches. Sinister spirits would release storms, floods, and pestilence,*

Martin Luther's parents, Hans and Margaretha Luder

and would seduce mankind to sin and melancholia. Luther's mother believed that they played such minor pranks as stealing eggs, milk, and butter; and Luther himself was never emancipated from such beliefs.

Strict discipline was the rule of the day. Luther later related his own childhood trials:

My father once whipped me so that I ran away and felt ugly toward him until he was at pains to win me back. [At school] I was caned in a single morning fifteen times for nothing at all. I was required to decline and conjugate and hadn't learned my lesson. My mother caned me for stealing a nut, until the blood came. Such strict discipline drove me to the monastery, although she meant it well. [1]

The Failure of Priestly Celibacy

Most of the leading Reformers were Catholic clerics before they converted to the new Protestant faith, and many of them had struggled over the issue of celibacy and with vows that were routinely ignored. This was true for Ulrich Zwingli, the great reformer from Zurich. His scandalous personal life became an issue when he was being considered as parish priest at the prestigious cathedral in Zurich. Rumors were rife that he had seduced the daughter of a prominent official. It was a known fact that Renaissance popes had mistresses and children, and that the Swiss Bishop of Constance earned some 400 florins a year by fining his priests 4 florins for every child they fathered, but the leaders at Zurich were not inclined to call a preacher whose moral life was the subject of gossip. In response to their questions, Zwingli did not deny the rumors, but he insisted that he did maintain certain standards: "My principle was to inflict no injury on any marriage. . .and not to dishonor any virgin nor any nun." Despite their misgivings, they extended the call to him, when they learned his closest rival had three concubines and six children.[2]

The Decline of Morals

While he was still living as a celibate monk, Luther lamented that the institution of marriage had become just as decadent as the Church itself. Marriage, in his eyes, was "universally in awful disrepute," demeaned by the widely circulated "pagan books that treat of nothing but the depravity of womankind and the unhappiness of the estate of marriage." He blamed the Catholic Church and also the Church Fathers for "never having written anything good about marriage." To counter the prevailing views, Luther spoke of the institution of marriage in grandiose terms—encompassing all of nature:

> *Marriage pervades the whole of nature, for all creatures are divided into male and female; even trees marry; likewise, budding plants; there is also marriage between rocks and stones.* [3]

The Superiority of Marriage Over Virginity

The Reformation was a time when the Christian family was reaffirmed, and the Roman Catholic ideal of celibacy was condemned. Luther was the most vehement. He scorned those who insisted that virginity was superior to the married state, and he did not mince words in making his case:

> *If you are able to remain chaste and be pure by your own strength, why then do you vow to be chaste? Keep it, if you can; but it is a mere nothing that you should want to boast about your vow.... Do you want to know to whom you have vowed to keep chastity? I'll tell you: the miserable devil in hell and his mother.* [4]

Impediments to Marriage

The medieval church had dozens of impediments to marriage—many of which Martin Luther rejected outright. He argued, for example, that marriage to the relative of a deceased wife's relatives was permitted except in the case of a mother or daughter. Likewise, he did not forbid a Christian from marrying heretics, Jews, or Turks. "Another impediment which Luther declared invalid was the enforced celibacy of priests and nuns, and of the blind and deaf. . . .In fact, the only real impediment to marriage, in his opinion, was impotence or physical unfitness for the sexual act." [5]

Advice for the Groom

> *After yu hast married thy wife, go thy waye into thy chamber, and abstaynyng thre dayes from her, geue thy selfe to prayer with her, and in the fyrst nyght thou shalt burne the liver of the fyshe, and the deuil shalbe driuen awaye. The seconde nighte thou shalte be admitted vnto the companye of saynetes. The third night shalt yu obtaine the blessyng of God, so that whole children shalbe borne of you. And after the third nighte be past, take thy wyfe vnto thee in ye feare of God, and moore for the desyre of children, than bodelye lust.* [6]

Juan L. Vives

An artist's depiction of Luther's marriage to
Katherine von Bora, June 13, 1525

Luther on Marriage

❧ *Marriage may be likened to a hospital for incurables which prevents inmates from falling into a graver sin.*

❧ *It is a grand thing for a married pair to live in perfect union, but the devil rarely permits this. When they are apart, they cannot endure the separation, and when they are together, they cannot endure the always seeing one another.*

❧ *If I were to marry again I would carve myself an obedient wife out of stone, for to find one of flesh and blood is not conceivable.*

❧ *Is it sinful for a man and a woman to desire each other for the purpose of marriage? This is ridiculous, a question that contradicts both Scripture and nature. Why would people get married if they did not have desire and love for each other? Indeed, that is just why God has given this eager desire to bride and bridegroom, for otherwise everybody would flee from marriage and avoid it.*

❧ *Married folk are not to act as they now usually do. The men are almost lions in their homes, hard toward their wives and servants. The women, too, everywhere want to domineer and have their husbands as servants.*

❧ *The world says of marriage, "Brief is the joy, lasting the bitterness." Let them say what they please; what God wills and created is bound to be a laughingstock to them.*

❧ *Many have wives, but few find wives. Why? They are blind; they fail to see that their life and conduct with their wives is the work of God and pleasing in his sight. Could they but find that, then no wife would be so hateful, so ill-tempered, so ill-mannered, so poor, so sick that they would fail to find in her their heart's delight and would always be reproaching God for his work, creation, and will.* [7]

Martin Luther's Marriage and Wedding Night

Luther's marriage to Katherine von Bora was the tabloid cover story of the sixteenth century. For some it was a dirty scandal; for others it was a monument to the Christian family. The story is familiar. Luther arranged to have a merchant who sold smoked herring to the convent of Nimbschem make a late-night delivery and on his return trip to bring out the nuns instead of the empty herring barrels. Katie was among them, and when no eligible bachelor was found for her, Luther agreed to marry her. They married in the summer of 1525, when he was forty-two and she was twenty-six. The courtship was secret, but that privacy did not extend into their marriage. Indeed, his first intimate moments with Katie were anything but private. Justus Jonas, Martin Luther's good friend, described the scene the following day: "I was present yesterday and saw the couple on their marriage bed. As I watched this spectacle I could not hold back my tears." Patrick O'Hare, one of Luther's harshest critics of the twentieth century, blamed Luther, not custom, for "the vulgarity to lift the covers of the nuptial bed and disclose its sacred secrets to the gaze of others." [8]

Martin Luther

The Morning After

Marriage changed Martin Luther's life in many ways—one of which he described as the shock of opening his eyes in the morning, after a night's sleep, to find pigtails on the pillow.

Occultic Fear of Impotence

Impotence was one of the "impediments" to marriage, according to Luther, and it was also considered valid grounds for divorce. It is not surprising, then, that this condition caused great fear among men.

> *A great fear of witchcraft still existed, and one of the most potent fears for the bridegroom was that he might fail to demonstrate his manliness due to an evil person's curse. The most common curse was* les nouements d'aiquilettes—*strips of leather, cotton, or silk which, when tied in knots by evil-wishers and*

Katie Luther

143

passed through the wedding ring, had the effect of preventing consummation until the knots were untied. The usual procedure for counteracting all such curses was for the man to urinate through his wedding ring. [9]

A Bachelor's Scorn for "Insane Lovers"

But always keep in mind what I seek to find in her; for I am none of those insane lovers who embrace also the vices of those with whom they are in love, where they are smitten at first sight with a fine figure. This only is the beauty which allures me, if she is chaste, if not too fussy or fastidious, if economical, if patient, if there is hope that she will be interested about my health. [10]

John Calvin to a friend

Reformation Wives

Reformation wives—as exemplified by Katie Luther—were often very independent and feisty. Katie was her husband's equal and did not hesitate challenging his views and decisions. She operated her own farm in Zuhlsdorf, and periodically left her husband home with the children in Wittenberg, while she took care of business there. But her primary responsibility was supervising a busy household. Martin, on one occasion, referred to her as "my kind and dear lord and master, Katy, Lutheress, doctoress, and priestess, of Wittenberg." Katherine Zell was another spunky Reformation woman. Her husband Matthew was a priest turned Reformer, and she became a full partner in the ministry— so much so that when he died she felt constrained to assure people at his funeral that, contrary to the rumors, she would not be taking over the pulpit. Nevertheless, her active involvement in ministry brought the accusation that she was "disturbing the peace," and she did not shrink from condemning the religious intolerance of her fellow Reformers.

Not all Reformation wives, however, enjoyed the support of their husbands. Argula von Stauffer paid a heavy price for her Reformed faith. "Her husband," wrote Luther, "treats her tyrannically…. She alone, among those monsters, carries on with firm faith, though she admits, not without inner trembling." [11]

Male Headship

Luther strongly defended male headship in a letter he wrote to an acquaintance whose wife had refused to move with him to another city, but had promised to receive counsel from Luther on the matter:

Grace and peace in Christ, and authority over your wife!

My dear Stephen:

Your lord and mistress has not yet come to see me, and this her disobedience to you displeases me greatly…. You should have remembered that you ought to obey God rather than your wife, and so you should not have allowed her to despise and trample underfoot that authority of the husband which is the glory of God, as Saint Paul teaches…. By your own fault you are now opening a window in this weaker vessel through which Satan can enter at will and laugh at you, irritate you, and vex you in every way. You are an intelligent man, and the Lord will enable you to understand what I write. At the same time you will recognize how sincerely I wish you two to come to an agreement and Satan to be driven off. Farewell in Christ. [12]

Martin Luther's Reflection on Katie

I am an inferior lord, she the superior; I am Aaron, she is my Moses. [13]

Divorce and Remarriage

Traditional Roman Catholic beliefs and practices concerning divorce and remarriage were forcefully challenged during the Reformation. The Catholic Church regarded marriage a sacrament and permitted divorce only on the grounds of adultery, and remarriage was not allowed. However, it was not difficult to get around this policy through an annulment based on a variety of impediments such as false representation. Protestants denied that marriage was a sacrament and took a more pragmatic view of divorce. "If marriages were made in heaven, they were also dissolved there." Martin Bucer, a leading Protestant Reformer, strongly opposed the Catholic position:

The Papists… oppose themselves to God when they separate [couples] for many causes from bed and board and yet have the bond of matrimony remain, as if this covenant [of marriage] could be other than the conjunction and communion not only of bed and board, but of all other loving and helpful duties…. God requires of [both spouses] so to live together and to be united in

Luther relaxing with his family

body and in mind with such an affection as none may be dearer and more ardent among all the relations of mankind…. The proper and ultimate end of marriage is not copulation or children…but…the communicating of all duties, both divine and humane, each to the other with utmost benevolence and affection. [14]

Luther, the Marriage Counselor

Luther once told the story that is reminiscent of the Gospel story of Jesus and the woman taken in adultery. In this case the woman was a wife and mother of four children, who became involved with another man. When her husband learned of her unfaithfulness, he reported her to the local officials and had her publicly whipped. Luther and two other ministers then counseled with the couple in an effort to get them reconciled. The husband agreed, but the wife was so mortified by her public disgrace that she ran away from home, never to be seen again. In this instance, Luther later reflected, "one should have pursued reconciliation before punishment." [15]

Luther on Nagging Wives

If a man can have his wife in bed, he ought not complain about her incessant nagging, for "he who wants a fire must endure the smoke." [16]

Luther, the Proud Father

Only a few months after he and Katie were married, Luther confided to a friend that "My Katherine is fulfilling Genesis 1:28." When baby Hans was born, Luther could not resist making a humorous but underhanded observation: "Kick, little fellow. That's what the pope did to me, but I got loose." He relished fatherhood, commenting, "These are the joys of marriage, of which the pope is not worthy." Luther's sentimentality, however, was always qualified by his realism. He humorously expressed such feelings in a letter to the woman he hoped would become his daughter Elizabeth's godmother:

Dear Lady,

God has produced from me and my wife, Katie, a little heathen. We hope you will be willing to become her spiritual mother and help make her a Christian. [17]

The "First Baby" of the Reformation

Martin and Katie had six children, all of whom became a deep source of pride to Protestants who still had painful memories of their Catholic past and the outward requirement of clerical celibacy.

When little Hans, the eldest, arrived on June 7, 1526, it was a day of great rejoicing for Luther's friends all over Germany…and the arrival of the first tooth at six months was a national event. [18]

Father teaching catechism

Luther and Dirty Diapers

Now observe that when that clever harlot, our natural reason (which the pagans followed in trying to be most clever), takes a look at married life, she turns up her nose and says, "Alas, must I rock the baby, wash its diapers, make its bed, smell its stench, stay up nights with it, take care of it when it cries, heal its rashes and sores, and on top of that care for my wife, provide for her, labor at my trade, take care of this and take care of that, do this and do that, endure this and endure that, and whatever else of bitterness and drudgery married life involves?

"What, should I make such a prisoner of myself? O you poor, wretched fellow, have you taken a wife? Fie, fie upon such wretchedness and bitterness! It is better to remain free and lead a peaceful, carefree life; I will become a priest or a nun and compel my children to do likewise." What then does Christian faith say to this? It opens its eyes, looks upon all these insignificant, distasteful, and despised duties in the Spirit, and is aware that they are all adorned with divine approval as with the costliest gold and jewels. It says, "O God…I confess to Thee that I am not worthy to rock the little babe or wash its diapers, or to be entrusted with the care of the child and its mother. How is it that I, without any merit, have come to this distinction of being certain that I am serving Thy creature and Thy most precious will. O how gladly will I do so, though the duties should be even more insignificant and despised. Neither frost nor heat, neither drudgery nor labor, will distress or dissuade me, for I am certain that it is thus pleasing in Thy sight." [19]

Martin Luther on the Blessing of Children

People who do not like children are swine, dunces, and blockheads, not worthy to be called men and women, because they despise the blessing of God—the Creator and Author of marriage. [20]

Luther's Instructions on Training Children

But as for those who will not learn, let them be told that they deny Christ and are no Christians, and let them not be admitted to the Sacrament…. Besides this, let their parents or masters refuse them food and drink, and tell them that the prince will have such rude people driven from the land…. Especially urge authorities and parents that they govern well and send the children to school, and admonish them how it is their duty to do this, and what an accursed sin they commit if they neglect it. For thereby they overthrow and desolate both God's kingdom and the world's, as the worst enemies both of God and man. Lay also great stress on this horrible injury they do, if they do not help to train children for pastors, preachers, clerks, &c., and that God will punish them terribly. For it is very necessary to preach on this subject. Parents and magistrates now sin in this matter more than we can say. The devil has also most evil designs therein. [21]

A hungry family preparing for the evening meal

Table Manners

Listen you children who are going to table. Wash your hands and cut your nails. Do not sit at the head of the table; This is reserved for the father of the house. Do not commence eating until a blessing is said. Dine in God's name And permit the eldest to begin first. Proceed in a disciplined manner. Do not snort or smack like a pig. Do not reach violently for bread, Lest you may knock over a glass. Do not cut bread on your chest…. Do not elbow the person sitting next to you. Sit up straight; be a model of gracefulness. Do not rock back and forth on the bench, Lest you let loose a stink…. If sexual play occurs at table, Pretend you do not see it…. Do not pick your nose…. Silently praise and thank God For the food He has graciously provided And you have received from His fatherly hand…. [22]

Hans Sachs, shoemaker

The Lively Luther Household

The Luther parsonage was often a frolicking center of activity. In addition to their own family, there were visitors and others needing long-term shelter—a home described by a guest as being "occupied by a motley crowd of boys, students, girls, widows, old women, and youngsters."

Where formerly sedate monks had walked about by twos with bowed heads and sober… dressed in the somber black robes of the order, the halls now echoed the laughter and chatter of children's voices, the hustle and bustle of a busy household, the vitality and exuberance of youth. [23]

118

A New Status for Women and Children

During the Middle Ages, children were sometimes sent away to be reared in monasteries when they were not more than toddlers. Girls were the most vulnerable because they were often regarded a financial liability to the family. This was an outrageous crime in the eyes of the Reformers:

> *The first generation of Protestant reformers died believing they had released women into the world by establishing them firmly at the center of the home and family life, no longer to suffer the withdrawn, culturally circumscribed, sexually repressed, male-regulated life of a cloister. And they believed children would never again be consigned at an early age to involuntary celibacy but would henceforth remain in the home, objects of constant parental love and wrath, until they were all properly married. [24]*

The Importance of Parenting

"There is no power on earth that is nobler or greater than that of parents," declared Luther, who viewed the father's role just as important as the mother's. Proper discipline was the key to good parenting. Permissiveness was condemned as the cause of much of society's ills, and Christian parents were admonished to recognize the seriousness of their task. Veit Dietrich, a Reformed pastor in Nuremberg, lamented the dire state of family affairs:

Family singing in the Luther household

> *Today you find few parents who once mention study or work to their children. They let them creep about idly, eating and drinking whenever they please, casually dressed in ragged pants and jackets. Through bad example and lax discipline, children learn to curse and swear, lie and steal. Parents aid and abet such ill breeding by laughing at small children when they curse or repeat bawdy rhymes. [25]*

Punishing Sin in Calvin's Geneva

John Calvin, with the help of the city council, sought to regulate morals in Geneva by instituting Old Testament Jewish laws. The law proscribed the death penalty for adultery, although most offenders were fined and sent to jail instead. In many of its regulations, the Geneva law code went far beyond any biblical statutes:

Dancing, gambling, drunkenness, the frequenting of taverns, profanity, luxury, excesses at public entertainments, extravagance and immodesty in dress, licentious or irreligious songs were forbidden and punished by censure or fine or imprisonment. Even the number of dishes at meals was regulated.... Reading of bad books and immoral novels was also prohibited.... Watchmen were appointed to that people went to church. The members of the Consistory visited every house once a year to examine into the faith and morals of the family. The Geneva court records for this period offer a fascinating glimpse of the offenses and their penalties:

Several women, including the prominent wife of the captain-general Ami Perrin, were imprisoned for dancing.

A young man was punished because he gave his bride a book on housekeeping with the remark: "This is the best Psalter."

Three children were punished because they remained outside the church during the sermon to eat cakes.

A child was whipped for calling his mother a thief and a she-devil.

A girl was beheaded for striking her parents.

A baker was executed for repeated adultery.

A man was imprisoned for four days because he persisted in calling his child Claude (a Roman Catholic saint) instead of Abraham, as the minister wished. [26]

John Calvin of Geneva

John Calvin and Family Struggles

John Calvin fathered no children of his own, but when he married the widowed Idelette de Bure, he brought her two little children into his home. Idelette died after nine years of marriage, and Calvin was left alone as a single father to care for the children. She had been concerned for their welfare as he testifies: "Since I feared that these personal worries might aggravate her illness, I took an opportunity, three days before her death, to tell her that I would not fail to fulfill my responsibilities to her children." But despite his efforts, he was not immune to the struggles that plague families in every age.

The children were approaching adolescence when she died, and they would have been expected to care for their own needs. Their environment in Geneva, apart from the religious atmosphere of their home and church, offered many worldly pleasures, and without their mother's close supervision they no doubt found it difficult to resist the temptations. Several years after Idelette died, her daughter Judith was convicted of adultery. So humiliated was Calvin over the scandal that he refused to leave the house for days. [27]

Secret Marriages Condemned

Protestant Reformers spoke out strongly against secret marriages, even as medieval churchmen had, but despite their protests, the practice continued. Johannes Brenz, a German Reformer, insisted that a "valid" marriage is one that is carried out in a "sensible, legal, and godly manner." Otherwise it was of Satan, and what Satan joins together, society can dissolve. Indeed, he argued that a secret marriage was nothing more than fornication instigated by the devil.

> *When two young people secretly and without the knowledge and will of their parents, in the disobedience and ignorance of youth, as if intoxicated, wantonly and deceitfully, sometimes aided and abetted by a matchmaker, lying flattery, or other unreasonable means, join themselves together in marriage, who would not agree that such a union has been brought about by Satan and not by the Lord God?* [28]

Contraception

Contraception is by no means a modern invention, but its use in earlier times was almost universally condemned by the Church—both Catholic and Protestant.

An Anabaptist family

> *A variety of contraceptive devices did exist in the sixteenth century, especially sponges and acidic potions, and they appear to have been widely used by prostitutes…. Church law and catechism condemned contraceptive potions and poisons as instruments of homicide….The first generation of Protestants was equally inflexible on the subject; although Luther expressed personal pleasure in his own marital bed and urged others to have no shame about sexual intercourse, as a theologian he excused sex largely as a means to the higher ends of procreation and avoidance of fornication. John Calvin brought up the subject of contraception in his* Commentary on Genesis *only to condemn* coitus interruptus *as homicide and threatened genocide.* [29]

Babies Begin from the "Seed" of the Father

Menno Simons, the "father" of the Mennonites, sought to bolster the principle of male headship by arguing that the father alone contributes the seed of a child, while the mother only incubates that seed:

> *Therefore I hope by the Lord's help and grace to explain to all unbiased and sensible readers with so forcible an argument from Scripture, and also from observable facts of God's ordinances, that men may see with one eye shut that procreative seed by which the human race*

124

The Luther family home, formerly an Augustinian cloister

exists and multiplies is to be sought with the fathers and not with the mothers.... You see, worthy readers... the origin and substance of the child comes from the father's body or loins, that women come of men, that mothers conceive seed from the fathers, that in the blood of the mother the fruit congeals with the seed of the father, and that in this manner mothers bear children unto the fathers, as is plain enough in the ... Scriptures. [30]

Anatomy of a Pregnant Woman

There were still many misconceptions about human reproductive organs during the Reformation period, as this "scientific" description indicates:

The breasts are cold and moist and filled with vessels, arteries, and nerves. Within each breast are cavities in which blood is transformed into white milk. The breasts are connected to the womb by two vessels through which the fetus is nourished and maintained. The womb lies deep within and is tightly sealed. During sexual intercourse it opens, and afterward it closes as tightly as possible.

The menstrual flow originates in the liver and discharges through a vessel in the front of the womb. The womb is a receptacle preordained by God the Lord, wherein a child is conceived, nourished, and assumes human form. Little receptacles or vessels hang on the womb. They gather the menstrual flow from the liver and discharge it when the time is right through the outer veins of the womb.... The womb also has two fleshly stems hanging on its sides. From these are suspended two little containers called vessels of seed. [31]

H. Vogtherr the Elder, Vienna, 1538

The Curse of Eve and Childbearing

Intolerance of "heresy" was one of the legacies left over from the Middle Ages that continued on for generations. Both Protestants and Catholics burned heretics at the stake and not just for gross theological error. Here is the story told by Patricia Gundry to a group of scholars—mostly men:

🙟 *In the sixteenth century in Scotland, Eufame MacLayne was pregnant. Most of you don't know what it's like to be pregnant. In the sixteenth century it was even less fun than now. Eufame was very big; she was carrying twins. When labor began, things got rough. Sometimes twins do not come the easy way. They can be in odd positions, causing long and difficult labors. Eufame, for whatever reason, requested a certain pain-killing herb be given to her. I do not know how much it helped, but she survived and so did her babies. However, someone found out what she had done. Painkillers were forbidden to women in childbirth. It was against God's law. He wanted women to suffer in labor. The Bible said so, their punishment for Eve's sin. So Eufame was brought before those who decided punishment. And they could not, of course, let her go free (there was also the possibility of witchcraft, you see, because she had not relied solely on the grace of God for relief from her pain). So her babies were taken from her arms and given to someone else's care. Eufame was tied to a stake. Bundles of wood were laid at her feet. The new mother Eufame was burned alive.* [32]

Wife-Beating

Strict laws and moral codes often benefited women, and nowhere was this more evident than in Reformation Europe's most tightly regulated city:

🙟 *Wife beaters in Protestant towns and territories were haled before the marriage court or consistory, and nowhere more speedily than in Geneva, which by century's end had gained the reputation of "the woman's Paradise."* [33]

A Case of Mutual Submission

Hermann von Weinsberg described his parents' efforts to compromise in their marriage in their sixteenth-century household in Cologne. They had frequent disagreements, and his father suggested a solution: "Wife, let's make a deal: one week you rule over the house and hold authority, and the next week I will rule and hold authority." Sometimes they lost track of the week, and if his mother insisted on having her way, his father would say: "Well, you rule today and this week, and I will rule next week." [34]

Testimony of a Holy Death

Protestants rejected the Roman Catholic sacrament of extreme unction, but they did not deny the importance of death rituals—especially the testimonies of those who were prepared to see their Maker. Loved ones at the death bed eagerly awaited the final words, as did John Calvin at the death of Idelette.

🙟 *She suddenly cried out in such a way that all could see that her spirit had risen far above this world. These were her words, "O glorious resurrection! O God of Abraham and of all of our fathers, the believers of all the ages have trusted on Thee and none of them have hoped in vain. And now I fix my hope on Thee." These short statements were cried out rather than distinctly spoken. These were not lines suggested by someone else, but came from her own thoughts.* [35]

Grieving a Beloved Wife

I have been bereaved of the best companion of my life, who, if our lot had been harsher, would have been not only the willing sharer of exile and poverty, but even of death. While she lived she was the faithful helper of my ministry. From her I never experienced the slightest hindrance. [36]

John Calvin

Idellette de Bure Calvin

Father and the Family Altar:
Puritan Family Relationships

CHAPTER

8   The Protestant emphasis on family life culminated with the Puritans. The purpose of the family was first and foremost to glorify God. God had established the family at creation, and the husband and wife, according to Isaac Ambrose, were to carry out God's purpose by "erecting and establishing Christ's glorious kingdom in their house." The home, then, was the foundation for all other institutions, and without a well-ordered home the Puritans were convinced there would be no well-ordered society. The family was seen as "a school wherein the first principles and grounds of government and subjection are learned"—"a true image of the commonwealth." Richard Baxter, the great Puritan divine, offered a slightly different slant: "A Christian family…is a church…a society of Christians combined for… better worshipping and serving God." [1]

The Puritan "focus on the family" sounds very modern to those who are concerned about declining family values in today's world. Puritans were convinced that the family was the basic institution of society, and that if the family failed so would the society. A godly family, headed by the father, was one that prayed and read the Bible together and made religion a natural part of everyday life.

The term "Puritan" is often used in derision to characterize someone who is a prude, but the Puritans were anything but prudish in matters of love and sex as is evident in their writings.

A New Perspective on Sex

The Roman Catholic perspective on sex had developed from the teachings of the Church Fathers and essentially viewed it as a physical act of the flesh that was sinful except for procreation. This view was challenged by certain of the Reformers, but it was left to the Puritans to

THE
SCHOOL
OF
MANNERS.
OR
RULES for Childrens
Behaviour:
AtChurch,at Home,atTable,
inCompany,inDiscourse,at
School,abroad, and among
Boys. With some other
short and mixt Precepts.

By the Author of the *English*
Exercises.

The Fourth Edition.

LONDON.
Printed for *Tho. Cockerill*, at the
ThreeLegs andBible against Gro-
cers-Hall in the *Poultrey*, 1701.

Title page of the children's book,
The School of Manners

offer a new perspective on marital intimacy by shifting the focus from procreation to companionship. Sexual intercourse was to be part of the very family life that glorified God. They challenged the Catholics "who hold that the secret coming together of man and wife cannot be without sin unless it be done for procreation of children," and insisted rather that "sex was not only legitimate" but "it was meant to be exuberant." Indeed, married couples were encouraged to engage in lovemaking "with good will and delight, willingly, readily, and cheerfully." John Milton summed up the biblical sanction for sexual enjoyment from a Puritan perspective:

> *Wisest Solomon among his gravest Proverbs countenances a kind of ravishment...in the entertainment of wedded leisures; and in the Song of Songs...sings of a thousand raptures between those two lovely ones far on the hither side of carnal enjoyment. By these instances, and more which might be brought, we may imagine how indulgently God provided against man's loneliness.* [2]

Crimes and Misdemeanors

The reputation the Puritans had for being prudish and "puritanical" regarding sex has been rightly challenged by revisionist historians, but that reputation is not entirely groundless. For Puritans, sex was a beautiful gift from God to be enjoyed by husband and wife in private. There was no place for the bawdy humor of a Martin Luther or of a medieval street play; nor was there any place for a public display of legitimate affection between the sexes. The New England Puritans regulated virtually every aspect of daily life, and no activity was more closely watched as that related to sexual morality.

> *Sunday Blue Laws were hardest on lovers. John Lewis and Sarah Chapman were arrested for sitting together on the Lord's Day, under an apple tree. Men who "saluted" their wives on Sunday were pilloried. And Captain Kemble, who "publicquely, lewdly—Lord's Day noon"—kissed his wife at his own front door, spent the rest of the day in stocks. Children born on the Sabbath were thought to have been conceived on the same day, and pious parents were accused by the ministers of making sinful, Lord's Day love. The wife of a Connecticut magistrate had twins on a Sunday, and she and her husband were as surprised as anyone. After this there was less talk, for the magistrate made the ministers back down—and only God kept tabs. Love and toil were stolen sweets on Sunday, and Elizabeth Eddy was fined ten shillings for hanging out clothes, and her mother ten more for catching eels. Less fortunate ladies were made to sit on the meeting-house "stool of repentance," with their sin written in Capitall Letters on a paper above their foreheads. Scarlet Letter girls wore their shame on their breasts, and stood on a sheet beside the pulpit.* [3]

Sex and the Puritan Conscience

Although sex in marriage was regarded a glorious gift from God, many Puritans struggled with impure thoughts which they sometimes confided to their diaries. One of the most noted diarists was the Reverend Cotton Mather, a Boston minister.

New England Puritans on their way to church

In 1695 we find him reflecting on the "manifold filthiness of my heart and life, and the horrible aggravations of that filthiness"; and when his uncle, the minister of Plymouth, was driven from his pulpit for fornication in 1697, Cotton was very much afraid that God's judgment might also light on him for his sins. He had clearly been tempted to extra-marital adventures. His wife died in December 1702, and by January 1703 he was praying that he might avoid the temptations that beset a widower…. The only solution to his problem was another wife, and in June he found a discreet and respectable widow two doors down the road, with a sweet temper, only one son, and "a very comely person." He married her and was soon happy in "the enjoyment of a most lovely creature."…After his second wife's death, by which time he was fifty-one, he decided to remain single, praying for "purity in the widowhood."… But within two years, he was tired of his widowhood, and he married again in 1715 to a woman who had been widowed only six months before…. In March of 1718, when he was fifty-seven, he wrote in his diary: The diseases of my soul are not cured until I arrive at the most unspotted chastity and purity. I do not apprehend that Heaven requires me utterly to lay aside my fondness for my lovely consort. But I must mourn most bitterly and walk humbly all my days for my former pollutions. I must abhor the least thought of regard unto any other person but this dearly beloved of my soul. [4]

Puritan Marriages

Puritans married fast and young—sometimes within weeks or months after becoming widowed, and often while they were in their teens. Cotton Mather's first wife was sixteen when she married and thirty-two when she died, leaving behind ten children.

It was customary for girls then to marry before they were sixteen. This was realistic in view of the slim life expectancy in those days—about thirty-three years. . . . One item on which a girl always worked for her hope chest was a huge pile of napkins—a necessity in those days of few forks. The New England Weekly Journal *in 1733 announced that "no maiden properly brought up would think herself prepared to marry until she had at least 10 pr. linen sheets.".... Puritans took marriage very seriously. Wives were well protected by law, and a man could be punished for using "harsh words" to his wife, while a woman was fined for a "shrewish tongue." The stability of a family was immensely important to the continuity of the new society that had ventured so far across so perilous an ocean.* [5]

Bundling

As strict as the Puritans were on issues of sexual morality, it was in colonial New England where the practice of bundling most flourished. There were ministers who preached against it, but most accepted it, according to Eleanor Early, as a perfectly normal aspect of the culture.

> *There was a curious New England custom in those days called Bundling, which was love-making under peculiar circumstances. . . . Boys and girls who bundled went to bed together, with their clothes on, and stayed until morning. Sometimes they got married afterward. And sometimes they didn't. Bundling was a cozy custom of rural New England, and hardly anybody thought it was wrong—except the Reverend Jonathan Edwards and his cultured associates. Very few ministers opposed it—and some even practiced it.... It was a lovers' custom as old as the first settlement, and until Mr. Edwards got excited about it, it was scarcely a matter for gossip. But after Mr. Edwards' first "hell-fire and conniption-fit sermon," his colleagues took up the subject. And one of them wrote a poem with twenty-seven verses dedicated to "Ye Youth of Both Sexes," that ended like this:*

Bundling with only the shoes off

> *Should you go on, the day will come*
>   *When Christ your judge will say,*
> *"In bundles bind each of this kind,*
>   *And cast them all away.*
>
> *"Down deep in hell there let them dwell,*
>   *And bundle on that bed.*
> *There burn and roll without control*
>   *'Till all their lusts are fed."*
>
> *The Reverend Samuel Peters of Hebron, Connecticut, wrote a History of the Colony in 1781, and in it he tells us that:*

> *"Notwithstanding the great modesty of the females is such that it would be accounted rudeness for a gentleman to speak before a lady of a garter, or her leg, yet it is thought but a piece of civility to ask her to bundle."*

> *If she was an honest, country bundling girl, she probably expected it. Boys came a long way to court. When they had done their day's chores and reached a girl's home, it was suppertime. And after supper, it was bedtime—and the fires went out, and the house grew cold. Then, in a big feather bed, there was warmth and loveliness—and the long, long night to talk!* [6]

A Bundling Song

A popular song in colonial New England summed up the Puritan perspective on bundling:

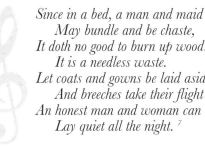

Since in a bed, a man and maid
May bundle and be chaste,
It doth no good to burn up wood.
It is a needless waste.
Let coats and gowns be laid aside,
And breeches take their flight
An honest man and woman can
Lay quiet all the night. [7]

Punishment for Fornication

Sex before marriage was regarded a serious crime among the Puritans of New England—even if the couple agreed to marry. When Samuel Hoskings and Elizabeth Cleverley of New Haven confessed their sin in 1642, they were whipped publicly. Then they went to the court to request permission to marry. They were granted that request, but not without further censure:

> *Samuel Hoskings and Elizabeth Cleverley, being desirous to join together in the state of marriage, and not being able to make proof of their parents' consent, but seeing they both affirm they have the consent of their parents and with having entered into contract, sinfully and wickedly defiled each other in filthy dalliance and unclean passages, by which they have made themselves unfit for any other, and for which they have both received public correction, upon these considerations granted them liberty to marry.* [8]

Wifely Subjection as True Freedom

Puritans did not question the traditional view that the husband held authority in the family and the wife was in subjection to him, but they did seek to give a different slant to this authority and subjection. John Winthrop, the governor of the Massachusetts Bay Colony, wrote that natural liberty "makes men grow more evil and in time…worse than brute beasts." But moral liberty "is the proper end and object of authority…it is a liberty to that only which is good, just, and honest." The prime example of moral liberty was that enjoyed by the Christian wife:

129

🖋 *The woman's own choice makes such a man her husband; yet being so chosen, he is her lord, and she is to be subject to him, yet in a way of liberty, not of bondage; and a true wife accounts her subjection her honor and freedom, and would not think her condition safe and free but in her subjection to her husband's authority.* [9]

"These pictorial church directories always take longer than we expect."

The Dangers of Denying Wives Liberty

John Cotton, a leading Puritan preacher, warned of the danger of a husband becoming heavy-handed and denying his wife liberty in the marriage relationship:

🖋 *It is good for the wife to acknowledge all power and authority to the husband, and for the husband to acknowledge honor to the wife; but still give them that which God hath given, else you will find you dig pits, and lay snares, and cumber their spirits, if you give them less; there is never peace where full liberty is not given, nor never stable peace where more than full liberty is granted.* [10]

Mistress Hopkins' Insanity

A woman's place was in the home—so said the Puritans—and if her husband allowed her to venture outside that realm he was endangering her and the well-being of the family. According to Governor Winthrop of the Massachusetts Bay Colony, Mistress Hopkins, the wife of the governor of Connecticut, was a case in point:

🖋 *Her husband being very loving and tender of her, was loath to grieve her; but he saw his error, when it was too late. For if she had attended her household affairs and such things as belong to women, and not gone out of her way and calling to meddle in such things as are proper to men, whose minds are strong . . . she [would have] kept her wits, and might have improved them usefully and honorably in the place God had set her.* [11]

"To My Dear and Loving Husband"

No American literature text is complete without selections from the poetry of Anne Bradstreet. Among other subjects, this New England Puritan housewife wrote of her love for her husband. Her marriage to Simon Bradstreet was one of mutual devotion and commitment, as is expressed in this private poem published after her death.

> *If ever two were one, then surely we*
> > *If ever man were lov'd by wife, then thee;*
> *If ever wife was happy in a man,*
> > *Compare with me ye women if you can.*
>
> *I prize thy love more than whole mines of gold,*
> > *Or riches that the East doth hold.*
> *My love is such that rivers cannot quench,*
> > *Nor aught but love from thee give recompense.*
>
> *Thy love is such I can no way repay,*
> > *The heavens reward thee manifold I pray.*
> *Then while we live, in love let's so persever,*
> > *That when we live no more, we may live ever.* [12]

A Disgraceful Divorce in the Family

A Puritan father instructing his family in psalm singing

Anne Bradstreet grew up Anne Dudley in a strict Puritan home. Her little sister Sarah grew up in the same home, but they went their very separate ways. Anne wrote a poem about two sisters, symbolizing the struggle between the spirit and the flesh, but it could also be seen as reflective of herself and Sarah.

> *In secret place where once I*
> *stood,*
> > *Close by the banks of*
> *lacrym flood,*
> *I heard two sisters reason on*
> > *Things that are past and things to come.*
> *One Flesh was called, who had her eye*
> > *On worldly wealth and vanity;*
> *The other Spirit, who did rear*
> > *Her thoughts unto a higher sphere….*

Both sisters made reputations in the Massachusetts Bay Colony. "Anne Bradstreet's harmonious marriage is known through her poetry; Sarah Keayne's stormy divorce is glimpsed through scattered letters." While she and her husband were abroad in England, Sarah's husband wrote to her father in Boston, vowing never to live with her again because she had "unwived herself"— implying she had committed adultery. To a Boston minister, he wrote:

> *[I have] hazarded my health & life, to satisfy the unsatiable desire & lust of a wife that in requittal impoysoned my body with such a running of a reines that would, if not (through mercie) cured, have turned unto french Pox…. It is clear & unfallible case that no poyson can be received from the bodie of a woman, but what shee first has received from the infected body of some other.*

With the help of her influential father, Sarah obtained a divorce from Benjamin Keayne, and not long afterward she was excommunicated from Boston's First Church on charges of "odious, lewd, & scandalous uncleane behavior with one Nicholas Hart of Taunton, an Excommunicate person." [13]

Excerpt from a Puritan Sermon

> *The husband is also to understand, that as God created the woman, not of the head, and so equall in authoritie with her husband: so also he created her not of Adam's foote that she should be trodden down and despised, but he took her out of the ribbe, that she might walke joyntly with him, under the conduct and government of her head.* [14]

A Puritan Love Letter

It was natural for Puritans to express their love for God in the same breath that they expressed romantic love, as this letter from a young minister, Edward Taylor, illustrates:

> *My Dove,*
>
> *I send you not my heart, for that I trust is sent to Heaven long since, and unless it hath woefully deceived me, it hath not taken up its lodgings in any one's bosom on this side of the royal City of the Great King, but yet most of it that is allowed to be layed out upon any creature doth safely and singly fall to your share.* [15]

A Puritan child decked out in her best dress

Punishment for Adultery

The Puritans in New England imposed severe penalties for adultery. In fact, in the early colonial period the penalty was death in most of the colonies, though it was not enforced rigorously.

> *By 1673, Connecticut had dropped the death penalty in favor of the gentler punishment of branding the letter "A" on the foreheads of offenders. Massachusetts, in 1694, formally abandoned the death penalty, but the adulterer had to stand on the gallows with a rope around his neck, undergo a severe whipping, and be obliged to wear the scarlet letter "A."*
>
> *On one occasion, a woman who had borne an illegitimate child was forced to stand in the Boston market place with the placard, "Thus I stand for my adulterous and whorish carriage."* [16]

Jonathan Edwards' Marriage

> *The real Puritans loved well and were not ashamed to enjoy it. Sarah's wedding dress expressed the mood. No white wraith mistily drifting toward some vague spiritual experience, she wore a pea green satin brocade with a bold pattern as she stepped joyfully toward her lover.... Edwards met her on July 28, 1727, wearing a new powdered wig and a new set of white clerical bands given him by his sister Mary.* [17]

Elisabeth Dodds

No Sex on the Sabbath

No one was exempt from the scrutiny of Sunday blue laws—not even New England's most celebrated minister, Jonathan Edwards. He was known for his strict code of morality, and was quick to censure others. On one occasion, when some of the young people in the community were caught reading a midwives manual, he read their names the next Sunday in church—making a public spectacle of their wicked behavior. But Edwards himself was not without his secret sins, as rumors had it in Northampton, Massachusetts.

> *Some ministers in those days [1730s] refused to baptize children born on Sunday because it was believed that children arrived on the same day of the*

Jonathan and Sarah Edwards' parsonage in Northampton, Massachusetts

Portraits of Jonathan and Sarah Edwards

week that they had been conceived. The village wits enjoyed their speculations about their sedate minister when on April 26, 1730, "towards the conclusion of the afternoon exercise," the Edwardses acquired another daughter, Jerusha. Six Edwards children were to arrive conspicuously on a Sunday. [18]

A Mother's Work Is Never Done

One of the most detailed records of home life among the Puritans in colonial New England is that of the Edwards household—Jonathan, Sarah, and their eleven children. In some respects this family was atypical, but it nevertheless offers a fascinating glimpse of everyday life:

The management of a large, busy household took leadership and efficiency. Mothers then had to be administrators, because the food and clothing depended on the mother's ability to produce it. Sarah had to learn to assign chores…one child would take a turn breaking ice in the lean-to next to the kitchen, to get water for the breakfast tea, while another child brought in the wood…. Another girl would be setting the table. Many households of the time were content to call a shot of hot buttered rum "breakfast," but the Edwardses sat down to large meals: bean porridge with ham bone, or cold corned beef and hot potatoes, or salt fish in cream. Cooking eggs was complicated because few houses had clocks. Eggs were sometimes timed by singing psalms (an eight-line verse was usually right for boiling an egg.) The first cure for scurvy wasn't discovered until 1747, and this diet deficiency disease weakened many people, but there was none of it in Sarah's house. A prudent mother was also skeptical of drinking water. Many mothers found it safer to give babies beer, though one eighteenth-century almanac advised that it was "best to have their beer a little heated." [19]

A Godly Legacy

The sins of the fathers (and mothers) extend from generation to generation, a proverb that is nowhere better illustrated than in the lives of two men of the eighteenth century:

One was a devout Christian minister whose name was Jonathan Edwards. He married a consecrated Christian girl, and out of their union, over a certain period of years, came 729 descendants. Of these 300 were ministers, 65 were authors of good books, 3 were U.S. congressmen, and 1 was vice-president of the United States. Almost 70 percent of them made a positive contribution to society....

The other man was an unbeliever named Max Jukes. He lived close to Jonathan Edwards, in the same period of time.... He married an unbeliever, and they produced over the same period of time 1,026 descendants, 300 of whom died early in life. One hundred went to prison for an average of 13 years each. Two hundred were public prostitutes. Another 100 were alcoholics. The family cost the state over 1 million dollars, and none made any significant contribution to society. [20]

The Importance of Children

It is no small mercy to be the parents of a Godly seed: and this is the end of the institution of marriage. [21]

Richard Baxter

Advice on Child Rearing

Children, in the minds of Puritans, were part of God's covenant family, and rearing godly children was a top priority.

The gentle rod of the mother is a very gentle thing, it will break neither bone nor skin: yet by the blessing of God with it, and upon the wise application of it, it would break the bond that bindeth up corruption in the heart.

John Eliot

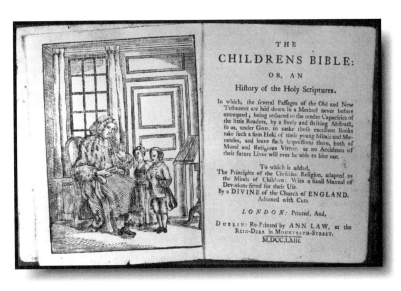

The Puritan version of *The Children's Bible*

Diverse children have their different natures; those parents are wise that can fit their nurture according to their nature. [22]

Anne Bradstreet

A Puritan Nursery Rhyme

> *In the burying ground I see*
> *Graves shorter there than I,*
> *From Death's clutch no age is free*
> *Young children too must die.* [23]

Haunted Christian Houses

Cotton Mather, a well-known Puritan preacher, insisted that prayerless houses are haunted houses. "If your Houses be not Warmed with your Prayers," he warned his parishioners, "the fierce Wrath of God abideth on them."

 The Curse of God is the Sauce in every dish, the Curse of God is the Cover to every Bed, in that lamentable Family. Houses molested with Devils, are not more miserable, than Houses destitute of Prayers. I have seen in an house, when the Devils have had Possession of a child, that when Family Prayer began, the Devils would make Hideous Roarings and Noises in the Room, as being under a Vexation threat, which was intolerable to them. Truly, The Devils have No Disturbance in Houses where Family Prayer is not maintained; prayerless houses are haunted houses, and the Fiends of Darkness reign, and ramp, there without controul. [24]

Puritan children at play

Home Alone in Colonial New England

For all the emphasis they placed on children and family life, the Puritans sometimes woefully neglected their little ones. This was due in part to their belief that any misfortune that came was by the design of God—sometimes as punishment for their sins. Never did it seem to occur to them that the misfortune was a result of their own neglect. When Cotton Mather's daughter Nanny was severely burned from falling into the fire, Mather lamented: "Alas, for my sins the just God throws my child into the fire." Some time later, two other daughters suffered painful burns. In this case his response was a sermon entitled, "What use ought parents to make of disasters befallen their children." On another occasion when his daughter Nibby was left home alone, he wrote in his diary that she would have burned to death if it had not been for "a person accidentally then passing by the window." Another family had a similar experience—this one ending in tragedy:

> After they had supped, the mother put two children to bed in the room where they themselves did lie, and they went out to visit a neighbor. When they returned...the mother [went] to the bed, and not finding her youngest child (a daughter about five years of age), and after much search she found it drowned in a well in her cellar....

The father, in this instance, blamed the death of the little girl on his having worked on the Sabbath. [25]

Naming a Child

Judge Samuel Sewall illustrates how religious faith and the Scriptures played a role in naming their children, as his diary entry after the christening of his daughter indicates:

> I named my little Daughter Sarah. Mr. Torrey said call her Sarah and make a Madam of her. I was struggling whether to call her Mehetible or Sarah. But when I saw Sarah's standing in the Scripture, viz: Peter, Galatians, Hebrews, Romans, I resolv'd on that suddenly. [26]

Pious Puritan Names

"Thankful"   "Sin Deny"   "Safe-on-High"   "Increase"

And then there were those **Barebones...**
"Praise God Barebones"
"Jesus Died For the Elect Only Barebones"
and
"If Thou Be Not Elected Thou Shalt Surely Be Damned Barebones"

Laziness and Original Sin

The Puritans taught their children early the value of hard work. There was no place for idleness in God's design for daily living. In the *Memoirs* of David and John Brainerd, missionaries to the Indians in

Puritan child-care aided by a go-cart

Colonial America, laziness in children was equated with original sin.

 The boy was taught that laziness was the worst form of original sin. Hence he must rise early and make himself useful before he went to school, must be diligent there in study, and promptly home to do "chores" at evening. His whole time out of school must be filled up with some service, such as bringing in fuel for the day, cutting potatoes for the sheep, feeding the swine, watering the horses, picking the berries, gathering the vegetables, spooling the yarn. He was expected never to be reluctant and not often tired. [27]

Wicked Little Children

The Puritans minced no words about the total depravity of the human heart, and children were not exempt. Story books reiterated the biblical warning that "the wages of sin is death," and that "there is none righteous, no not one." In James Janeway's *The Fairchild Family*, death scenes were common—and not just ordinary deaths. In one instance the Fairchild children, in punishment for their naughtiness, were taken to the gallows where they were forced to look at the body of a man hanged for his crime. Mr. Fairchild made no effort to spare their sensitivities as he turned it into a moral lesson for them to contemplate. But their own sinfulness is far deeper than outward naughtiness, as daughter Lucy's prayer illustrates:

My heart is so exceedingly wicked, so vile, so full of sin, that even when I appear to be tolerably good, even then I am sinning. When I am praying, or reading the Bible, or hearing other people read the Bible, even then I sin. When I speak, I sin; when I am silent, I sin. [28]

Sin in the Cradle

Rearing godly children began with discipline in the cradle, and parents who failed in this duty were setting the stage for incorrigible offspring, as one Puritan writer suggested:

> *The young child which lieth in the cradle is both wayward and full of affections; and though his body be but small, yet he hath a great heart, and is altogether inclined to evil.... If this sparkle be suffered to increase, it will rage and burn down the whole house.... Therefore parents must be wary and circumspect.... They must correct and sharply reprove their children for saying or doing ill.* [29]

Despairing Over the Young Generation

The Puritans, like Christians before and since, worried about their unruly youngsters and at times almost despaired of the hope for the next generation, as Henry Lawrence wrote in 1928:

Children playing on the Sabbath are drowned, from *Divine Examples of God's Severe Judgment Upon Sabbath Breakers,* 1671

> *The wild waywardness of the young generation seems to have been no less disturbing two or three centuries ago than it is today. The departures of youth from the standards established by age were a favorite subject of lamentation among the elders of early New England. And great calamity that befell from smallpox to Indian massacre, was obviously a sign of God's displeasure with the growing wickedness, especially that of the youngsters. If they were not rescued and brought back to the good old ways, the wrath of the Almighty was certain to explode in the near future, inflicting remarkable damage on old and young alike.*
>
> *"Do your children and family grow more godly?"* inquires a Puritan divine in 1657. *"I find greatest trouble and grief about the rising generation. Young people are little stirred here; but they strengthen one another in evil by example and by counsel. Much ado have I with my own family."* [30]

"Grown-up" Sins

The wayward youth—as raucous as they might be—were not the only ones in colonial New England straying into sin. The quarterly court records for Essex County, Massachusetts, from 1680 to 1682 show that even in this straight-laced Puritan community there was a problem with sexual immorality, anti-social behavior, and vice.[31]

Speeding Tickets in Old Boston

❧ *Speeding was a big problem in Old Boston—until the Selectmen established a fine of 3 shillings and 4 pence for galloping a horse inside the city limits.*[32]

Offense	Times Mentioned
Fornication	34
Debt	32
Drunkenness	18
Trespass	14
Theft	11
Beating Another (assault)	9
Breach of the Sabbath	6
Living Away from Wife	5
Lying	5
Swearing	5
Running Away from Master	4

Fatal Attraction in Colonial New England

Cotton Mather was not the type one would associate with a "fatal attraction" scenario. His stern glare and his frizzy white wig hardly gave him the appearance of a dashing and debonair ladies' man. Nor would his self-abasement ("loathing himself continually") tend to lend itself to ardent romance. But he was a respected minister and public servant, and Prudence Prynne was determined to snare him. She boldly declared her love to him barely two months after he had buried his first wife—his "Lovely Consort," who had given birth to their nine children. Prudence confessed in a letter her long-held affection for him and requested permission to visit him. Mather quickly recognized his attraction for this young woman half his age, but he feared it was temptation from the devil. Moreover, "Her reputation has been under some Disadvantage," he confided to his diary. "She has gott a bad Name among the Generality of the People." He, nevertheless, permitted her to visit him repeatedly—until the neighborhood gossip got back to him. Though smitten by her, he was determined not to risk his good reputation, as he painfully expressed in his diary:

❧ *I sett myself to make unto the Lord Jesus Christ, a Sacrifice of a Person, who, for many charming Accomplishments, has not many equals in the English America.... I struck my Knife into the Heart of my Sacrifice by a Letter to her mother."*

But Prudence and her mother were not so easily appeased. After a visit to Salem, he wrote:

❧ *In my absence, the young Gentlewoman to whom I have been so unkind many Weeks or Months ago, writes and comes to my Father, and brings her good Mother with her and charms the Neighbors into her Interests; and renews her Importunities that I would maker her mine.*

So alarmed was Mather that he went to Prudence and her mother and persuaded them "to furnish me with their Assertions, That I have never done any unworthy Thing; but acted most honorably and righteously toward them, as became a Christian, and a Minister." But only weeks later when Prudence "learned that her ex-lover was hot on the trail of a charming young widow, she burst into a jealous rage and threatened to relate in public the unedifying details of her recent relations with the godly widower." According to Mather, she threatened "that she will be a Thorn in my Side, and contrive all possible Wayes to vex me, affront me, disgrace me, in my Attempting a Return to the married state with another Gentlewoman." In August, eight months after the death of his first wife, Mather married his new love, an "irreproachable widow." He reestablished his reputation, and Prudence got lost in history. [33]

Cotton Mather

Christmastime in the Bay Colony

When the governor of Massachusetts, in December of 1722, made a motion in the Legislature to "Let us adjourn the Court over Christmas Day," pandemonium broke out. "One might suppose he had said, 'Let us set apart this day for the worship of the Devil.' Indeed, many a sturdy Puritan seems to have believed that Christmas was the Devil's own holiday." Celebrating Christmas was illegal in the Bay Colony, as the law of 1659 specified:

For preventing disorders arising in several places within this jurisdiction, by reason of some still observing such festivals as were superstitiously kept in others countries to the great dishonor of God and Offense of others; It is therefore ordained by this court and the authority thereof, that whosoever shall be found observing any such days as Christmas and the like, either by forbearing labor, feasting, or any other way upon any such account as aforesaid, every such person so offending shall pay for each such Offense, five shillings as a fine to the Country. [34]

Saturday Night Baths and Sunday Night Suppers

The Puritan family was bound together and regulated by a weekly routine that maintained the ebb and flow of life through good times and bad times. The Sabbath, of course, was the focal point of the week.

From the beginning of the New Englander's Sabbath, at sunset on Saturday evening, the housewife must have found that portion of sacred time anything but a period of rest. The Saturday evening meal must be hastened, that the dishes might be washed in secular time. Personal ablutions were held to be labor not unbefitting the holy day, and from the earliest times in the New England colonies, the Saturday evenings were devoted, first to an hour's catechizing, and then to the conscientious scrubbing…of each person in the family, beginning with the youngest and concluding with the oldest members of the household…. The house mistress had not only to see that all was in readiness for this great weekly ablution, but that none for whom she was responsible should escape it. Nothing but a case of severe illness was allowed to excuse any inmate of a self-respecting household…. It was fortunate for the madam that Puritan usage required that as little cooking as might be should be done on the Sabbath, for otherwise time and strength would both have failed her; but the sacred hours ended with the setting of the sun, and after this there was cooked and served the best meal of the week, which was made an occasion of real festivity, and enjoyed with keen zest imparted by long anticipation…. During this privileged time after the "Sunday night supper," the young folks separated into groups, unrebuked by their elders. The children played games, elderly men talked of theological dogmas, politics and crops, and women of their household employments and clothes. [35]

Broken Marriages and Hurting Children: The Wesley Family Woes

The Wesley family is a painful example of how Christian family life sometimes goes awry. Susanna and Samuel Wesley had a rocky marriage, and their children fared little better in their own relationships. Yet, out of this "dysfunctional" family came two boys who grew up and made a profound impact on society and spiritual values. The story of the Wesleys extends far beyond one isolated family.

It is a story for all generations that tells the struggle of one family in its efforts to live above the standards of a decaying and decadent society all around them. And in many ways their story reflects the good and the bad side of eighteenth-century life in England. The era of the Wesleys is critical in the history of Christian family life because it spans the period of the societal upheaval known as the Industrial Revolution—an era that had profound effects on the family that continue to the present day. The rise of industrialism turned the once cohesive family into a fractured unit of related people who struggled to maintain a livelihood often separated by space and time and varying interests and responsibilities. This was the Wesleyan era.

> *John Wesley grew up in a world of rapid change, very much like ours in some respects and very different in others. The whole way of work was changing in eighteenth-century England. Revolutions in smelting, spinning, and distilling created whole new industries. The world of science was unfolding—the first chemical tables, the first comprehensive biological classification system, the first experiments with the physics of electricity, of photographic materials, and the steam engine, emerged during Wesley's life. Meanwhile, the cities collected the debris of society. Poverty, gin, and filthy living conditions in the city contrasted with the refined life of the new city gentry and new country gentry.... Instead of welfare or any other relief for the poor, the government gave punishment for the crime of poverty—confinement to a work house.... Personal health and cleanliness were deplorable. The plague, smallpox, and countless diseases we call minor today had no cures.* [1]

A Lost Generation of Children

How society treats its children is a revealing reflection on the society itself, and in this realm eighteenth-century England did not fare well.

A scene depicting the debauchery in England

❧ *Nowhere is the hope of a people more unmistakably or more creatively expressed than in its protection, nurture and guidance of the Kingdom of Childhood: how then fared children in this age of "expiring hopes"? Their death rate tells its own tragic tale…. In the period immediately preceding the Great Revival three out of four of all children born of all classes, died before their fifth birthday…. Years earlier, Thomas Coram, agitating for the establishment of the Foundling Hospital, had referred to the large numbers of "exposed" children, and declared that he had himself witnessed "the shocking spectacle of innocent children who had been murdered, and thrown on dunghills…. The few who survive are generally turned "into the streets to beg or steal"—some being "blinded, or maimed and distorted in their limbs, in order to move pity," thus becoming "fitter instruments of gain" to "vile, merciless wretches…." The incredible bestialities practiced in the earlier half of the eighteenth century upon friendless children become more understandable when it is remembered that this was par excellence "the Gin Age" of English history…. During the national "orgy of spirit drinking" (1720–51), crude gin was being sold from thousands of rimy dens [for] a penny a pint.* [2]

An Era of Darkness without Light

✿ *A new century [the 1700s] was dawning but it seemed as if in the spiritual sky of England the very light of Christianity was being turned by some strange and evil force into darkness.* [3]

William Fitchett

A Godless Society

Christian moralists in every age fear that theirs is the most evil age ever. So it was in the age of the Wesleys.

> In 1738, the year of Wesley's "conversion," Bishop Berkeley in his Discourse Addressed to Magistrates and Men in Authority, *declared that morality and religion in Britain had collapsed* "to a degree that has never been known in any Christian country." "Our prospect," he averred, "is very terrible and the symptoms grow worse from day to day. The accumulating torrent of evil, "which threatens a general inundation and destruction of these realms," Berkeley attributed chiefly to "the irreligion and bad example of those . . . styled the better sort." Then, pleading with all State officials to mend their ways and consider well the future of their country, he continued: "The youth born and brought up in wicked times with any bias to good from early principle, or instilled opinions, when they grow ripe, must be monsters indeed. And it is to be feared that the age of monsters is not far off." [4]

A Godly Heritage

One of the factors that paved the way for John and Charles Wesley to become great Christian leaders in the church and in society was their godly heritage. In a godless society around them, they could draw strength from their own ancestry of Christian values. Bartholomew Wesley was their great grandfather, born in 1599, and educated at Oxford in medicine and divinity. He served as a faithful and plain-speaking vicar in rural Anglican parishes, but was "driven from his living immediately after the Restoration," though he continued "preaching whenever a safe opportunity presented itself."

Bartholomew's son John (the grandfather of John and Charles) followed his father into the ministry, where he faced even greater opposition. While he was still at Oxford, he formed a "gathered church" separate from the Church of England. His continued association with dissenters forced his resignation from his Anglican parish, but he could not be silenced. He was plagued by "terrible temptations about fulfilling his call to preach the Gospel." As a result he was "four times cast into prison." "His manifold and heavy trials,—all the result of his unflinching adherence of the testimony which he held,—soon prepared him for an early grave." One of his sons was Samuel—the Reverend Samuel Wesley, the father of John and Charles.

On their mother's side, their grandfather was Dr. Samuel Annesley, the son of the Reverend John Annesley and his wife Judith. "From the moment of his birth, his parents, in solemn vows and prayers, had consecrated him to the Lord 'for the work of the ministry.' " Like their ancestors on their father's side, Samuel Annesley was a Dissenter, and for that he suffered greatly, but when political tensions eased he became a well-known and highly respected leader of the Puritans—sometimes referred to as "a second Saint Paul." [5]

THE EPWORTH WESLEY FAMILY

NAME	BIRTHPLACE	BORN	DIED
Samuel Wesley, Sr.	Whitchurch	late in 1662	4/25/1735
Susanna	London	1/20/1669	7/23/1742
Children			
1. Samuel, Jr.	London	2/10/1690	11/6/1739
2. Susanna	South Ormsby	1691	4/1693
3. Emilia (Harper)	South Ormsby	1/1692	1771
4. Annesley } twins	South Ormsby	1694	1/31/1695
5. Jedediah	South Ormsby	1694	1/31/1695
6. Susanna (Ellison)	South Ormsby	1695	12/7/1764
7. Mary (Whitelamb)	South Ormsby	1696	11/1734
8. Mehetabel (Wright)	Epworth	1697	3/21/1750
9. Not known whether boy or girl	Epworth	1698	soon died
10. John	Epworth	5/18/1699	soon died
11. Benjamin	Epworth	1700	soon died
12. & 13. Unnamed twins	Epworth	5/17/1701	soon died
14. Anne (Lambert)	Epworth	1702	?
15. John	Epworth	6/17/1703	3/2/1791
16. Son smothered by nurse	Epworth	5/8/1705	5/30/1705
17. Martha (Hall)	Epworth	5/8/1706	7/19/1791
18. Charles	Epworth	12/18/1707	3/29/1788
19. Kezziah	Epworth	3/1709	3/9/1741

The Wesley family birth and death record

"Cheaper by the Dozen"

Susanna, "the mother of the Wesleys," would be completely forgotten today were it not for the fact that two of her sons grew up to be famous and that she personally had such a significant role in their godly upbringing. But they were only two out of nineteen children that she bore in twenty-one years (including two sets of twins)—though a mere nine of them survived to adulthood. Today that many children in one family seems like a remarkable feat, but in an age before birth control was widely accepted or easily accessible, nineteen births was not so unusual.

And the fact that she was reared in a family of twenty-four children—"a quarter of a hundred"—may have made her large brood seem less remarkable, though her father was married twice, and her own mother apparently gave birth to only twenty-three of the twenty-four children. [6]

Pain in Childbearing

Susanna Wesley was delivered of all her babies by a midwife. We know that Samuel Jr.'s birth was a difficult one and that Charles came prematurely, but other than that we know nothing of Susanna's many accouchments. Her husband Samuel, in a letter to the archbishop, lists among his misfortunes "one child at least per annum and my wife sick for half that time." We must remember in this connection that at that time asepsis and anesthesia were unknown. [7]

Rebecca Lamar Harmon

Eighteenth-Century Marital Code

The eighteenth-century jurist Sir William Blackstone summarized the marital legal code of his day by quipping: "the husband and wife are one, and the husband is that one." [8]

Beyond the Honeymoon

Susanna and Samuel met when she was a young girl and Samuel, seven years her senior, was visiting her home to talk religion with her father. Samuel quickly recognized her interest in spiritual matters, and some years later when she was twenty, they married. Though they were both very strong-willed individuals, their early years of marriage were apparently graced with harmony—as long as Susanna accepted her proper place in the hierarchy of their marriage. Early in their marriage, Samuel alluded to his view of headship in a love poem about his wife—a poem that ends with an amazing testimony of mutuality:

The Epworth rectory where John and Charles grew up

> *She graced my humble roof, and blest my life,*
> *Blest me by a far greater name than wife;*
> *Yet still I bore an undisputed sway,*
> *Nor wasn't her task, but pleasure, to obey….*
> *Nor did I for her care ungrateful prove,*
> *But only used my power to show my love.*
> *Whate'er she asked I gave, without reproach or grudge,*
> *For still she reason asked, and I was judge;*
> *All my commands, requests at her fair hands,*
> *And her requests to me were all commands.* [9]

Strong Wills and Marital Breakdown

Samuel's poetic testimony of marriage bliss was not a reality behind the closed doors of the church rectory—at least as he and Susanna progressed into the second decade of their marriage. The most publicized marital spat occurred one evening during family prayers when Susanna refused to say "amen" to Samuel's prayer for the king. William of Orange was widely considered a usurper of the throne of the Stuart line of royalty, and Susanna expressed her political opinion through silence on this occasion. Since William had been on the throne during the entire span of their decade-long marriage, Samuel should not have been surprised. But the issue went beyond politics to that of wifely submission. So outraged was he that he put their marriage on the line: "We must part, for if we have two kings we must have two beds." Then, according to Susanna, "he immediately kneeled down and imprecated the divine vengeance upon himself and all his posterity if ever he touched me more or came into a bed with me before I had begged God's pardon and his, for not saying amen to the prayer for the King."

Samuel left home, and Susanna was philosophical: "I am more easy in the thought of parting because I think we are not likely to live happily together." She was convinced that he, not she, was in the wrong:

The Reverend Samuel Wesley

> *I have successfully represented to him the unlawfulness and unreasonableness of his Oath; that the Man in that case has no more power over his own body than the Woman over hers; that since I am willing to let him quietly enjoy his opinions, he ought not to deprive me of my little liberty of conscience.*

Samuel finally returned home after King William III fell off his horse and died and Queen Anne ascended the throne. Since he and Susanna were no longer divided politically and he could assume that she would say "amen" to his prayers for the queen, he could go to bed with her without losing face—and that is apparently exactly what he did. Nine months later came the birth of John, referred to as "the child of his parents' reconciliation." [10]

A Brand from the Fire

John Wesley became a legend among his followers in England before he died, and the one account of his life that was most repeated was the story of the fire in the Epworth rectory and the miraculous rescue of five-year-old John—the illustration of which was widely distributed and "hung up in many a collier's home." The night of the fire made an impression John would never forget as he later recorded in his journal:

> *This was a Thursday night, February 9, 1709, I believe between 11:00 and midnight, which completely destroyed the building. All were quickly evacuated except for me. As my rescue came none too soon, I have frequently thought of myself (to use those words of the*

prophets) as a "brand plucked from the burning." From that moment on, my mother seemed to take special pains to see that I was wholly committed to God. [11]

Susanna's Method of Child Discipline

Susanna was convinced that rearing a large brood of children required very strict discipline—especially considering the evil influences that were present in every aspect of eighteenth-century English life. She wrote out her rules for posterity, at her son John's request, ten years before she died:

Young John Wesley rescued from the Epworth house fire

The children were always put into a regular method of living, in such things as they were capable of, from their birth; as in dressing, undressing, changing their linen, and so on.... When turned a year old (and some before), they were taught to fear the rod and to cry softly; by which means they escaped abundance of correction they might otherwise have had; and that most odious noise of the crying of children was rarely heard in the house.... As soon as they were grown pretty strong, they were confined to three meals a day.... They were never suffered to choose their meat, but always made to eat such things as were provided for the family.... In order to form the minds of children, the first thing to be done is to conquer their will and bring them to an obedient temper.... The children of this family were taught, as soon as they could speak, the Lord's Prayer, which they were made to say at rising and bedtime constantly, to which as they grew bigger, were added a short prayer for their parents and some collects; a short catechism and some portion of Scripture, as their memories could bear. They were very early made to distinguish the Sabbath from other days, before they could well speak or go.... They were quickly made to understand they might have nothing they cried for and instructed to speak handsomely for what they wanted. [12]

Susanna's Methods of Home Schooling

Susanna, as her letters attest, was well educated. Her father recognized her intelligence and eagerness to learn, and readily took on the challenge of educating her himself. She, in turn, was determined that her children would also enjoy a good education, which in that era offered no alternative but to teach them herself.

Susanna Wesley, the home-school teacher

None of them were taught to read till five years old, except Kezzy…. The day before a child began to learn, the house was set in order, everyone's work appointed them, and a charge given that none should come into the room from nine till twelve, or from two till five, which, you know, were our school hours. One day was allowed the child wherein to learn its letters…. Samuel… learned the alphabet in a few hours… and as soon as he knew the letters, began at the first chapter of Genesis. He was taught to spell the first verse, then to read it over and over, till he could read it offhand without any hesitation, so on to the second, and so on, till he took ten verses for a lesson, which he quickly did…. There was no such thing as loud talking or playing allowed of; but everyone was kept close to his business for the six hours of school: and it is almost incredible what a child may be taught in a quarter of a year by a vigorous application. [13]

A Private Audience with Mother

Time alone for parent and child is difficult in a big family, but Susanna was well-organized, and private time was a high priority for her: "On Monday, I talk with Molly; on Tuesday with Hetty; Wednesday with Nancy; Thursday with Jacky; Friday with Patty; Saturday with Charles; and with Emily and Suky together on Sunday." [14]

Susanna's Commitment to Her Children

No one can, without renouncing the world, in the most literal sense, observe my method; and there are few, if any, that would entirely devote above twenty years of the prime of life in hopes to save the souls of their children, which they think may be saved without so much ado; for that was my principal intention, however unskillfully and unsuccessfully managed. [15]

Susanna Wesley

A Mother of Missionaries

When Governor Oglethorpe of the Georgia Colony asked John Wesley if he would be willing to come to the New World as a missionary to the Indians, John replied that his father had recently died and he felt obligated to care for his mother. Oglethorpe persisted, asking if he would come if his mother consented. John agreed, but dreaded going home to ask his mother. Her response was classic:

"Yes, John, you may go. If I had twenty sons I should be glad to have them all so engaged, though I should never see them more." With her blessing, both John and Charles served as missionaries though, unfortunately, with little success. [16]

The Pain of Waiting for Marriage

Emilia Wesley, John's oldest sister, who was later abandoned by her husband, wrote a letter of advice to her little brother—advice on love and marriage, based on her own experience:

Susanna preaching to Epworth parishioners

> *Whether you will be engaged before thirty or not I cannot determine; but if my advice is worth listening to, never engage your affections before your worldly affairs are in such posture that you may marry very soon.... Were I to live my time over again and had the same experience I have now, were it for the best man in England I would not wait one year. I know you are a young man encompassed with difficulties that has passed through many hardships already...but believe me, if you ever come to suffer the torment of a hopeless love all other afflictions will seem small in comparison of it. [17]*

Romantic Love

Customs, beliefs, and feelings about romantic love have changed over the course of Western history, and, as historian Harry Stout points out, the eighteenth century was pivotal.

> *Historians have identified the mid-eighteenth century as the crucial point of transition in which a new culture of romantic love began to replace traditional matrimony determined by community and parental involvement. The same forces of mobility and marketplace anonymity that were transforming religion and creating an unprecedented focus on the self were transforming the family and relations between the sexes. "Falling in love" was becoming to marriage and the family what being "born again" was to religion and the church. In both cases, the experience was intensely subjective and personal, transcending understanding and rationality and appealing to the passions for corroboration and "assurance." Trends begun in the 1750s continued into the nineteenth century, leading to the triumph of Victorian sentimentalism in the family and of highly emotional "great revival" in Anglo-American evangelical Protestantism. Both were expressions of the same transformations. With the public square increasingly devoid of extended family, community, and national churches, the private self and its experience became the locus of meaning. [18]*

John Wesley's "Unholy Desire"

In 1737, just a year after he arrived in Georgia to serve as a missionary to the colonists and the native Americans, John Wesley, then thirty-four years old, was suddenly consumed by "an unholy desire." Her name was Sophy Hopkey, the wealthy eighteen-year-old niece of Savannah's leading magistrate. To Wesley, she was a young woman whose "soul appeared to be wholly made up of mildness, gentleness, long-suffering," and who professed to be a devout Christian. Sophy's aunt and uncle were eager for a relationship between her and Wesley to develop, so as to divert her attention from another suitor, whose criminal record distressed them. Wesley was hesitant to declare his love, but apparently did make more than one feeble marriage proposal to her. He later vacillated, however, convinced that he was "not strong enough to bear the complicated temptations of a married state."

During his months of vacillation, Sophy became impatient, and agreed to marry another man who had suddenly appeared in her life. Wesley opposed the marriage, but to no avail. The couple eloped to South Carolina to be married, without the customary publishing of banns. The groom was not a regular churchgoer, and Sophy's attendance became sporadic. When Wesley denied her communion, she and her husband sued him on the grounds that he had defamed her and denied her the Lord's Supper. Wesley initially defended himself, but then concluded the time was right for him to move on. "The hour has come for me to fly for my life," he confided to his journal; "and as soon as evening prayers were over, about eight o'clock, the tide then serving, I shook off the dust of my feet, and left Georgia...." [19]

"I Went to the Garden of Love"

 I went to the Garden of Love
And saw what I never had seen:
A Chapel was built in the midst,
Where I used to play on the green.

And the gates of the Chapel were shut,
And "Thou shalt not" writ over the door;
So I turned to the Garden of Love
That so many sweet flowers bore;

And I saw it was filled with graves
And tomb-stones where flowers should be;
And priests in black gowns were walking their rounds,
And binding with briars my joys and desires.

William Blake, *Songs of Experience* (1794)

John Wesley's Heart-Breaking Love Triangle

Twelve years after his "love affair" with Sophy Hopkey, John Wesley was once again "in love"— this time with Grace Murray, a Methodist class leader. Robert Tuttle has pieced together the story of heartbreak from Wesley's diaries and journals:

Charles Wesley and his wife Sally

On Monday, July 24, 1749, Grace Murray and I, along with the rest of our company, returned to Bristol, having just completed my third journey into Ireland…. It must have been then that some of the women, apparently jealous of the close relationship between Grace and myself, sought (and not without some success) to cast doubt in her mind concerning my attachment…which caused Grace to renew her correspondence with Mr. Bennett….

On August 23 we left London, arriving in Epworth three days later, where Grace again met John Bennett. I interviewed him myself. I could readily see that Grace would force my hand. On September 6, having reached Newcastle, I asked her plainly: "Which will you choose?" Her reply: "I am determined by conscience, as well as inclination, to live and die with you." Thinking the matter settled, we both wrote to Mr. Bennett the next day…. My letter to Mr. Bennett was misdirected, but a copy was sent to my brother in Bristol, who quickly journeyed to Leeds, where he was informed by two (who should have known better), however innocently, that Grace was engaged to Bennett and that I was resolved to marry a woman who was already promised to another…. He left Whitehaven on September 28, journeyed to Hindley Hill, where he found Grace, and took her back to Newcastle. I arrived at Hindley Hill (having lost my way) two hours later. I need add no more, than that if I had more regard for her I loved than for the work of God I should now have gone straight to Newcastle, and not back to Whitehaven. I knew this was giving up all…. On October 3, my brother succeeded in persuading two bewildered, half-reluctant persons to marry…. Instead of preventing me from *marrying one betrothed to another, he had coerced poor John Bennett (who was perhaps the innocent party) into marrying the one promised to me....*

Thurs. [October] 5.—About eight, one came in from Newcastle, and told us, "They were married on Tuesday." My brother came an hour after. I felt no anger, yet I did not desire to see him. But Mr. Whitefield constrained me. After a few words had passed, he accosted me with, "I renounce all intercourse with you, but what I would have with an heathen man or a publican." I felt little emotion. It was only adding a drop of water to a drowning man, yet I calmly accepted his renunciation, and acquiesced therein. Poor Mr. Whitefield and John Nelson burst into tears. They prayed, cried, and entreated, till the storm passed away. We could not speak, but only fell on each other's neck.

J[ohn] B[ennett] then came in. Neither of us could speak, but we kissed each other and wept. [20]

John Wesley's Troubled Marriage

A little more than a year after his muddled love affair with Grace, John Wesley was again determined to get married. This time it was the widowed Molly Vazeille, and fearing Charles' interference again, they married without giving notice according to Methodist rules. The marriage quickly soured. Molly, who had been married to a London merchant, was used to more material wealth than John could provide, and John was not willing to alter his heavy travel schedule. They lived together "only occasionally" for the next two decades, and then Molly moved to Newcastle to live with her married daughter—"never to return." John's response: "I did not desert her; I did not send her away; I will never recall her." [21]

Daughters of Desolation

The Wesley daughters fared no better in their marriages than did their famous brother. Despite the sacrificial efforts of their mother to bring them up properly, they made very poor choices in their relationships. All the godly home-schooling lessons in the world could not overcome the marital discord they observed in the home, and one after another their own relationships went awry.

Emilia was the oldest daughter, and she deeply resented her father, lashing out at him in letters to her brothers and blaming him for the "intolerable want and affliction" the family faced financially. She did not marry until she was in her forties, and when she did, it was a

Susanna Wesley

poor choice. Her husband abandoned her and their small child a few years after their marriage.

Susanna, the second daughter to survive to adulthood, married a man whom her mother described as "little inferior to the apostate angels in wickedness." Their marriage lasted long enough to produce four children, but eventually they separated.

Hetty, the fourth daughter, ran away with a man who falsely promised to marry her. Having "ruined" her reputation, she hurriedly married a man she hardly knew, probably "to legitimize a baby she was expecting in less than four months." Her husband became a heavy drinker and treated her cruelly, and she had a miserable life with him.

Martha, the second to the youngest of the daughters, married a minister who was highly recommended by her brothers. They had ten children before he ran off to the West Indies with a mistress.

Kezzy, the youngest of the girls, never married, but she "was no less pathetic a figure than most of her sisters." After a painful love affair with a scoundrel who later married her sister Martha, she fell in love with a man and became engaged. But Kezzy became ill and died at the age of thirty-two before they were able to marry. [22]

Second-Guessing Mother Wesley's Conversion

When was Susanna Wesley converted? Apparently she did not have a life-changing emotional experience in youth that is characteristic of the evangelical conversion experience, but as an adult she repeatedly reaffirmed her faith in God, and through her ministry there was a revival in the parish during her husband's absence. Despite her spiritual depth, however, her sons did not regard her truly converted until three years before her death at the age of seventy when she finally came under the saving influence of "Methodism." This was a deeply flawed perspective, according to a nineteenth-century Wesley biographer:

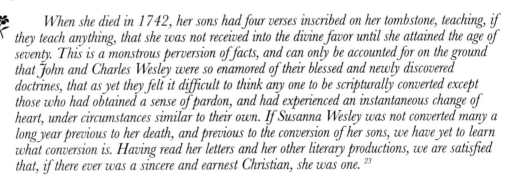

When she died in 1742, her sons had four verses inscribed on her tombstone, teaching, if they teach anything, that she was not received into the divine favor until she attained the age of seventy. This is a monstrous perversion of facts, and can only be accounted for on the ground that John and Charles Wesley were so enamored of their blessed and newly discovered doctrines, that as yet they felt it difficult to think any one to be scripturally converted except those who had obtained a sense of pardon, and had experienced an instantaneous change of heart, under circumstances similar to their own. If Susanna Wesley was not converted many a long year previous to her death, and previous to the conversion of her sons, we have yet to learn what conversion is. Having read her letters and her other literary productions, we are satisfied that, if there ever was a sincere and earnest Christian, she was one. [23]

Susanna Wesley's Epitaph

HERE LIES THE BODY
OF
MRS. SUSANNA WESLEY
YOUNGEST AND LAST SURVIVING
DAUGHTER
OF DR. SAMUEL ANNESLEY.

In sure and steadfast hope to rise,
And claim her mansion in the skies,
A Christian here her flesh laid down,
The cross exchanging for a crown.

True daughter of affliction, she,
Inured to pain and misery,
Mourn'd a long night of griefs and fears,
A legal night of seventy years.

The Father then reveal'd His Son,
Him in the broken bread made known;
She knew and felt her sins forgiven,
And found the earnest of her heaven.

Meet for the fellowship above,
She heard the call, "Arise, My love!"
"I come!" her dying looks replied,
And lamb-like as her Lord, she died. [24]

"A Whimsical Epitaph"

John Wesley began publishing *The Arminian Magazine* in 1778, which became a popular magazine among his followers—in part because of the humorous and light-hearted items it sometimes contained. The following is an example:

> *To be jocular in death is preposterous; nor is it less-so to inscribe low jests on the Monuments of the dead. We insert the following as a remarkable instance of this sort of buffoonery, found, in a country Church-yard, on the tombstone of one Katharine Gray, who in her lifetime had been a dealer in earthen-ware.*
>
> *To understand this ridiculous piece, you are to follow the letters, till they make up a word; not regarding whether they be great or small; nor how they are divided or pointed.*

Solution to "A Whimsical Epitaph"

Beneath this stone lies Katharine Gray,
chang'd from a busy life to lifeless clay.

By earth and clay she got her pelf,
and now she's turn'd to earth herself.

Ye weeping friends let me advise,
abate your grief and dry your eyes.

For what avails a flood of tears;
who knows but in a run of years,
in some tall pitcher or broad pan,
she in her shop may be again. [25]

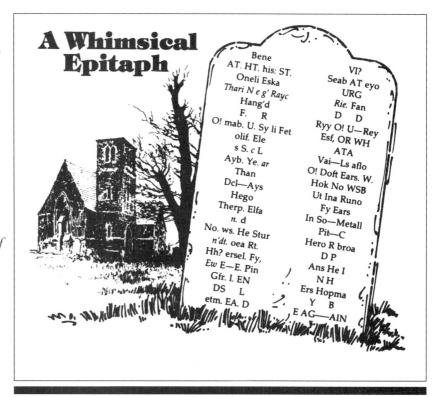

Until Death Do Us Part

John Wesley throughout his adult life was married to his ministry as Sophy, Grace, and Molly were painfully aware and he maintained his active preaching schedule until he died at eighty-eight. What was the secret of his longevity? He offered the following reflections on his eighty-fifth birthday:

First, doubtless to the power of God, fitting me for the work to which I am called, as long as He pleases to continue me therein; and, next, subordinately to this, to the prayers of His children. May we not impute it as inferior means,

1. To my constant exercise and change of air?

2. To my never having lost a night's sleep, sick or well, at land or at sea, since I was born?

3. To my having slept at command so that whenever I feel myself almost worn out I call it and it comes, day or night?

4. To my having constantly, for about sixty years, risen at four in the morning?

5. To my constant preaching at five in the morning for above fifty years?

6. To my having had so little pain in my life; and so little sorrow, or anxious care?

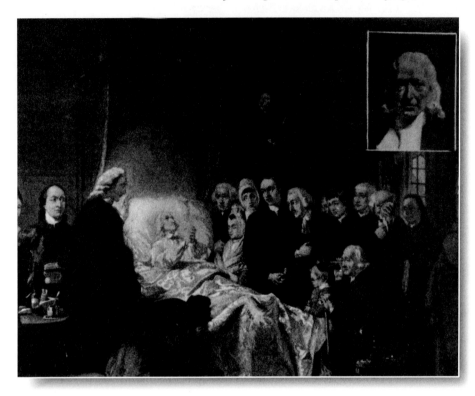

John Wesley on his deathbed

The day after his birthday was Sunday, and he maintained his regular preaching schedule, with three sermons at three different locations: "At eight I preached at Misterton, as usual; about one to a numerous congregation at Newby, near Haxey; and about four at my old stand in Epworth market place, to the great congregation." [26]

Nobody Knows the Trouble I've Seen: Slave Family Struggles

CHAPTER

African-American slave families were sometimes barely families at all. Family members were often cruelly separated, never to see each other again. Slave women were raped by their masters, and slave men were accused of rape when they were innocent. It was a life of trials and hardship. Yet, there are amazing examples of strong family bonds—bonds of love that challenge both black and white families today who may be struggling against the evils of an oppressive system that works against close family ties. But the single most important factor that sustained many of these slave families was their Christian faith. Although the Bible was turned into a tool of repression by the masters—not only to defend the institution of slavery in general but to enforce specific servile behaviors—slaves nevertheless found true Christianity to be a liberating force in their personal and family lives.

Slave Living Conditions

Sometimes slave families were fortunate enough to live in houses with floors and roofs that did not leak, but very often the living conditions were not fit for human beings. Josiah Henson, who grew up as a slave in Maryland, gives a graphic description of the housing provided free of charge on the plantation:

A slave cabin on a Southern plantation

❧ *We lodged in log huts, and on the bare ground. Wooden floors were an unknown luxury. In a single room were huddled, like cattle, ten or a dozen persons, men, women, and children. All ideas of refinement and decency were, of course, out of the question.*

159

There were neither bedsteads, nor furniture of any description. Our beds were collections of straw and old rags, thrown down in the corners and boxed in with boards; a single blanket the only covering.... The wind whistled and the rain and snow blew in through the cracks, and the damp earth soaked in the moisture till the floor was as miry as a pig sty. Such were our houses. In these wretched hovels were we penned at night, and fed by day; here were the children born and the sick neglected. [1]

Surviving the System through Family Ties

For slaves, family ties offered an escape from the oppression of everyday life, and families were often brought closer together by their struggle for survival.

     The family, while it had no legal existence in slavery, was in actuality one of the most important survival mechanisms for the slave. In his family he found companionship, love, sexual gratification, sympathetic understanding of his sufferings; he learned how to avoid punishment, to cooperate with other blacks, and to maintain his self-esteem. However frequently the family was broken, it was primarily responsible for the slave's ability to survive on the plantation without becoming totally dependent on and submissive to his master. . . . The rearing of children was one of the most important of these [traditional family] functions. Since slave parents were primarily responsible for training their children, they could cushion the shock of bondage for them, help them to understand their situation, teach them values different from those their masters tried to instill in them, and give them a referent for self-esteem other than their master. [2]

Slave Songs and Spirituals

Many of the slave songs and spirituals were plaintive cries to God for help and understanding—often sung in the first person, as in the well-known spiritual, "Nobody knows the trouble I've seen; nobody knows but Jesus." Biblical themes and characters became part of the slave struggles as in "Roll, Jordan, Roll," and "Go Down Moses." Allusions to family were also common, sometimes in a generic sense as in "Sometimes I Feel Like a Motherless Child," but frequently family and friends were referred to by name.

     [Negro spirituals] were composed in the fields, in the kitchen, at the loom, in the cabin at night, and were inspired by some sad or awe-inspiring event. The death of a beloved one, even one of the master's family, the hardness of a master or his cruelty, the selling of friends or relatives, and the heart-rending separations, a camp-meeting, a great revival, the sadness and loneliness of old age—...any of these might be sources of inspiration.

The pain and anguish of the present—especially the heartbreak of family separation—was alleviated only by the powerful hope of reuniting again in the life hereafter:

A slave auction notice "Negroes for Sale"

♪ *When we all meet in Heaven,*
There is no parting there;
When we all meet in Heaven,
There is no more parting there.
See wives and husbands sold apart,
Their children's screams will break my heart—
There's a better day a coming,
Will you go along with me?
There's a better day a coming,
God sound the jubilee. [3]

Slave Family Separations

The slave auction was the most dreaded ordeal a slave family endured. Many masters sought to keep families together, but no family was safe from the terror of being separated by a bill of sale—never to be reunited again. One of the most heart-rending testimonies is Father Henson's early recollections of his mother's indescribable anguish:

My brothers and sisters were bid off first, and one by one, while my mother, paralyzed by grief, held me by the hand. Her turn came, and she was bought by Isaac Riley of Montgomery County. Then I was offered to the assembled purchasers. My mother, half distracted with the thought of parting forever from all her children, pushed through the crowd, while the bidding for me was going on, to the spot where Riley was standing. She fell at his feet, and clung to his knees entreating him in tones that a mother only could command, to buy her baby as well as herself, and spare to her one, at least, of her little ones. Will it, can it be believed that this man, thus appealed to, was capable not merely of turning a deaf ear to her supplication, but of disengaging himself from her with such violent blows and kicks, as to reduce her to the necessity of creeping out of his reach, and mingling the groan of bodily suffering with the sob of a breaking heart? As she crawled away from the brutal man I heard her sob out, "Oh, Lord Jesus, how long, how long shall I suffer this way!" I must have been then between five and six years old. I seem to see and hear my poor weeping mother now. This was one of my earliest observations of men; an experience which I only shared with thousands of my race, the bitterness of which to any individual who suffers it cannot be diminished by the frequency of its recurrence, while it is dark enough to overshadow the whole after-life with something blacker than a funeral pall. [4]

A Want Ad for a Runaway Mother

Emeline Chapman's escape on the Underground Railroad from Washington D.C. to Syracuse was not prompted because of the hard work and poor living conditions of slavery, but rather the fear of separation. She had learned that she was about to be sold on the auction block, and the horror of being separated from her babies gave her no other choice, she was convinced, than to run—leaving behind her husband and her older children. The anguish of this separation is related in a letter written from one official of the Underground Railroad to another, who refers to her by her alias Susan Bell:

Syracuse, Oct. 5, 1856

Dear Friend Still:—I write to you for Mrs. Susan Bell, who was at your city some time in September last. She is from Washington city. She left her dear little children behind (two children). She is stopping in our city, and wants to hear from her children very much indeed…. She wants to know if Mr. Biglow has heard anything about her husband. If you have not written to Mr. Biglow, she wishes you would. She sends her love to you and your dear family. She says that you were all kind to her, and she does not forget it. You will direct your letter to me, dear brother, and I will see that she gets it. [5]

$300 REWARD

~

<u>RAN AWAY</u> from the subscriber on Saturday, the 30th of August, 1856, my <u>SERVANT WOMAN</u>, named <u>EMELINE CHAPMAN</u>, about 25 years of age; quite dark, slender built, speaks short, and stammers some; with two children, one a female about two and a half years old; the other a male, seven or eight months old, bright color. I will give the above reward if they are delivered to me in Washington.

Mrs. Emily Thompson Capitol Hill, Washington, D.C.

The slave auction block

The Farewell of a Virginia Slave Mother

*Gone, gone—sold and gone,
   To the rice-swamp dank and lone. . . .
From Virginia's hills and waters,—
   Woe is me, my stolen daughters!*

*Gone, gone—sold and gone,
   To the rice-swamp dank and lone.
There no mother's eye is near them,
   There no mother's ear can hear them;*

Never, when the torturing lash
    Seams their back with many a gash
Shall a mother's kindness bless them,
    Or a mother's arms caress them. . . .

Gone, gone—sold and gone,
    To the rice-swamp dank and lone.
By the holy love He beareth—
    By the bruised reed He spareth—
Oh, may He, to whom alone
    All their cruel wrongs are known,
Still their hope and refuge prove,
    With a more than a mother's love,
Gone, gone—sold and gone,
    To the rice-swamp dank and lone,
From Virginia's hills and waters,—
    Woe is me, my stolen daughters. [6]

John Greenleaf Whittier

A Brother's Anguish for His Sister

When he was a youth, Austin Steward witnessed the cruel beating of his sister by an overseer, and later in life expressed the pain and guilt that he had endured on that occasion.

The God of heaven only knows the conflict of feeling I then endured; He alone witnessed the tumult of my heart, at this outrage of manhood and kindred affection. God knows that my will was good enough to have wrung his neck; or to have drained from his heartless system its last drop of blood! And yet I was obliged to turn a deaf ear to her cries for assistance which to this day ring in my ears. Strong and athletic as I was, no hand of mine could be raised in her defense, but at the peril of both our lives. [7]

A runaway slave trying to protect his family

No Roots

The horrors of slavery were nowhere more graphically described than in *Uncle Tom's Cabin* by Harriet Beecher Stowe, the "little woman" who Lincoln credited for starting the Civil War. The book sold some 300,000 copies in its first year of publication and a million copies before the war even began. Stowe wrote about the poor living conditions and the inhuman treatment of slaves, but the theme that seemed to grip her the most was the breakup of families. She herself had grown up in a minister's home, the daughter of the famous Lyman Beecher, and the sister of one of the nineteenth century's most celebrated preachers, Henry Ward Beecher. Family ties were strong, and her own seven children grew up knowing exactly who they were and what their family heritage was. Not so with Topsy, one of Stowe's memorable characters, whose new mistress inquired about her family.

Harriet Beecher Stowe and title page of *Uncle Tom's Cabin*

> Sitting down before her, she began to question her. "How old are you, Topsy?" "Dunno, Missis," said the image, with a grin that showed all her teeth. "Don't know how old you are? Didn't anybody ever tell you? Who was your mother?" "Never had none!" said the child with another grin. "Never had any mother? What do you mean? Where were you born?" "Never was born!" persisted Topsy, with another grin.... "You mustn't answer me in that way, child; I'm not playing with you. Tell me where you were born, and who your father and mother were." "Never was born," reiterated the creature, more emphatically; "never had no father nor mother, nor nothin'. I was raised by a speculator, with lots of others. Old Aunt Sue used to take care of us...." [8]

A Letter from a Slave Mother to a Free Daughter

> *Warton, Warton County, March 13, '59*
>
> *My Dear Daughter, Your very kind and affectionate letters dated at St. Louis, One in January the other in February has been received and contents partickularly notist, I had them read often creating in me both Sorrow and Joy. Joy that you were living & a doing wel so far as the*

comforts of this world are concerned and you seem to have a bright prospect in the World to come, this the brightest of all other prospects, If a Person should gain the whole world & lose there Soul they have lost all, My Dear Daughter you say a great deal to me about instructing your Brother in his duty, I endeavor to set a good example before him it is all that I can do. John is a good disposed Boy & a favorite with his Master.... In your first letter you spoke of trying to purchase me & your Brother, the proposition was made to you to exchang Property of equal value, or to take One Thousand Dollars for me, & Fifteen Hundred for your Brother.... I know of nothing on this earth that would gratify me so much as to meet with My Dear & only daughter, I fear that I should not be able to retain my senses on account of the great Joy it would create in me, But time alone will develup whether this meeting will tak plase on earth or not Hope keeps the soul alive, but my Dear Daughter if this should not be our happy lot, I pray God that we may be able to hold fast to the end, & be the Happy recipients of the promise made to the faithful. There will be no parting there but we shall live in the immediate presence and smiles of our God....

May God guide and protect you through Life, & Finally save You in Heaven is the prayer of your affectionate mother, Elizabeth Ramsey [9]

Slave Courtship

Although the slave community was often perceived as an atmosphere where promiscuity and non-consensual sex predominated, in many instances there was a strong code of Christian morality often upheld by the slave mother. This was true for Lucy Ann Dunn of North Carolina.

I was in de little Baptist church at Neuse where I first seed big black Jim Dunn and I fell in love with him den I reckons. He said dat he love me den too, but it was three Sundays before he asked to see me home.

We walked dat mile home in from of my Mammy, and I was so happy dat I ain't thought it half a mile home. We et corn bread and turnips for dinner and it was night before he went home. Mammy wouldn't let me walk with him to de gate, I knowed, so I just set dere on de porch and says goodnight.

He come every Sunday for a year and finally he proposed. I had told Mammy dat I thought dat I ought to be allowed to walk to the gate with Jim and she said all right, iffen she was settin' dere on de porch lookin'. [10]

Immorality Punished

When slave children, especially young girls, strayed from the moral principles of their families, they often faced the glare and anger of their elders—even in situations where guilt might not have been clearly established. The case of Harriet Jacobs, who was raised under the Christian influence of her grandmother, is an example. She had been taught to read and write as a child, a privilege that allowed her to record her struggles as a slave—including the deep humiliation she endured when she faced her relatives with the news of her pregnancy at age fifteen:

165

Humble as were their circumstances, they had pride in my good character. Now, how could I look them in the face? My self-respect was gone! I had resolved that I would be virtuous, though I was a slave. . . . I thought I could bear my shame if I could only be reconciled to my grandmother. I longed to open my heart to her. I thought if she could know the real state of the case, and all I had been bearing for years, she would perhaps judge me less harshly. . . . I knelt before her, and told her things that had poisoned my life; how long I had been persecuted; that I saw no way of escape; and in an hour of extremity I had become desperate. I told her I would bear any thing and do any thing, if in time I had hopes of obtaining her forgiveness. I begged of her to pity me, for my dead mother's sake. And she did pity me. She did not say, "I forgive you"; but she looked at me lovingly, with her eyes full of tears. She laid her old hand gently on my head, and murmured, "Poor child! Poor child!" [11]

Cursing the Mistress

The anger that slaves felt toward their masters (and mistresses) was sometimes vented through rhymes and songs that used Christian terminology but reflected a bitterness that mocked the professed religion of the slaveholders.

*My old mistress promised me,
    Before she dies she would set me free.
Now she's dead and gone to hell,
    I hope the devil will burn her well.* [12]

Atrocities Endured by Slave Families

It is remarkable that so many Southern slaves became Christians and accepted the religion of their white masters—considering not only the physical but the emotional abuse they were forced to endure. But for many slaves, their faith involved far more than a religion; it involved a person. "Nobody knows the trouble I've seen; nobody knows but Jesus."

A weary, sun-scorched field hand

Regardless of the circumstances under which their womenfolk were sexually abused, black men reacted with deep humiliation and outrage, a reaction that at least some slaveholders intended to provoke. One Louisiana white man would enter a slave cabin and tell the husband "to go outside and wait 'til he do what he want to do." The black man "had to do it and couldn't do nothing 'bout it." (This master "had chillen by his own chillen.") Other husbands ran away rather than witness such horrors. Recalled one elderly former slave, "what we saw couldn't do nothing 'bout it. My blood is bilin' now at the thought of dem times." It would be naive to assume that the rape of a black wife by a white man did not adversely affect the woman's relationship with her husband; her innocence in initiating or sustaining a sexual encounter might have shielded her from her husband's wrath. The fact that in some slave quarters mulatto children were scorned as the master's offspring indicates that the community in general hardly regarded this form of abuse with equanimity. [13]

Picking cotton in the Old South

The Secret Pain of a Plantation Mistress

The humiliation and pain felt by African slave women who were sexually exploited by their masters was often secretly shared by the plantation mistress, as is seen in this diary entry of Mary Bodkin Chesnut in 1861:

God forgive us, but ours is a monstrous system, a wrong and an iniquity! Like the patriarchs of old, our men live all in one house with their wives and their concubines; and the mulattoes one sees in every family partly resemble the white children. Any lady is ready to tell you who is the father of all the mulatto children in everybody's household but her own. Those, she seems to think, drop from the clouds. My disgust sometimes is boiling over. [14]

Slave Marriage and the Law

"The relation between slaves," wrote a North Carolina judge in 1858, "is essentially different from that of man and wife joined in lawful wedlock…[for] with slaves it may be dissolved at the pleasure of either party, or by the sale of one or both depending on the caprice or necessity of the owners." [15]

Slave Wedding Ceremony

Slave marriage ceremonies were sometimes conducted in such a way as to reinforce the slaves' subservience to the master, as in this rite formulated by the Reverend Samuel Philips of Andover, Massachusetts:

> *I then agreeable to your Request, and by the Consent to your Masters & Mistresses, do Declare, that you have License given you to be conversant and familiar together, as Husband and Wife, so long as God shall continue your places of abode as aforesaid; and so long as you shall behave yourselves as it becometh Servants to doe: For you must, both of you, bear in mind, that you Remain Still as really and truly as ever, your Master's Property, and therefore it will be justly expected, both by God and Man, that you behave and conduct your-selves, as Obedient and faithfull Servants towards your respective Masters & Mistresses for the Time being.* [16]

Let No Man Put Asunder

Slaves were fully aware of the fact that their wedding vows were not the same as the wedding vows of white folks. They "knew very well that weddings were supposed to reach the climax with 'Till death do you part,' and they were bound to react grimly to the absence of such words in their own ceremonies. Not many blacks could have thought it clever when a white minister offered 'Until death or distance do you part.'" Matthew Jarrett, who had grown up in slavery in Virginia, reflected on this double standard in marriage vows:

> *We slaves knowed that them words wasn't bindin'. Don't mean nothin' lessen you say, "What God has jined, caint no man pull asunder." But dey never would say dat. Jus' say, "now you married."* [17]

A slave wedding ceremony

Slave Mothers

It was often left to the slave mother to teach her children Christian ethics and morality, as was so frequently attested to by their children. When the Reverend Lucius Holsey was growing up under slavery, it was his "intensely religious" mother who instilled in him moral lessons of life. Henry Box Brown's mother was the one who taught him "not to steal, and not to lie, and to behave myself in other respects." They also warned their children of the dangers of rebelling against their masters. William Webb reflected on how his mother "taught me there was a Supreme Being that would take care of me in all my trials; she taught me not to rebel against the men that were treating me like some dumb brute, making me work and refusing to let me learn." [18]

The Slave Father

Christian parenting was very difficult in the slave community, especially in relation to the father's role. The slave father may have read or heard biblical admonitions directed at fathers, but he was often powerless to put them into practice.

For the Negro child, in particular, the plantation offered no really satisfactory father image other than the master. The "real" father was virtually without authority over his child, since discipline, parental responsibility, and control of rewards and punishments all rested in other hands; the slave father could not even protect the mother of his children except by appealing directly to the master. Indeed, the mother's own role loomed far larger for the slave child than did that of the father. She controlled those few activities—household care, preparation of food, and rearing of children— that were left to the slave family. For that matter, the very etiquette of plantation life removed even the honorific attributes of fatherhood from the Negro male, who was addressed as "boy" until when the vigorous years of his prime were past, he was allowed to assume the title of "uncle." [19]

Slave Family Prayers

Despite their limitations as a provider and leader in the home, slave fathers often took part in family religious activities and led the family in prayer.

A slave prayer meeting

The slave's constant prayer, his all-consuming hope, was for liberty. Fathers opened family religious observances with prayers for freedom which held out the slender thread of hope to their children. Jacob Stroyer's father, for example, disturbed over the cruel punishment of his son, knelt one night and prayed: "Lord, hasten the time when these children shall be their own free men and women." The prayer raised Jacob's spirits, and he wrote that at the time "my faith in father's prayer made me think that the Lord would answer him at the farthest in two or three weeks." W. H. Robinson recalled that all of the slaves "prayed for the dawn and light of a better day"…many looked long and eagerly for freedom but died without the sight. [20]

Praying Slaves

Masters sometimes objected to community and family prayer meetings because they knew all too well that their slaves prayed for freedom and rest from their weary labors. But no master had the power to stop their prayers, as a former slave testified as he reflected back over his life.

> *My master used to ask us children, "Do your folks pray at night?" We said "No," 'cause our folks had told us what to say. But the Lord have mercy, there was plenty of that going on. They'd pray, "Lord, deliver us from under bondage."* [21]

A Harmonious Christian Marriage

Married life was very difficult in the slave community because the highest degree of loyalty was to be given to the master—not to the spouse. Yet, the expression of love displayed between the husband and wife was often a powerful testimony that the bonds of slavery need not demean the bonds of love—especially marital love that was rooted in the Christian faith. This was the scene in the boyhood home of a former slave.

> *I loved my father. He was such a good man. He was a good carpenter and could do anything. My mother just rejoiced in him. Whenever he sat down to talk she just sat and looked and listened. She would never cross him for anything. If they went to church together she always waited for him to interpret what the preacher had said or what he thought was the will of God. I was small but I noticed all of these things. I sometimes think I learned more in my early childhood about how to live than I have learned since.* [22]

A Slave Catechism

If slaves were given religious instruction at all, it was typically the type of instruction that was specifically designed to treat them like children and make them compliant. This slave catechism was intended to serve that purpose.

Q. Who keeps the snakes and all bad things from hurting you?
A. God does.
Q. Who gave you a master and a mistress?
A. God gave them to me.
Q. Who says that you must obey them?
A. God says that I must.
Q. What book tells you these things?
A. The Bible.
Q. How does God do all His work?
A. He always does it right.
Q. Does God love to work?
A. Yes, God is always at work.
Q. Do the Angels work?
A. Yes, they do what God tells them.
Q. Do they love to work?
A. Yes, they love to please God.
Q. What does God say about your work?
A. He that will not work shall not eat.
Q. Did Adam and Eve have to work?
A. Yes, they had to keep the garden.
Q. Was it hard to keep that garden?
A. No, it was very easy.
Q. What makes the crops so hard to grow now?
A. Sin makes it.
Q. What makes you lazy?
A. My wicked heart
Q. How do you know your heart is wicked?
A. I feel it every day.
Q. Who teaches you so many wicked things?
A. The Devil.
Q. Must you let the Devil teach you?
A. No, I must not. [23]

A slave revival meeting

Church Attendance

Christianity is a faith that sets the captive free—a truth that was not lost on slaveowners who feared their slaves might take the biblical offer of freedom too literally. Yet, there were plantation owners who were truly concerned about the spiritual welfare of their slaves.

 Frequently, while in the first flush of his own conversion, a planter required all of his slaves to attend church. Both master and slave might attend

Sunday worship on the plantation

a camp meeting, fervently pray to be saved, be converted, and then moan, shout, cry, faint, and be baptized at the same time. These planters or members of their families taught in the plantation Sabbath schools, held prayer meetings with the blacks at the end of each day, built plantation chapels, hired itinerant white ministers, or preached to the slaves every Sunday themselves. [24]

Slaves Sharing Their Christian Faith

Sometimes slaves took it upon themselves to bring their owners to true faith in Christ. Amanda Smith, a great nineteenth-century evangelist, got her start as an evangelist while living under the tutelage of her mother and grandmother as a slave on a plantation in Maryland.

When "the spirit of the Lord got hold of my young mistress, my mother was awfully glad the Lord had answered her and grandmother's prayer. As I have heard my mother tell this story she has wept as though it had just been a few days ago." So strong was the influence of these slave women that the young mistress "wanted to go to the colored people's church." Her family "would not have that. So they kept her from going. Then they separated my mother and her. They thought maybe mother might talk to her, and keep up the excitement.... About a quarter of a mile away was the great dairy, and Miss Celie used to slip over there when she got a chance and have a good time praying with mother and grandmother." [25]

Mamma Jeffries' Baptism

Baptism was the most celebrated event in the religious life of slaves, and it often marked a radical change in the individual. Isaiah Jeffries' mother was converted when he was a boy, and his recollections paint a picture of the excitement and ecstasy in this dear woman's life.

When I to be a big boy, my Ma got religion at de Camp meeting at El Bethel. She shouted and sung fer three days, going all over de plantation and de neighboring ones, inviting her friends to come to see her baptized and shouting and praying fer dem. She went around to all de people dat she had done wrong and begged dere forgiveness. She sent fer dem dat had wronged her, and told dem dat she was born again and a new woman, and dat she would forgive dem. She wanted everybody dat was not saved to go up wid her…. My Ma took me wid her to see her baptized, and I was so happy dat I sung and shouted wid her. All de niggers joined in singing. [26]

A Real Woman

The nineteenth-century "cult of true womanhood" placed women on a pedestal by emphasizing their purity and virtue, but it also idealized her as weak and needing to be protected by her husband or a chivalrous man. One of the most riveting orations against such stereotyping came from Sojourner Truth, speaking at a women's rights convention in 1851.

Working together

That man over there says women need to be helped into carriages and lifted over ditches, and to have the best place everywhere. Nobody every helps me into carriages or over puddles, or gives me the best place—and ain't I a woman?

Look at this arm! I have ploughed and planted and gathered into barns, and no man could head me—and ain't I a woman?

I could work as much and eat as much as a man when I could get it and bear the lash as well. And ain't I a woman?

I have borne thirteen children, and seen most of 'em sold off to slavery, and when I cried out with my mother's grief, none but Jesus heard me—and ain't I a woman? [27]

Slave Obituary

In 1863, James Melvin, an overseer, sent a death notice to his employer, Audley Britton, which clearly reflects the Christian family bonds that were part of the slave community:

[Old Bill] breathed his last on Saturday the 31st, Jan. about 8 1/2 o'clock in the morning. He appeared prepared for Death and said he was going to heaven and wanted his wife to meet him there. When he took sick he told all it would be his last sickness—I was very sorry to lose him. [28]

"I Have a Dream"

I have a dream…. It is a dream deeply rooted in the American dream…. I have a dream that one day in the red hills of Georgia, sons of former slaves and the sons of former slave owners will be able to sit down together at the table of brotherhood. [29]

Martin Luther King, Jr.

Faith of Our Mothers: Victorian Family Life

CHAPTER

11

The Victorian era is named for Queen Victoria, who had a profound influence on her age not only in Britain and its empire but also America and elsewhere in the world. Victoria was the reigning monarch of the British Empire for more than sixty-three years, from June 1837 until January 1901, but she was more than a queen. She saw herself first and foremost as a wife and mother, and she vowed that her family life would be a model of the Christian home. Although she was the ruling monarch, she was determined to have a proper Christian marriage and dutifully submit to her husband Albert as head of the home. She was outraged by the attitude of women who championed "this mad, wicked folly of 'Women's Rights' with all the attendant horrors on which her poor sex is bent." Albert, she lamented not long after their marriage, "is in my house and not I in his. But I am ready to submit to his wishes as I love him so dearly." Albert's perspective was somewhat different. To a physician who knew his wife well, he wrote:

 *Victoria is too hasty and passionate…. She will not hear me out but flies into a rage and overwhelms me with reproaches of…want of trust, ambition, envy, etc., etc. There are, therefore, two ways open to me: (1) to keep silence and go away (in which case I am like a schoolboy who has had a dressing down from his mother and goes off snubbed); (2) I can be still more violent (and then we have scenes…which I hate, because I am sorry for Victoria in her misery, besides which it undermines the peace of the home).* [1]

Prince Albert eventually found his place in the marriage as far more than a mere subject of the queen, in part because Victoria was determined to make her marriage work. One of the stories that illustrates the struggle toward this goal has a touch of humor:

 *When, in wrath, the Prince one day had locked himself into his room, Victoria, no less furious, knocked on the door to be admitted. "Who is there?" he asked. "The Queen of England," was the answer. He did not move, and again there was a hail of knocks. The question and the answer repeated many times; but at last there was a pause, and then a gentler*

knocking. "Who is there?" came once more the relentless question. But this time the reply was different. "Your wife, Albert." And the door was immediately opened. [2]

A Royal Flush

Queen Victoria and her "beloved" Prince Albert wasted no time in starting a family. Their first child was born during their first year of marriage, and Victoria was pregnant with her seventh on her tenth anniversary. Together they reared nine children who survived to adulthood.

Victorian Holidays

The Victorian emphasis on the family, combined with a penchant for extravagance, set the stage for festive and lavish holiday celebrations. It was Prince Albert who popularized the custom of the Christmas tree in England. "At Windsor small trees—one for each member of the family—were placed on decorated tables and hung with cakes, sweets and toys." [3]

≈ 1840	**Victoria**
≈ 1841	**Albert**
≈ 1843	**Alice**
≈ 1844	**Alfred**
≈ 1846	**Helena**
≈ 1848	**Louise**
≈ 1850	**Arthur**
≈ 1853	**Leopold**
≈ 1857	**Beatrice**

The "Cult of True Womanhood"

Queen Victoria's role as wife and mother had a powerful influence on her age, but there were many other factors—particularly in America—that made the nineteenth century "the great age of the home." At no other time in history had there been such a clear demarcation between the home and the economic world outside—the former the woman's domain and the latter the man's. Gender roles were strictly defined, and the home became a woman's domain where her husband found solace from the struggles of an uncertain world. Family life in the Victorian period was influenced by what became known as the "cult of true womanhood." The woman—more specifically, the mother—was put on a pedestal and idealized. Her virtues were "piety, purity, submissiveness, and domesticity." She was the "queen of the home" and motherhood was her vocation. Her role in society, in the church, and in the family was critical because she was viewed as the "keeper" of the home and of the faith. Men, of course, were still the leaders at home and certainly in society and in the church, but they delegated the day-to-day functioning of family and faith to their wives. [4]

Beyond the Puritan Past

The spiritual ancestors of the Victorians were the Puritans, but like most children of the second and third generation, the Victorians set out on a course of their own. Some traditions, however, were retained:

Puritan family worship formed the basis for evangelical Protestant worship during the Victorian period. Although the content of devotion would change during the nineteenth century, its structure remained the same. The family met in the morning and evening to recite prayers, sing psalms, and read from the Bible.

But the nineteenth century was very different than the preceding centuries. The Industrial Revolution had forever changed the family and home life.

As men and women drifted farther apart in the workplace, the social roles of the sexes became more distant…. The period of the Puritan father overseeing the family economy with the support of wife, children, and apprentices had become a distant memory. Now it was the mother who according to cultural norms would be expected to nurture the family. [5]

A Victorian etching of the royal family and the Queen's mother standing around their candlelit Christmas tree

Family Morning Devotions

Sarah Hale, a religious reformer and the editor of *Godey's Lady's Book* became the foremost authority of feminine values and tastes in Victorian America. She wrote articles and poems that encouraged women to pursue their primary calling as wives and homemakers, and she gave them ideas and advice to beautify their homes—most importantly by making it a Christian home where God is worshiped every morning before the workday begins:

What a fount of strength what a draught of joy
*   That morn's devotion yields!*
It girds the souls with righteousness,
*   Or, from temptation shields;*
It adds the pearl of priceless worth
*   Where Life's rich gifts abound*
And scatters flowers of Paradise
*   The lowliest home around. [6]*

Motherly Prayers

As mothers assumed the spiritual nurture of the family, the content and style of domestic religion shifted away from what might be characterized as a masculine model of faith to that of a more feminine model:

By mid-century, teaching children how to pray fell within the domain of the mother. Victorian mothers were reluctant to induce the fear of eternal damnation that typified Calvinist prayer and preferred to present prayer as a comforting activity.... Like a mother's loving reassurance, prayers at home were personal, individual, and founded on affection. Children were not to be frightened by God's wrath. They were taught to say a prayer to Jesus before going to bed.... In the maternal understanding of religion, mothers and children had direct access to God. They did not need the mediation of the priest-father or the minister.... The changing nature of home Sabbath activities justly epitomizes the maternal dimension of Victorian domestic religion. The Sabbath, which had once been a time of contemplation of the divine, became child-oriented and mother-directed. [7]

Morning devotions around the breakfast table

Woman's Priesthood in the Home

Before this altar crowned with peace,
This centre of our spirit home,
Let every strife and question cease
And fruitful faith and concord come.

For here the last deliverance stands,
To loose the palsied spell of fear;
And woman with unfettered hands
Keeps thine accepted priesthood here. [8]

Julia Ward Howe

178

Designing "Christian" Homes

Until the Victorian period, there was little thought given to designing homes in order to enhance the family's Christian faith. Churches, yes. But houses were houses, and the architect's design had no relation to religious beliefs and morals. The Puritans typically lived in one or two rooms, with no apparent need for privacy or specialized work space for family members. For the Victorians, however, home design became part of "an evolving Protestant perspective"—especially in America. Leading avant-garde architects "were crucial in asserting the equation of Protestantism with Christianity, Christianity with civilization, and civilization with America."

 As one rose in social rank and financial stability, interior layout and design became more complicated. The living room was broken into a formal parlor for receiving guests, an informal family sitting room, a library for father, and a boudoir for mother. A kitchen, scullery, serving room, pantry, coal pit, china closet, larder, store room, and wood porch now served where a sole kitchen had previously…. Men and women had their own areas. Adults were separated from children, just as private family space was separated from public space. Rooms were decorated to point out their purpose—lady's boudoir with chintz and delicate colors, a library with dark oak and leather chairs, and a drawing room with "more beauty and elegance than any other apartment in the house…." The library and parlor were essential in conveying to the visitor the respectability and status of the family. [9]

A depiction of a "Christian house" in *The American Woman's Home* by Catherine Beecher and Harriet Beecher Stowe

Victorian Home Decor Revisited

Like other First Families, the Clintons quickly gave a new face to the White House by their choice of furnishings and decor, in their case, Victorian—much to the chagrin of a *Time* magazine reporter, in an article entitled, "Clinton Family Values." What is wrong with Victorian decor?

 Mid nineteenth-century American decor was in its, shall we say, bawdy-house phase…. The Victorians never met a swag or tassel they didn't like; if one patterned fabric was good, surely four would be better. [10]

Decorating a "Happy Home"

Embroidered fabric wall plaques known as "samplers" decorated Christian homes in the Victorian era. As soon as a young girl's hand was steady enough to guide a needle, she was encouraged to compose a poem or choose a Bible verse for her own sampler, often bordered with a floral design. Sometimes these "samplers" were more elaborate and mass produced, as in the case of "The Happy Home," produced by the Religious Tract Society, "that brightened the walls of many a humble home."

The Ideal Christian Home

John Ruskin (1819–1900), the leading social critic of his day, had a profound influence on the tastes and taboos of Victorian England. He was raised in an evangelical family and memorized large portions of Scripture in preparation for the ministry, but while studying at Oxford his interests turned instead to the arts and social issues—including the home and family. Preserving the family structure was crucial not only for the individuals involved but for society at large.

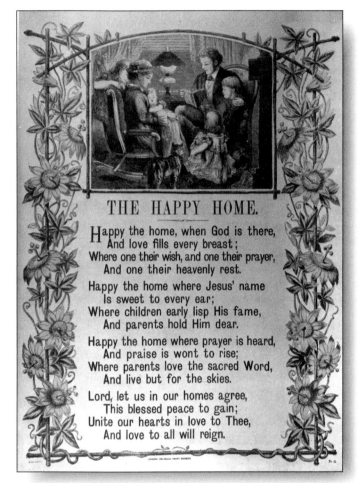

THE HAPPY HOME.

Happy the home, when God is there,
  And love fills every breast;
Where one their wish, and one their prayer,
  And one their heavenly rest.

Happy the home where Jesus' name
  Is sweet to every ear;
Where children early lisp His fame,
  And parents hold Him dear.

Happy the home where prayer is heard,
  And praise is wont to rise;
Where parents love the sacred Word,
  And live but for the skies.

Lord, let us in our homes agree,
  This blessed peace to gain;
Unite our hearts in love to Thee,
  And love to all will reign.

A Victorian Religious Tract Society wall hanging

The man's power is active, progressive, defensive. He is eminently the doer, the creator, the discoverer, the defender. His intellect is for speculation and invention; his energy for adventure, for war, and for conquest, whenever war is just, whenever conquest necessary. But the woman's power is for rule, not for battle; and her intellect is not for invention or creation, but for sweet ordering, arrangement and decision.... This is the true nature of home—it is the place of peace; the shelter, not only from all injury, but from all terror, doubt, and division. In so far as it is not this, it is not home; so far as the anxieties of the outer life penetrate into it, and the inconsistently minded, unknown, unloved, or hostile society of the outer world is allowed by either husband or wife to cross the threshold, it ceases to be home; it is then only a part of that outer world which you have roofed over and lighted fire in. But so far as it is a sacred place, a vestal temple, a temple of the hearth ...it vindicates the name and fulfills the praise of home. [11]

Separation of the Sexes

Alfred Lord Tennyson, writing in *The Princess* in 1847, spoke for many men and women when he penned the following lines that clearly delineated sex roles in society:

> *Man*
> *for the field*
> *and woman*
> *for the*
> *hearth;*
> *Man*
> *for the sword*
> *and for the*
> *needle she;*
> *Man*
> *with the head*
> *and woman*
> *with the heart;*
> *Man to*
> *command and*
> *woman to obey;*
> *All else confusion.* [12]

A depiction of the mother's influence over the heart and the father's over the intellect from Samuel Goodrich's *Fireside Education*

The Domineering Wife

The much-touted marriage ideal of wifely submission to the husband was probably no more a reality in the Victorian era than in any other era of history. Then, as in centuries gone by, it provided good subject matter for humor. Here Mark Twain parodies marital bliss in his story, "The McWilliamses and the Burglar Alarm," with Mr. McWilliams lamenting his domestic situation:

> *When we were finishing our house, we found we had a little cash left over, on account of the plumber not knowing it. I was for enlightening the heathen with it, for I was always unaccountably down on the heathen somehow; but Mrs. McWilliams said no, let's have a burglar alarm. I agreed to this compromise. I will explain that whenever I want a thing, and Mrs. McWilliams wants another thing, and we decide upon the thing that Mrs. McWilliams wants—as we always do—she calls that a compromise.* [13]

Prudishness

If the Victorian era in England stood for anything, it was politeness—especially in the manner of speaking.

🌹 *Women no longer became pregnant—they were "in an interesting condition." Ladies nibbled on "bosom of chicken." The term "miscarriage of justice," if used by a young girl brought instance admonition from her mother.*

Repressed sexuality was displaced to such innocuous areas as furniture. Chairs were constructed with broad shoulders and wasp waists, and piano legs were so human in appearance that they were covered with skirts by embarrassed ladies, who by this ploy made them still more noticeable. Victorians approached sexuality like a dog a hot piece of meat—too hot to touch, yet too desirable to turn away from. [14]

Love, Sex, and Delicate Ladies

Our Victorian ancestors are often remembered for their pretentiousness—for covering over the ugly side of life with a veneer of elegance and refinement, and for pretending to be what they were not. As such, love and courtship were very different than they had been in earlier generations. The exuberant sex life of the Puritans and the practice of bundling were offensive to Victorian sensibilities. The perfect young maiden was portrayed as delicate and weak; her valiant, manly beau was her strength and security, protecting her from physical and emotional peril. A traveler from London gave the following description of the well-bred Victorian lifestyle he found in New England:

Clothes for the
well-dressed lady

🌹 *In America it is not the desire of women to be in robust health. If a young lady languish with snowy cheeks, and if she has a tremulous voice, she may be expected to break a score of hearts. When she goes out, it is in a softly-cushioned carriage, with servants to wrap her carefully from the benignant influences of out-of-doors, so the vulgar wind and sunshine have not a stray peep at that exquisite skin of hers.*

Eleanor Early paints a similar portrait of the period:

 This was in the days of Queen Victoria's widowhood, and Godey's Lady's Book, when young ladies simpered on plush divans, and swooned on Brussels carpets; and had vapors and the megrims, and thought their legs a sin. Their swains wore sideburns, and wrote sugary verse. And then they all got married…. It was elegant to be delicate. Languid ladies embroidered violets on center-pieces, and wild roses on sofa cushions…. Their swains could span their waists with both hands—though this was a liberty seldom vouchsafed. [15]

Childhood Innocence

In the changing middle-class family structure of Victorian times, children became prototypes of innocence—especially in children's literature and child-rearing manuals. Lydia Maria Child, a religious reformer, challenged her readers of *Mother's Book* in 1831, that "it is the first duty of a mother to make the Bible precious and delightful to her family." But at the same time she could write sentimentally about the nature of children.

 They come to us from heaven, with their little souls full of innocence and peace, and, as far as possible, a mother's influence should not interfere with the influence of angels. [16]

"Buds of Life from Heaven"

The sentimentalized innocence of children is illustrated by this stanza of "The Little Children," published in 1872 in *Godey's Lady's Book*:

Buds of life from Heaven,
Little children come
To be nursed and ripened
In a human home.
Screen the flower, unfolding,
From the blight of sin:
Watch the rich fruit growing
Lest the worm creep in. [17]

A mother teaching her daughter the Scriptures

The Death of a Child

In romanticizing childhood, the Victorians often focused on death and dying and heaven. Children were innocent, and the only way for them to never lose their innocence was to die and go to heaven.

Child characters were dying in record numbers in fiction even as actual child mortality was declining.... For Victorian writers, children were the guardians of virtue. So it followed that the fictional children dying of these mysterious wasting diseases would go to heaven. For heaven was theirs by right and not by God's mercy. [18]

The death of a child was the theme of James Russell Lowell's memorable poem written in 1849.

"The First Snow-Fall"

The snow had begun in the gloaming,
    And busily all the night
Had been heaping field and highway
    With a silence deep and white.

    Every pine and fir and hemlock
        Wore ermine too dear for an earl,
    And the poorest twig on the elm-tree
        Was ridged inch deep with pearl.

From sheds new-roofed with Carrara
    Came Chanticleer's muffled crow,
The stiff rails were softened to swan's-down
    And still fluttered down the snow.

    I stood and watched by the window
        The noiseless work of the sky,
    And the sudden flurries of snow-birds,
        Like brown leaves whirling by.

I thought of a mound in sweet Auburn
    Where a little headstone stood;
How the flakes were folding it gently,
    As did robins the babes in the wood.

Up spoke our own little Mabel,
    Saying, "Father, who makes it snow?"
And I told of the good All-father
    Who cares for us here below.

Again I looked at the snow-fall
    And thought of the leaden sky
That arched o'er our first great sorrow,
    When that mound was heaped so high.

    I remembered the gradual patience
        That fell from that cloud like snow,
    Flake by flake, healing and hiding
        The scar that renewed our woe.

And again to the child I whispered,
    "The snow that husheth all,
Darling, the merciful Father
    Alone can make it fall!"

    Then, with eyes that saw not, I kissed her;
        And she, kissing back, could not know
    That my kiss was given to her sister,
        Folded close under deepening snow. [19]

A New Style of Discipline

Gone were the days of harsh discipline—at least in the child-rearing manuals. Susanna Wesley's prescription for "breaking the will" of a child was no longer in vogue. Victorians had a much softer touch than did their ancestors in matters of corporal punishment and verbal correction. They idealized childhood, while at the same time not utterly discarding the belief in original sin. The "Christian scheme" involved "recognizing the child's inherent depravity" and striving to "educate him at once for earth and heaven."

The advantage of such a view of the child was that the parent was not surprised at any evidence of sinfulness, rather expected it and set about, with love and patience, to correct it. The mother should preside over a happy but an orderly kingdom. That doctrine that children should be "reasoned into obedience and subjection" was usually rejected. It imposed too great a strain on parents and children alike and replaced obedience with disputation. Children should obey their parents because they believed them to be reasonable, loving, and just. Mothers were advised to be tolerant of the mirth and noise of children, of their exuberant animal spirits—"how delightful to all young creatures is freedom!"—and to try to enter sympathetically into the child's own world, a world of fantasy and make-believe where fact and fiction were often quite mixed up in youthful imaginations. [20]

A Victorian family on their way to chapel

Loving Discipline of a Father

D.L. Moody is remembered as a great evangelist who made a profound impact on religious life in the Victorian era. But it was D.L. Moody as "Dad" that most influenced his children. "In his home," wrote his son William, "grace was the ruling principle and not law, and the sorest punishment of a child was the sense that the father's loving heart had been grieved by waywardness or folly." Moody's son Paul confirmed this portrayal of their father. On one occasion when he had stayed up past his bedtime with a friend, Moody scolded him harshly:

> ≈ *I retreated immediately and in tears, for it was an almost unheard-of thing that he should speak with such directness or give an order unaccompanied by a smile. But I had barely gotten into my little bed before he was kneeling beside it in tears and seeking my forgiveness for having spoken so harshly. He never, he said, intended to speak crossly to one of his children.*

Moody left a legacy for his children—not primarily as a great evangelist, but as a loving father. Years later Paul reflected on that night when his father came to his room:

> ≈ *Half a century must have passed since then and while it is not the earliest of my recollections I think it is the most vivid, and I can still see that room in the twilight and that large bearded figure with the great shoulders bowed above me, and hear the broken voice and the tenderness in it. I like best to think of him that way. Before then and after I saw him holding the attention of thousands of people, but asking for the forgiveness of his unconsciously disobedient little boy for having spoken harshly seemed to me then and seems now a finer and a greater thing, and to it I owe more than I owe to any of his sermons. For to this I am indebted for an understanding of the meaning of the Fatherhood of God, and a belief in the love of God had its beginnings that night in my childish mind.* [21]

Letter to a Wayward Son

Loving parental discipline does not ensure good behavior in children, as Dwight and Emma Moody knew all too well. When their wayward son Will was in college, Emma wrote him a letter pouring out her deep concerns for his spiritual condition, admonishing him of the danger of "being in any college without reliance on the help of Christ." In another letter she anguished over the temptations of alcohol and sexual immorality:

Dwight and Emma Moody in 1869

My thoughts have so often gone to you with the prayer also that you might be kept from sin. I know so much more about the temptations than if I had always lived quietly at home & as I have known in College you don't know how I have yearned after you & prayed that you might be kept. I have a horror of strong drink and its dreadful power but I have as great a dread of a sin that I know young men fall a victim to as often & now as I write I know you won't laugh or make light of my earnest prayer for you that you may be kept from the first steps either in drink or in impurity. You are not stronger than other men & temptations are ready. Don't depend on yourself but look to the same source for help in overcoming that we go to for you. May God keep & bless my dear boy![22]

A Boy Named "Mahershallalashbaz"

In 1866, B.J. Armstrong, an Anglican vicar from East Dereham, England, penned the following entry in his diary:

25 December. Married a young parishioner of the name of Mahershallalashbaz Tuck. He accounted for the possession of so extraordinary a name thus: his father wished to call him by the shortest name in the Bible, and for that purpose selected Uz. But, the clergyman making some demur, the father said in pique, "Well, if he cannot have the shortest he shall have the longest."[23]

The Other Side of Victorian Childhood

A family impoverished by alcohol

The Victorians had an uneasy conscience concerning childhood. The middle-class mother doted on her children, while her breadwinning husband worked long hours to assure they would enjoy a comfortable home environment and lifestyle previously unknown to regular folks. But there was another side of family life in nineteenth-century America. Industrialization had dealt a harsh blow to the poor, who often lived in crowded, dilapidated tenement houses and worked twelve- to fourteen-hour days in the factories. Children were not spared long working hours and the harsh realities of life, and adding to their misery was the prevalence of alcoholism—especially among their factory-working fathers. Their plight stirred reform-minded Victorians who took up the cause of the less fortunate through benevolent societies, through legislation, and through verse. The alcoholic father, the helpless mother, and the dying child were common themes in Victorian literature, as in this poem by Henry Clay Work:

187

"Come Home Father"

Father, dear father, come home with me now,
The clock in the steeple strikes one.
You said you were coming right home from the shop
As soon as your day's work was done.

Our fire has gone out, our house is all dark,
And Mother's been watching since tea,
With poor brother Benny so sick in her arms,
And no one to help her but me.
Come home! Come home! Come home!
Please, father, dear father, come home.

Father, dear father, come home with me now,
The clock in the steeple strikes two;
The night has grown colder, and Benny is worse,—
But he has been calling for you….

Father, dear father, come home with me now,
The clock in the steeple strikes three.
The house is so lonely—the hours are so long
For poor weeping Mother and me.

Yes we are alone—poor Benny is dead,
And gone with the angels of light
And these were the very last words he said:
"I want to kiss papa good night."
Come home! Come home! Come home!
Please, father, dear father, come home.

Hear the sweet voice of the child
Which the night winds repeat as they roam!
Oh, who could resist this most plaintive of prayers?
Please, father, dear father, come home! [24]

The Call to Service

For some Victorian women, the calling as wife and mother held no compelling appeal. They saw the plight of a needy world, and they wanted to be involved. Florence Nightingale, known for her pioneer ministry in nursing, was one such woman. She lamented the role restrictions she found in the church and in proper Victorian society. In 1851, she wrote:

 I would have given her [the church] my head, my heart, my hand. She would not have them. She did not know what to do with them. She told me to go back and do crochet in my mother's drawing room; or, if I were tired of that, to marry and look well at the head of my husband's table. You may go to the Sunday School, if you like, she said. But she gave me no training even for that. She gave me neither work to do for her, nor education for it.

The solution for many Victorian women, both married and single, was to seek their own avenues of service in ministries of every description. But the universal preeminent calling for women remained marriage and motherhood. [25]

A Queen's Coronation

It was a queen for whom the Victorian era was named, but the real queen, according to DeWitt Talmage, was not a monarch in England but the nameless mother who in life and death gave herself for her family. As for women's rights, he believed the ultimate "right" of a woman was the right to "reach heaven" after a life of sacrifice. In an article entitled, "The Queens of the Home," Talmage wrote:

The Victorian drawing room

Some of you will have no rest in this world. It will be toil and struggle and suffering all the way up…. But God has a crown for you…. He is now making it, and whenever you have a pang of body or soul, he puts another gem in that crown; until…God will say…"The crown is done; let her up, that she may wear it."…Angel will cry to angel, "Who is she?" and Christ will say… "She is the one that came up out of great tribulation…. She suffered with Me on earth, and now we are going to be glorified together." [26]

Norman Rockwell's America:
Reflections of Contemporary Christians

12

Many older Christians today reflect back on pleasant memories of an era a generation or two ago, when life was simple and delightfully depicted in a Norman Rockwell painting—an era before television and the mass media began to take the place of regular family devotions and interaction around the dinner table. It was an era of robust farm families and small-town values—when the church was often the center of community activities. Life was less than idyllic in that era, but today's family has much to gain by learning lessons from the family life of this bygone era.

The Victorian era faded away as the sun rose over the horizon of the twentieth century. It was a new day. Modern technology was the product of the Industrial Revolution, and life would never be the same again. The Wright brothers tested their first glider at Kitty Hawk, North Carolina in 1900, and in 1903 they made their first successful airplane flight. That same year Henry Ford organized the Ford Motor Company, and within a few years his "Model T" was coming off the assembly line. It was an exciting time to be alive, but it was also a time of apprehension. How would this modern era with all its technology affect the family—especially the Christian family?

A "speakeasy," an illegal bar of the Roaring Twenties

The early decades of the twentieth century witnessed profound changes in social customs, and many Christians feared that long-held moral standards and good taste were becoming extinct. The days of Victorian politeness and prudity were long gone, and new fads were shaking the very foundation of the Christian family. "Speakeasies" and sensual women were the symbols of decadence. "Americans," writes Betty DeBerg, "were unsettled and threatened by the revolution in manners and morals."

> *The modernization of sex and the revolution in manners was most widely symbolized by the flapper, the "thoroughly modern" woman of the twentieth century who smoked, drank, danced, wore short skirts, and petted with young men in automobiles, and bobbed her hair.* [1]

A Call for Mothers

In the 1920s, the *King's Business,* a Christian magazine, issued a summons for women to return to the home:

WANTED—MORE MOTHERS.

We are short on homes; real homes. We are short on mothers; real mothers…. God designed woman as the homemaker but somehow she seems to have gotten sidetracked. [2]

The Ballot Box, Birth Control, and Family Breakdown

In 1920, the editor of the Missouri Synod *Lutheran Witness* warned of the ominous affects of women's suffrage and birth control:

> *Many women will be so busy about voting and political office that the home and children will have no attraction for them and American mothers and children, like Christian charity, will be a rarity…. The new woman hates children and is madly exerting her ingenuity in frustrating the ends of matrimony.* [3]

Billy Sunday's Verdict on the American Family

Billy Sunday was America's most celebrated evangelist during the early decades of the twentieth century. But he was more than an evangelist. He was a fiery critic of American morals and social values, and he minced no words and spared no sensitivities in making his case. The breakdown of the family was one of his familiar themes. Douglas Frank summarizes Sunday's lurid portrait of the American family:

> *The American home was an unsightly mess; if Jesus had come to it, He would have found beer in the refrigerator, playing cards on the table, "nasty music on the piano," and cigarettes (location unspecified). The husband was all too often a "cigarette-smoking, cursing, damnable libertine" who played poker, spent his money on his own pleasures…abused his wife, growled at and beat his children, taught his sons to smoke, drink, and chew. The wife tended to spend money on "fool hats and card parties" and cosmetics, driving the husband away with her*

"badly cooked meals" while her children ran the streets, *"learning to be hoodlums,"* looking like *"a rummage sale in a second-hand store; with uncombed hair, ripped pants, buttons off, stockings hanging down."* Instead of praying with their children, parents were taking them to *"dancing schools and haunts of sin,"* serving them liquor, letting them *"gad about the streets with every Tom, Dick and Harry, or keep company with some little jack rabbit whose character would make a black mark on some piece of tar paper."* It was no wonder to Sunday that criminals in prison *"blame their mothers for their being where they are."* [4]

A smoking, worldly, woman of the 1920s

Small-Town American Religion

Christian parents were as fearful as preachers were about the changing morals and values of the next generation. This fear, as Mark Senter reminds us, is delightfully portrayed in the Broadway musical classic, *The Music Man:*

Main Street America: Sauk Center, Minnesota

 The parents of River City typified the values of the average evangelical church member at the turn of the century. They were more concerned with issues of conventional morality than national progress. Sloth, drinking beer from a bottle, reading dime novels, memorizing jokes out of Captain Billy's Whiz Bang, and using words like "swell" and "so's your old man" alarmed the people of Meredith Wilson's comedy, while they were urged to maintain a discreet distance from the likes of Tommy Djilas whom Mayor Shinn described as a wild kid whose father was one of the day laborers living south of town. [5]

Amish Family Values

Most Christians families during the first half of the twentieth century were unable to slow the rush of progress and change. They longed for "the good old days" and for traditional values, but they could not escape the onslaught of modernity. Not so with the Amish. They settled in tight-knit communities around the country, where their faith and family values were protected from the world outside.

 The home is the pulse of Amish life. It is the Alpha and Omega (the beginning and the ending) of their lives, and the few God-given years between are a symphony of homespun learning and hard work, mixed with impromptu fun and frolic. The children learn to speak Pennsylvania Dutch at home. Amish church services are held in their homes. Get-togethers and group singings take place in their homes. Courtship and marriage take place in their home. Even the viewings and funeral services for the departed are held at home. [6]

Amish men passing the time of day

An Amish Kitchen

Amish family life revolves around the kitchen, the most important room of the house:

 Contrasted with our modern, all-electric kitchen is the Amish kitchen. This is huge in size, and features a large old stove almost in the center, with an eight-board family table a few

194

yards away. Most of the activity centers around the polished black stove, from the baking of bread, pies, and succulent meals, to the heating of water for baths, and oh yes, the feet warming in the oven after the chores in sub-zero weather. [7]

Amish Courtship

Unlike modern dating that has been revolutionized by the automobile and the movie theater, Amish courtship follows the customs that have been carried down through the centuries:

Courting time after evening chores

Amish dating is called "running around." When a boy (or girl) is old enough, usually sixteen, he attends the Sunday evening "singings" and this soon makes him eligible for dating. After three or more dates a young man may ask his girl, "Do you want to go for steady, or for so?"

Boys often have their first date arranged for them after a singing. This is known as "getting propped up." A young man going steady will tell his bashful friend, "Let me prop it up for you." He arranges for the date and thus saves the beginner some embarrassment.

After chores are done on Sunday evening, the young folks prepare for the singing. The young man dresses in his best, brushes his hat and suit, and makes sure that his horse and "rig" are neat and clean. He may take his sister to the singing, or if he takes his girl he will arrange to pick her up about dusk, perhaps at her home or at the end of a lane or at a crossroad. In some localities the young folks meet in crossroad villages to pair off in couples. Considerable secrecy pervades the entire period of courtship.

Other occasions when young folks get together are husking bees, weddings, apple schnitzins (apple peeling and cutting parties), and frolics. [8]

Nostalgia for the Happy Family

Foremost among the myths [of the family] is what may be called the "legend of the Waltons": The nostalgic saga of the ideal "extended" family embracing three or more generations in its magic circle—a Norman Rockwell vision of a golden age from which we have sinfully fallen away to our present age of nuclear fission. [9]

Ashley Montagu

Rules for Little Women

The determination to hold the line on modernity and changing morals during the mid-twentieth century was embodied in the person of John R. Rice, a fiery fundamentalist radio preacher and the author of a widely circulated book, *Bobbed Hair, Bossy Wives, and Women Preachers*. He feared the "new woman" and her influence on the home and family values, and he insisted that "bobbed hair" was "a sign of woman's rebellion against husband, father and God"—even worse than the worldly sins of wearing "lipstick, rouge and painted fingernails"—and girls were not excluded:

Is it a sin for little girls to have bobbed hair? The Bible does not separately discuss that question as far as I know. But a girl should be subject to her father and should have the "symbol of authority" on her head. In our own home I felt that since my girls would grow to be women, they had better begin to feel like women and act like women. So all of my six daughters have long hair. And how beautiful it is! And when the matter is settled while they are young, and the character is fixed into the lines of womanly behavior and womanly thought and ideals, then I do not expect a great clash and struggle after they are women. Why should not girls be taught that long hair is a glory, as God has said? Why should they not revel in the thought of being women, wives and mothers? [10]

What Is a Good Family?

We found it easy in days past to define a good family. In my childhood, I knew what a good family was just from hearing my parents talk. "He comes from a good family" usually meant "from one like ours." The term "good family" was used in praise, for instance, when someone would say about a local marriage, "Isn't it wonderful? They both come from good families." And the phrase "good family" was spoken in sorrow when a young person deviated in some way from the work or faith values of the family. Then someone was sure to comment sadly, "Isn't it too bad? He comes from such a good family...."

A good family, then, was one that was self-sufficient, didn't ask for help from others, supported its institutions, was never tainted with failure, starved before it went on welfare, and met all the criteria of good families as determined by community and church.

People paid little attention to what went on inside a family—whether there was good communication, emotional support, or trusting relationships. People were only concerned about whether a family met the more obvious, visible family standards set by society. [11]

Dolores Curran

A Godly Heritage

Billy Graham was raised in a Christian home, where God held the place of honor from the first day of his parents' marriage. His father Franklin Graham proposed to his sweetheart, Morrow, in 1912, but it was not until the fall of 1916 that she was ready to tie the knot.

Before setting out for their five-day honeymoon in the mountains, she carefully tucked her Bible into her suitcase—"I just wouldn't have felt like a clean person without my Bible with me." On their wedding night, at last standing alone together in a bleak and sallow-lit hotel room, Franklin immediately had his bride kneel beside him on the worn linoleum and proceeded to conduct the two of them in an extended and slightly wavery prayer there by the side of the bed, "dedicating our marriage and our family to the Lord." [12]

Billy Graham at six months held by his mother Morrow Graham

Graham-Style Family Devotions

From the time Billy Graham was a small child, Bible study, prayer, and family devotions were a central part of the Graham home:

He grew up…in a regimen of diligent pieties in his household; by the time he was ten, he had memorized all the 107 articles in the Shorter Catechism. "We had Bible reading and prayer right after supper, even before I cleaned up the kitchen," says Mrs. Graham. "We all got down on our knees and prayed, yes we did, sometimes from twenty to thirty minutes. That was the main event of the day in our house."…On Sundays, Billy was forbidden to read the comics in the newspaper, to play ball, to venture into the woods—the only diversions during that day being the perusal of Scripture and religious tracts, with Mrs. Graham collecting the children into the front room in the afternoon to sit together listening, on their radio console, to Charles Fuller's "Old Fashioned Revival Hour." [13]

Feeling His Father's Belt

Billy Graham's parents maintained strict discipline for their growing son. Mischief and misdemeanors were dealt with, according to the biblical proverb, as his mother recalls:

Billy was always full of pranks; sometimes he carried things a bit too far, and off came his father's belt. Mr. Graham never punished in anger or desperation, but when he did see the necessity for correction, I winced. At such times I had to remind myself of another Proverb: "Withhold not correction from the child: for if thou beatest him with the rod, he shall not die"

197

(Proverbs 23:13). More than once I wiped tears from my eyes and turned my head so the children wouldn't see, but I always stood behind my husband when he administered discipline. I knew he was doing what was biblically correct. And the children didn't die. [14]

Definition of a Family

Even the best of families struggle with pain and problems and personality flaws that may not be evident to the world outside. The family of the late Francis Schaeffer is no exception. Schaeffer is known as one of the great philosophers and apologists of the evangelical world, who, with his wife Edith, founded the L'Abri community in Switzerland. But what was their family life like? In his book *Portofino* (described as an "autobiographical novel"), Franky, their son, writes in first person about boyhood in a fundamentalist Presbyterian missionary family to Switzerland that struggled with its own secret sins, including a father who fell into black rages and broke dishes and terrorized the family. Edith Schaeffer describes the family less graphically, but in terms we all recognize:

A family—for better or for worse, for richer or for poorer, in sickness and in health! Dirty diapers, chicken pox, measles, mumps, broken dishes, scratched furniture, balls thrown through the windows, fights, croup in the night, arguments, misunderstandings, inconsistencies, lack of logic, unreasonableness, anger, fever, flu, depressions, carelessness, toothpaste tops left off, dishes in the sink, windows open too far, windows closed tight, too many covers, too few covers, always late, always too early, frustration, economics, extravagance, discouragement, fatigue, exhaustion, noise, disappointment, weeping, fears, sorrows, darkness, fog, chaos, clamorings—families!

A family—for better or for worse, for richer or for poorer, in sickness and in health! Softness, hugs, children on your lap, someone to come home to, someone to bring news to, a telephone that might ring, a letter in the post, someone at the airport or station, excitement in meeting, coming home from the hospital with a new person to add…beloved old people, welcomed babies…families! [15]

Down on the farm—
an Iowa barn in the 1950s

A Father's Prayer

Build me a son, O God, who will be strong enough to know when he is weak and brave enough to face himself when he is afraid; one who will be proud and unbending in honest defeat, but humble and gentle in victory. Build me a son whose wishes will not replace his actions—a son who will know Thee and that to know himself is the foundation stone of knowledge. Send him, I pray, not in the path of ease and comfort but the stress and spur of difficulties and challenge; here let him learn to stand up in the storm, here let him learn compassion for those who fail.

Build me a son whose heart will be clear, whose goal will be high; a son who will master himself before he seeks to master others; one who will learn to laugh, yet never forget how to weep; one who will reach into the future, yet never forget the past, and after all these things are his, this I pray, enough sense of humor that he may always be serious yet never take himself too seriously. Give him humility so that he may always remember the simplicity of true greatness, the open mind of true wisdom, the meekness of true strength; then I, his father, will dare to whisper, "I have not lived in vain." [16]

General Douglas MacArthur

Importance of Fatherhood

By profession I am a soldier and take pride in that fact. But I am prouder to be a father. My hope is that my son, when I am gone, will remember me not from battle, but in the home, repeating with him one simple prayer, "Our Father which art in heaven." [17]

General Douglas MacArthur

A Father's Counsel from the Grave

Rosalynn Carter's carefree childhood in Plains, Georgia, was shattered when her father died of leukemia at the age of forty-four. As an eighth-grader, she was confused and flooded with guilt and shaken in her Christian faith:

I had prayed and prayed for him to get better, and because of those prayers, I'd expected him to get better. But he hadn't. . . . I felt sorry for myself and didn't understand why this had to happen to me. Had I been so bad? Didn't God love me anymore? I had doubts about God, and I was afraid because I doubted. That was long before I knew that God is a loving God who cares for us and loves us, who suffers when we suffer and who knows that we are going to have doubts and that we're not always going to do what is right, but he loves us anyway.

But even while she was doubting the love of God, her own father seemed to loom larger in her thinking:

199

In a curious way, my father affected me even more after he died than while he was alive. It seemed more important than ever to do what he had expected me to do. Whenever I was faced with a decision or even a temptation, I would think about whether Daddy would like it or not. The things he had talked about when I was little loomed large in my mind. I had heard him say many times how ugly women looked when they smoked cigarettes, so I never smoked. And I didn't dare take a drink. I had heard too much at home and in church about the "wicked" things that could happen to you if you drank. Curiously, we did have a bottle of whiskey in our house. My father bought it the day I was born because, he said, his father had always kept one in the house for medication…. The year after my daddy died our Uncle Will got sick and Mother gave him the last drink from the same bottle…fourteen years later! [18]

Bedtime Prayers

Bedtime prayers were a memorable part of Margaret Jensen's childhood, as she writes in *First We Have Coffee:*

Every detail of school and play came up on the bedtime screen. Nothing was hidden from Mama. As she tucked me in, she always said, "Look at me, Margaret. Is there anything you need to tell me before we talk to God?" Knowing her secret line to God, the confession poured out, and forgiveness followed. Sleep was sweet. [19]

Prayer for the Home

Peace, unto this house, I pray,
*   Keep terror and despair away;*
Shield it from evil and let sin
*   Never find lodging room within.*
May never in these walls be heard
*   The hateful or accusing word.*

Grant that its warm and mellow light
*   May be to all a beacon bright,*
A flaming symbol that shall stir

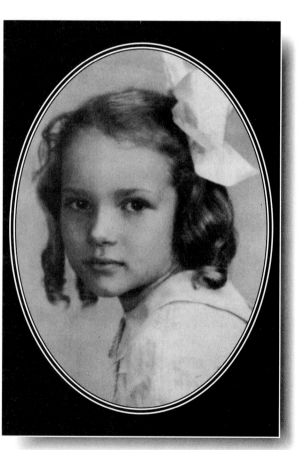

Rosalynn Carter at age six

The beating pulse of him or her
Who finds this door and seems to say,
  "Here end the trials of the day."

Hold us together, gentle Lord,
  Who sits about this humble board;
May we be spared the cruel fate
  Of those whom hatreds separate;
Here let love bind us fast, that we
  May know the joys of unity.

Lord, this humble house we'd keep
  Sweet with play and calm with sleep.
Help us so that we may give
  Beauty to the lives we live.
Let Thy love and let Thy grace
  Shine upon our dwelling place. [20]

Edgar A. Guest

Family Counsel from the Father of a Family Counselor

James Dobson, founder of Focus on the Family, was on the fast track to success in 1969, when he received a sobering letter from his father. "Although my activities," writes Dobson, "were bringing me professional advancement and the trappings of financial success, my dad was not impressed. He had watched my hectic lifestyle and felt obligated to express his concern. He did so in a lengthy letter which included the following paragraph":

Young James Dobson with his father

I have observed that the greatest delusion is to suppose that our children will be devout Christians simply because their parents have been or that any of them will enter into life in any other way than through the valley of deep travail of prayer and faith.

204

Failure at this point for you would make mere success in business a very pale and washed-out affair indeed. But this prayer demands time, time that cannot be given if it is all signed and conscripted and laid on the altar of career ambition.

"Those words," writes Dobson, "written without accusation or insult, hit me like the blow of a hammer. My father reminded me that my number-one responsibility is to evangelize my own children, as he had me." [21]

The Laughter of a Child

The laugh of a child will make the holiest day more sacred still. . . . Fill the vast cathedral aisles with symphonies sweet and dim . . . but know, your sweetest strains are discords all, compared with childhood's happy laugh—the laugh that fills the eyes with light and every heart with joy. O rippling river of laughter, thou art the blessed boundary line between the beasts and men; and every forward wave of thine doth drown some fretful fiend of care. O Laughter, rose-lipped daughter of joy, there are dimples enough in thy cheeks to catch and hold and glorify all the tears of grief. [22]

Robert G. Ingersoll

Growing Up in the Parsonage

Gloria Gaither credits her parents for giving her a stable and loving childhood. Her father was a minister, and there were many tender moments and many times of laughter in the parsonage that she called home.

My parents surrounded me with the Gospel and nestled me in their love for it. I often happened in on my father as he sat alone with the Bible, tears streaming down his cheeks at the beauty of some revelation. In our home, prayer was a natural response to problems and crises as well as good news and celebrations. My parents were verbal about their relationship with God, with each other, with us children, and with others. "I love you" was heard daily, not only when we were having family hugs, but also when we were having family worship.
My parents also gave me a sense of humor, and believe me, survival in a parsonage often depended on our ability to laugh. Daddy, for example, doubled over with laughter when we told him he had declared that "Judas is a carrot," and we all got a hearty chuckle from the prayer meeting in which a dear old saint testified that "my head hurt and I asked the Lord to take it away—and he did!" [23]

A Mother's Dedication of Her "Samuel"

As a young girl she dreamed of becoming a missionary, but when she was nine years old her father died, and she had no choice but quit school and find a job to support her mother and five younger brothers and sisters. Then, at sixteen, she married, but she never gave up her dream. She reached out to her neighbors in Philadelphia, and passed that vision on to her son, Tony Campolo, who has not only been active in mission work but has also become a noted author and speaker. In a tribute to his mother, he writes:

Tony Campolo (center)
with his family

As I grew up, she told me that I was her "Samuel" and that, like that character in the Bible, I had been presented to the Lord for service. Nothing in my life motivated me to give my life to missions more than her constant reminder that she had raised me for this calling....

Years later, as a sociologist, I learned the famous concept of "Cooley's Looking-Glass Self." According to Charles Cooley, one of the founders of American sociology, what you think of yourself is for the most part determined by what you think the most important person in your life thinks of you. When I was a child, the most important person in my life was my mother, and there was never any doubt as to what she thought of me. In her eyes, I was the greatest child who ever lived, and that faith in me was one of her greatest gifts....

Mom never took a course in parenting. She never heard those neo-Freudian theories about child rearing. I am sure that the "experts" in the field of child psychology could find many flaws in her practices. All I know is that she was always there. And she believed in me. And she modeled for me that missionary work is the best thing anyone can do. That's not a bad legacy for the daughter of Italian immigrants who had to drop out of school when she was nine years old. I hope that somehow she knows her dream lives on. [24]

A Prayer for Children

Father, hear us, we are praying,
   Hear the words our hearts are saying,
We are praying for our children.

Keep them from the powers of evil,
   From the secret, hidden peril,
From the whirlpool that would suck them
   From the treacherous quicksand pluck them.

From the worldling's hollow gladness
   From the sting of faithless sadness,
Holy Father, save our children.

> *Through life's troubled waters steer them,*
> *Through life's bitter battle cheer them,*
> *Father, Father, be Thou near them.*
> *Read the language of our longing,*
> *Read the wordless pleadings thronging,*
> *Holy Father, for our children*
> *And wherever they may bide,*
> *Lead them Home at eventide.* [25]

Amy Carmichael

The Graham Prodigal Sons

Billy Graham's own family life with his wife Ruth and their five children was very different than the home in which he was raised. With Billy often away conducting crusade evangelism, Ruth spent much of her child-rearing years as a single mother. She wrote a book about these years of struggle—especially with her two sons, Franklin and Ned. The title speaks for itself: *Prodigals—And Those Who Love Them.*

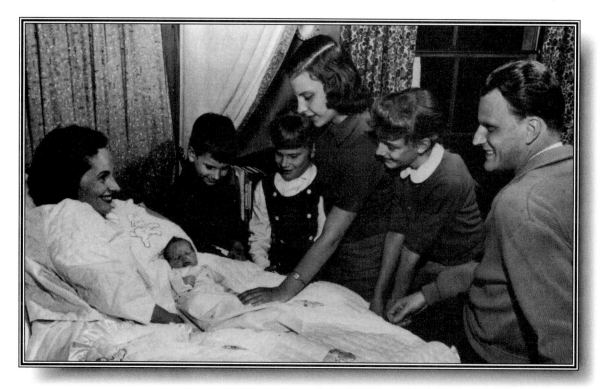

The Graham family admiring the latest addition, Nelson (Ned), born January 17, 1958

🎀 *As Franklin grew older, I'd get calls from the police. I'd get calls from the headmaster of his school. Franklin once said, "My Mom's hair is white because of me." To which I replied, "Don't take all the credit, son. Age has something to do with it."*

There's quite a gap in age between Franklin and my fifth child, Ned. He was a loving child, but he also went through a period where he was involved with drugs. Looking back on it, it seems like just a few weeks ago. But it dragged on for years. [26]

Ruth Graham's Child-Rearing Advice

From her own heart-breaking trials as a mother, Ruth Graham speaks from her heart to other parents. One night when she was lying awake worrying about Ned, she reached for her Bible and turned to Philippians 4, where she read: "In nothing be anxious, but in everything by prayer and supplication with thanksgiving let your requests be made known unto God." Through this experience she offers advice to others:

🎀 *Suddenly I realized the missing ingredient to my prayers had been thanksgiving. So I sat there and thanked God for all that Ned was and all he had meant to me through the years.... When we're most concerned, we should start thanking the Lord for the lessons He is teaching us through the tough times. And invariably, it's during those tough times that the Scriptures really come to life. Prayer is so important. Our children never outreach God's reach. This doesn't mean they won't go astray. This doesn't mean they won't mess up their lives. But sometimes we forget God is omnipotent, omnipresent, omniscient, and eternal. Our children can run but God knows where they are, and God's watching over them. I remember praying, "Lord, help me discipline this boy." He could get into more mischief when he was little. God never speaks out loud to me, but I know when He's spoken. "Love him more," He told me. And that's exactly what Franklin needed. The most important thing we can do for our children is to have two parents who love and respect one another, who love and respect the Lord, and who love and respect their children as people. And I think we should keep rules to a minimum.* [27]

Family Security

Joni Eareckson Tada grew up in a Christian family where she felt safe and secure under the protection of her parents. That security was shattered when as a teenager she was paralyzed in a diving accident. She was suddenly forced to trust in God as though she were alone in the raging seas of life.

🎀 *Each night as my parents put me to bed, I was reminded of God's care. Over my bed hung a plaque of a little girl in a tiny rowboat out on the ocean. She was surrounded by a dark night sprinkled with stars. Under the scene were the words, "Dear God, my little boat and I are on Your open sea. Please guide us safely through the waves, my little boat and me." As I gazed at the plaque, it amazed me that the girl was apparently not afraid. "Wow!" I thought. "That little girl really trusts God—but I wonder where her parents are? I'm glad mine are here."* [28]

Prayer of a Child

E. Stanley Jones often repeated the prayer of a little girl who was the daughter of missionary friends of his in India:

> *God bless Mama and Papa, my brothers and sisters, and all my friends. And now, God do take care of Yourself, for if anything should happen to You, we'd all be in the soup.* [29]

Epilogue

As I reflect back on the generations of family life that have gone by since biblical times, I am awed by my incredible family heritage. The record of my own family tree goes back only a few generations, but in a very real sense it goes back to the very beginning of time. It goes back to Adam and Eve in the Garden, where God revealed the human family—male and female becoming one flesh—as the pinnacle of creation. But as we know, family breakdown was only a temptation away. It was the tree of knowledge of good and evil that in a real sense turned into the family tree for all generations—a family tree of good and evil.

The family tree that runs through the Old Testament is one that is diseased by the blight of sin, and though the tree is grafted by a branch out of the stump of Jesse— the cross of Christ—the blight remains. From generation to generation through the early centuries on through the Middle Ages and Reformation and to the present time, the tree is never again truly healthy. There are leaves and sometimes whole branches that seem to be free from blight—but never entirely so. In certain seasons the tree appears less hearty than in others—almost dying—but it somehow always weathers the onslaught and continues

The "home place"—the Stellrecht family dressed in their Sunday best, with the author's father crouched in center right

growing and adding more leaves and branches for another season.

And despite its disease and blight, this family tree offers shade and shelter and security in the storms of life. With all its defects, it is who we are—our heritage and our future. One day, though, it will turn into a tree of life—no blight and no scars to remind us of its hollow core and rotting branches. The perfect family tree of creation will once again reappear as the perfect family tree throughout eternity.

I am humbled and gratified that somewhere amid the leaves and branches of this gigantic tree—blighted though it is—I can find my own family line, coming out of hearty German Lutheran stock. My grandparents on my father's side emigrated to America around the turn of the century. They settled on a farm near other family members in northern Wisconsin, and today there is a region west of Spooner and Shell Lake where the name Stellrecht is more common than the name Smith. My father was the fourth son in a family of eight children, and all five boys acquired farms close by the "home place."

My father died in 1989, and at his funeral I read the following eulogy:

In Memory of Percy W. Stellrecht

Dad was born on December 28, 1900, the fourth son of Christ and Luisa Stellrecht who had moved to this country from Germany, and after living in Minnesota for a time, settled on a farm several miles west of Spooner.

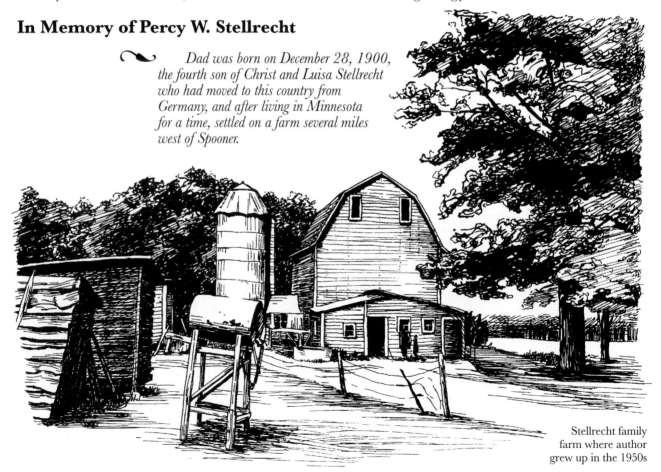

Stellrecht family
farm where author
grew up in the 1950s

As a young child, Dad visited Germany with his family. It was a trip that did not produce entirely happy memories—especially as he later recalled the meager food rations he was allotted.

Dad attended school through the eighth grade in the community. He was apparently a good student, and as children we often went to him for help with our homework.

Dad worked with his folks on the home place until he was twenty-six and was able to buy his own 160-acre farm just two miles away. He fixed up the house and soon began constructing other buildings. It was there where he "batched" for the next twelve years—until he married Mom, Jennie Carlton, a school teacher who had grown up only five miles away from the Stellrecht home place. They were married on August 19, 1938 at the Carlton farm and then went on a honeymoon in Mom's 1937 Chevy to Yellowstone National Park.

In the years that followed, as we five children came along, the house and the farm work expanded. In 1949, Dad supplemented the work of Dick and Colonel (our team of horses) with a tractor. The following year, we really went modern when we got electricity and indoor plumbing.

As children we have fond memories of life on the farm. There were long days of hard work, but there were also times of relaxation. We attended the Green Grove Alliance Church and often spent Sunday afternoons with a picnic dinner at a lake. Dad especially enjoyed these times, but in many ways his life was his farming—dairy farming throughout most of his life and beef cattle in the later years.

But he was known most for strawberries and vegetables that he raised and then sold in Spooner. Indeed, "Percy's strawberries" were almost considered a delicacy by some people and we still hear people comment about how they enjoyed that flavor.

Dad continued farming after Mom's death in 1969, and even after his cancer surgery in 1972. In fact, he was still selling his strawberries and vegetables in town when he was in his late seventies. By the time of his eightieth birthday party, though, his health was declining, and for the past five-and-a-half years, he has resided at the Spooner Nursing Home.

It was hard for Dad to leave the farm, but he seemed contented during his final years in the nursing home and became a favorite of many of the staff members there. He lived a long life and will be remembered fondly by all of us.

Growing Up on the Farm

When I was growing up in the 1940s and 1950s, life was much harder in many ways than it is today. We dreamed about the appliances and home furnishings and gadgets pictured in the Sears and Roebuck catalog, but they were beyond the reach of a poor farm family. Our "bathroom" was an outhouse, and we took our Saturday night baths in the kitchen in a big washtub right near the old wood

Author in 1948 (age 3) with father
who is fixing her wagon

stove. We washed our clothes with a ringer washer, and milked the cows by hand. It was a simple life back then, and I can sometimes still smell the fresh-mowed hay, hear the bumblebees buzzing in the clover, and see the Holstein cows grazing in the south pasture.

The Legacy of a Little Country Church

My faith pilgrimage began in the tiny Green Grove Alliance church—a church that made an incredible difference in my life, as I tell in my book, *Women in the Maze*:

> *The setting was a rural community in northern Wisconsin in the 1930s. Enter two "lady preachers"—Miss Salthammer and Miss Cowan— convinced that they were called by God to plant a church where there was no Gospel ministry. In the years that followed they did just that. First they opened a Sunday School and then they initiated church services. They evangelized, visited the sick, taught classes and preached sermons. Finally when the little church was on solid footing, they moved on to plant other churches, and a succession of male pastors took over the work. Miss Salthammer and Miss Cowan occasionally returned to my community to teach vacation Bible school, and it was through this ministry that I became acquainted with them. I thought they were rather odd characters, and it has not been until recent years that I have begun to appreciate them for who they were and for the incredible sacrifice they made. Their pay was rarely in cash—more often a trunk load of potatoes or turnips—and they lived and died in poverty. Indeed, when Miss Cowan died, she was buried in a pauper's grave. The county paid for her burial because no one else—not even the people of my little country church—came forward with the money.*
>
> *Today I often wonder if I would be a follower of Christ had it not been for their sacrificial service.* [1]

School Days

There was no kindergarten in those days for us country kids, and for me, first grade began at the Gaslyn Creek School—a tiny one-room schoolhouse where I learned alongside David and Jeannine, my older brother and sister—and some twenty other children. My most vivid memory of that year was in the dead of winter when the school bus became stuck in a snow drift, and my father came and pulled us out with his team of horses.

Gaslyn Creek School class picture, with author seated in front to the right of the school sign

Hard work was taken for granted, but there were fun and relaxing times as well. I was a "tomboy" and loved climbing trees and building "camps" with Jonnie my younger brother. I spent hours hiking through the woods with my little sister Kathy, and Buzzy my goat—the only pet I could ever call my own. Church hay rides and sledding parties were the social highlights of the year, and at Christmas-time, we all had our own little Christmas trees to decorate. In junior high and high school the French horn became my consuming focus—second only to church. As a youth, I took my faith and my "call" to ministry very seriously.

A Call to Missions

In the *Postscript* to my book *From Jerusalem to Irian Jaya,* I reflect on those who, for one reason or another, did not follow the call of God to overseas missions, and I share my own pilgrimage:

> One of those stories began in the 1950s in a farming community in northern Wisconsin. The setting was a summer Bible camp where missionary Delmer Smith of the Christian and Missionary Alliance was the featured speaker. There in the rustic pavilion under his moving messages a thirteen-year-old farm girl caught a vision for missions, and at the closing meeting she stood to commit her life to God as a foreign missionary. Through her high school years that followed, foreign missions was her life's goal. Nothing, she vowed, would deter her.
>
> Following her high school graduation her life was busy and eventful. Bible college, Christian liberal arts college, university, marriage, family, teacher career. One followed on another. But as the years slipped by, the prospect of embarking on an overseas mission career became less and less a reality.
>
> Only three miles away from her childhood home another young farm girl was growing up—her cousin, Valerie Stellrecht. They attended the same schools and the same little country church. Valerie, too, felt called to foreign missions. She, too, enrolled at the St. Paul Bible College to prepare for her life's calling. And she, too, longed for marriage and family. But her sense of calling to the foreign field came first. Valerie graduated from Bible college and soon thereafter bade farewell to her family and loved ones and set out alone for Ecuador, where she continues to serve today with the Christian and Missionary Alliance.
>
> Two young women whose lives paralleled each other's in so many respects. Two young women who felt called to foreign missions. Valerie went. I stayed home. [2]

Happy Memories and a Blighted Family Tree

Reflecting back on my childhood and youth, I tend to think only of the happy times that spanned the hot, sunny summer days to the shivering winter mornings when I huddled in front of the warm-air register. Life was simple back then, and I had few worries. My mother had a sharp temper and the wooden spoon was never far out of her reach, but I remember mostly her good humor and fun—and her fierce love for her five children. I've somehow forgotten the bad times—except for that awful evening of September 23, 1969, when the phone rang in my New Jersey apartment and Jonnie told me that Mom had been killed in a car accident—on Carlton Road, only three miles from home, a stone's throw away from the Carlton farm on which she had grown up. The grief was indescribable. Thankfully, there were happy memories to cling to.

But if my mind gravitates to the happy memories, I know all too well that my family, like all families, had our share of scandals and secrets. The disease and blight on the family tree did not escape us. There was a grandfather who sexually abused a granddaughter, an aunt who committed suicide leaving four young children behind, another aunt who divorced (a real scandal in those days), a cousin with the shame of an unwed pregnancy, and many more things we tried to hide from the neighbors. Our family was part of the blighted family tree that has come down through the generations since Adam and Eve.

The family tree continues to grow. On July 13, 1974, I gave birth to a son, Carlton Rand Tucker, who carries the names from both sides of the family. Today he is a young man, continuing on with the faith and with the family traditions—a branch for the next generation.

Ruth A. Tucker

Ruth A. Tucker holds a Ph.D. in history from Northern Illinois University and makes her home in Grand Rapids, Michigan. For twelve years she has served as a visiting professor of missions at Trinity Evangelical Divinity School in Deerfield, Illinois, and also teaches part-time at Calvin College, Fuller Theological Seminary, and Moffat College of the Bible in Kenya. A widely-traveled retreat and conference speaker, she also is the author of eleven books, including the Gold Medallion Award-winning *From Jerusalem to Irian Jaya* and *Private Lives of Pastors' Wives*.

Notes

INTRODUCTION

1. Mary Stewart Van Leeuwen, *Gender and Grace: Love, Work and Parenting in a Changing World* (Downers Grove, IL: InterVarsity, 1990), 10-11.

CHAPTER 1

1. Alexander Whyte, *Bible Characters* (New York: Fleming H. Revell, n.d.) 23-24.
2. Elie Wiesel, *Messengers of God: Biblical Portraits and Legends*, trans. by Marion Wiesel (New York: Random House, 1976), 14-15.
3. Cited in Herbert Lockyer, *All the Women of the Bible* (Grand Rapids: Zondervan, 1985), 57.
4. Mark Twain, "Eve's Diary," in Ruth Shelden, ed., *The Ways of God and Men* (New York: Stephen Daye, 1950), 19-25.
5. Elaine Pagels, *Adam, Eve, and the Serpent* (New York: Random House, 1988), 63.
6. Cited in Diane Kelsey McColley, *Milton's Eve* (Urbana: University of Illinois, 1983), 92-93.
7. Nancy Tischler, *Legacy of Eve* (Atlanta: John Knox, 1977), 11.
8. Cited in Mary Ann Jeffreys, "Colorful Sayings of Colorful Luther," *Christian History*, Issue 34, 27.
9. Eileen Power, *Medieval Women* (New York: Cambridge University, 1975), 34.
10. Jeffrey L. Sheler, "The Gospel on Sex," *U.S. News & World Report*, June 10, 1991, 61.
11. Gilbert Bilezikian, *Beyond Sex Roles* (Grand Rapids: Baker, 1985), 49.
12. Elisabeth Elliot, "The Essence of Femininity," in John Piper and Wayne Grudem, eds., *Recovering Biblical Manhood and Womanhood* (Wheaton, IL: Crossway, 1991), 397.
13. John A. Phillips, *Eve: The History of an Idea* (San Francisco: Harper & Row, 1984), 77.
14. Antonia Fraser, *The Weaker Vessel* (New York: Vintage, 1985), 147.
15. Ruth A. Tucker and Walter L. Liefeld, *Daughters of the Church: Women and Ministry from New Testament Times to the Present* (Grand Rapids: Zondervan, 1987), 185, 221.
16. Fraser, *Weaker Vessel*, 247.
17. Fannie MacDowell Hunter, ed., *Women Preachers* (Dallas: Berachah, 1905), 26.
18. Cotton Mather, *Tabitha Rediviva* cited in Rosemary Ruether & Rosemary Keller, *Women and Religion in America* (New York: Harper & Row, 1983, vol. 2), 339.
19. Cited in Fraser, *Weaker Vessel*, 71.
20. Cited in Laurel Thatcher Ulrich, *Good Wives* (New York: Oxford, 1980), 113.
21. Whyte, *Bible Characters*, 34.
22. Fraser, *Weaker Vessel*, 79-80.
23. H.V. Morton, *Women of the Bible* (New York: Dodd, Mead & Company, 1956), 14-15.
24. Cited in Lockyer, *All the Women of the Bible*, 58.
25. Fulton Oursler, *The Greatest Book Ever Written* (Garden City, NY: Doubleday, 1951), 10.
26. Wiesel, *Messengers of God*, 41, 47-49.
27. Cited in Dolores Curran, *Traits of a Healthy Family* (Minneapolis: Winston, 1983), 10.
28. D.L. Moody in *Bible Characters* (Chicago: Thomas Jackson, 1902), 17.
29. S.T. Martyn, *Women of the Bible* (Philadelphia: Cowperthwait, 1868), 20-21.
30. Herbert Lockyer, *All the Women of the Bible*, 171-172.
31. Joel Belz, "Cain and Abel Got the Headlines," *World*, May 9, 1992, 3.
32. John R. Levison, *Portraits of Adam in Early Judaism* (Sheffield, England: Sheffield Academic Press, 1988), 164-190.
33. Martin Luther, *Table Talk*, trans. by William Hazlitt (Philadelphia: United Lutheran Publication House, n.d.), 298.
34. Herbert Lockyer, *All the Women of the Bible*, 171-172.
35. Philip Schaff, *History of the Christian Church* (Grand Rapids: Eerdmans, 1979), VI, 729-730.

CHAPTER 2

1. Mary Stewart Van Leeuwen, *Gender and Grace: Love, Work and Parenting in a Changing World* (Downers Grove, IL: InterVarsity, 1990), 171-172.
2. Philip Yancey, *I Was Just Wondering* (Grand Rapids: Eerdmans, 1989), 156-157.
3. James B. Hurley, *Man and Woman in Biblical Perspective* (Grand Rapids: Zondervan, 1981), 42.
4. Bernard I. Murstein, *Love, Sex, and Marriage Through the Ages* (New York: Springer, 1974), 35.
5. Murstein, *Love, Sex, and Marriage*, 35.
6. Murstein, *Love, Sex, and Marriage*, 37.
7. Philip Yancey, *Disappointment with God* (Grand Rapids: Zondervan, 1988), 66-67.
8. Murstein, *Love, Sex, and Marriage*, 37.
9. Murstein, *Love, Sex, and Marriage*, 38.
10. Hurley, *Man and Woman in Biblical Perspective*, 33-34.
11. David Briggs, "Clay Tablets," *Grand Rapids Press*, August 29, 1993, B2.
12. Henri Daniel-Rops, *Daily Life in the Time of Jesus* (New York: Hawthorn Books, 1962), 118.
13. Ann Landers column, June 9, 1992.
14. William E. Phipps, *Assertive Biblical Women* (Westport, CT: Greenwood, 1992), 14-15.
15. Cited in George C. Baldwin, *Representative Women* (Philadelphia: American Baptist Publication Society, 1855), 82-83.
16. Alexander Whyte, *Bible Characters from the Old and New Testaments* (Grand Rapids: Kregel, 1990), 201.
17. Cynthia Maus, *The Old Testament and the Fine Arts* (New York: Harper & Row, 1954), 249.
18. Elie Wiesel, *Sages and Dreamers* (New York: Summit Books, 1991), 61-63.
19. Whyte, *Bible Characters*, 209-210.
20. Charles Swindoll, *You and Your Child* (New York: Bantam, 1980), 87-95.
21. Wiesel, *Sages and Dreamers*, 99, 112.

CHAPTER 3

1. Elliott Wright, *Holy Company: Christian Heroes and Heroines* (New York: Macmillan, 1980), 76.
2. Harriet Beecher Stowe, *Footsteps of the Master* (New York: J.B. Ford, 1877), 52.
3. Denis O'Shea, *Mary and Joseph* (Milwaukee: Bruce Publishing, 1949), 32-35.
4. O'Shea, *Mary and Joseph*, 36-38.
5. Philip Schaff, *History of the Christian Church* (Grand Rapids: Eerdmans, 1979), 5, 840-842.
6. Henri Daniel-Rops, *Daily Life in the Time of Jesus* (New York: Hawthorn Books, 1962), 126.
7. Ruth A. Tucker, *Multiple Choices: Making Wise Decisions in a Complicated World* (Grand Rapids: Zondervan, 1992), 33.
8. O'Shea, *Mary and Joseph*, 32-38.
9. A.C. Bouquet, *Everyday Life in New Testament Times* (New York: Charles Scribner's Sons, 1954), 147-148.
10. O'Shea, *Mary and Joseph*, 84-85.
11. O'Shea, *Mary and Joseph*, 382.
12. Charles Leach, *Mothers of the Bible* (New York: Fleming H. Revell, 1900), 58.
13. Bouquet, *Everyday Life in New Testament Times*, 146-147.
14. Ruth A. Tucker and Walter L. Liefeld, *Daughters of the Church: Women and Ministry from New Testament Times to the Present* (Grand Rapids: Zondervan, 1987), 169.
15. Marina Warner, *Alone of All Her Sex: The Myth and the Cult of the Virgin Mary* (New York: Alfred A. Knopf, 1976), 29.
16. Edgar Hennecke, *New Testament Apocrypha* (Philadelphia: Westminster, 1959), 393.
17. Cynthia Maus, *Christ and the Fine Arts* (New York: Harper & Row, 1959), 113.
18. Charles E. Miller, *Mother and Disciple* (New York: Alba House, 1989), 63.
19. Philip Yancey, *Disappointment with God* (Grand Rapids: Zondervan, 1988), 109.
20. Daniel-Rops, *Daily Life in the Time of Jesus*, 480.
21. Marjorie Holmes, *Three from Galilee* (San Francisco: Harper & Row, 1985), 155-156.
22. O'Shea, *Mary and Joseph*, 86.
23. Paul K. Jewett, *Man as Male and Female* (Grand Rapids: Eerdmans, 1975), 110.
24. Dorothy Pape, *In Search of God's Ideal Woman* (Downers Grove, IL: InterVarsity, 1976), 63.
25. Daniel-Rops, *Daily Life in the Time of Jesus*, 374.
26. Jean Cantinat, *Mary in the Bible* (Westminster, MD: Newman, 1965), 182.

CHAPTER 4

1. Lloyd deMause, "The Evolution of Childhood," in Lloyd deMause, ed. *The History of Childhood* (New York: Atcom, 1974), 43-44.
2. Evelyn and Frank Stagg, *Woman in the World of Jesus* (Philadelphia: Westminster, 1978), 46, 49.
3. Stagg, *Woman in the World of Jesus*, 53.
4. Rodney Clapp, "Is the Traditional Family Biblical?" *Christianity Today*, September 16, 1988, 24.
5. *The Message*, Paraphrased New Testament by Eugene Peterson, cited in the *Grand Rapids Press*, August 28, 1993, B1.
6. Cynthia Maus, *Christ and the Fine Arts* (New York: Harper & Row, 1959), 302.
7. Francis Greenwood Peabody, *Jesus Christ and the Social Question* (New York: Grosset & Dunlap, 1900), 147-148.
8. T. DeWitt Talmadge, *From Manger to Throne* (New York: The Christian Herald, 1893), 414-415.
9. Mary Stewart Van Leeuwen, *Gender and Grace: Love, Work and Parenting in a Changing World* (Downers Grove, IL: InterVarsity), 49.
10. James B. Hurley, *Man and Woman in Biblical Perspective* (Grand Rapids: Zondervan, 1981), 88.
11. Hurley, *Man and Woman*, 109.

12. C. John Sommerville, *The Rise and Fall of Childhood* (New York: Random House, 1990), 49-50.
13. Daniel-Rops, *Daily Life in the Time of Jesus*, 350.
14. A. C. Bouquet, *Everyday Life in New Testament Times* (New York: Charles Scribner's Sons, 1954), 28.
15. John Pollock, *The Apostle: A Life of Paul* (Wheaton, IL: Victor, 1972), 4-5.
16. Cited in Herbert Lockyer, *All the Women of the Bible* (Grand Rapids: Zondervan, 1985), 245-246.
17. Lockyer, *All the Women of the Bible*, 244-245.
18. William J. Petersen, *The Discipling of Timothy* (Wheaton, IL: Victor, 1980),10-14.
19. Patricia Gundry, *Woman Be Free!* (Grand Rapids: Zondervan, 1977), 72-73.
20. Bouquet, *Everyday Life in New Testament Times*, 146-147.
21. Philip Greven, *Spare the Child: The Religious Roots of Punishment and the Psychological Impact of Physical Abuse* (New York: Alfred A. Knopf, 1991), 54.
22. Edith Deen, *Great Women of the Christian Faith* (San Francisco: Harper & Row, 1959), 293-294.
23. Pollock, *The Apostle: A Life of Paul*, 237-238.

CHAPTER 5

1. Philip Schaff, *History of the Christian Church* (Grand Rapids: Eerdmans,1979), II, 787.
2. Michael Green, *Evangelism in the Early Church* (Grand Rapids: Eerdmans, 1970), 219.
3. F.F. Bruce, *The Spreading Flame* (Grand Rapids: Eerdmans, 1979), 190.
4. Schaff, *History of the Christian Church*, III, 112.
5. Schaff, *History of the Christian Church*, II, 788.
6. Steven Ozment, "Re-inventing Family Life," *Christian History*, Issue 39, 22.
7. Steven Ozment, *Protestants: The Birth of a Revolution* (New York: Doubleday, 1992), cited in *Christian History*, Issue 39, 23.
8. Richard B. Lyman, Jr., "Barbarism and Religion," in Lloyd deMause, *The History of Childhood* (New York: Atcom, 1974), 86.
9. Steven Ozment, *When Fathers Ruled: Family Life in Reformation Europe* (Cambridge, MA: Harvard University, 1983), 188.
10. Jean LaPorte, *The Role of Women in Early Christianity* (New York: Edwin Mellen, 1982), 27-28.
11. Bernard I. Murstein, *Love, Sex and Marriage Through the Ages* (New York: Springer, 1974), 104.
12. John Chrysostom, "The Wife's Domain" in *Christian History*, Issue 17, 34.
13. Schaff, *History of the Christian Church*, II, 366.
14. Lyman, "Barbarism and Religion," in deMause, *The History of Childhood*, 90-91.
15. Michael J. Gorman, *Abortion in the Early Church* (Downers Grove, IL: InterVarsity, 1982) 55.
16. Anne Yarbrough, "Christianization in the Fourth Century: The Example of Roman Women," *Church History*, June 1976, 156.
17. *The Martyrdom of Perpetua and Felicitas, Christian History*, Issue 17, 32.
18. Lyman, "Barbarism and Religion," in deMause, *The History of Childhood*, 89.
19. Brian L. Harbour, *Famous Parents of the Bible* (Nashville: Broadman, 1983), 26.
20. Lyman, "Barbarism and Religion," in deMause, *The History of Childhood*, 87.
21. Augustine, *The Confessions of Augustine in Modern English*, ed. by Sherwood E. Wirt (Grand Rapids: Zondervan, 1986), 46-47.
22. V. Raymond Edman, *The Light in Dark Ages* (Wheaton, IL: Van Kampen Press, 1949) 46.
23. Lyman, "Barbarism and Religion," in deMause, *The History of Childhood*, 75.
24. Susan G. Bell, ed., *Women from the Greeks to the French Revolution* (Stanford, CA: Stanford University, 1973), 90-91.
25. Paulinus the Deacon, "The Life of St. Ambrose," in *The Western Church Fathers* (New York, 1965), 150-151.

26. Deen, *Great Women of the Christian Faith* (San Francisco: Harper & Row, 1959), 11; Jean LaPorte, *The Role of Women in Early Christianity* (New York: Edwin Mellen, 1982), 81, 85.

27. *Christian History*, Issue 17, 35; trans. by Elizabeth A. Clark.

CHAPTER 6

1. Philip Hughes, *A Popular History of the Reformation* (Garden City, NY: Doubleday, 1960), 19.

2. Frances and Joseph Gies, *Life in a Medieval Village* (New York: Harper & Row, 1990), 91.

3. Frances and Joseph Gies, *Marriage and the Family in the Middle Ages* (New York: Harper & Row, 1987), 242.

4. *The Babees' Book: Medieval Manners for the Young* (New York: Cooper Square Publishers, 1966), 24-25.

5. Eileen Power, *Medieval Women* (New York: Cambridge University, 1975), 67.

6. Gies, *Life in a Medieval Village*, 115.

7. Gies, *Life in a Medieval Village*, 115.

8. Gies, *Life in a Medieval Village*, 115.

9. Marjorie Rowling, *Life in Medieval Times* (New York: G.P. Putnam's Sons, 1979), 65.

10. Rowling, *Life in Medieval Times*, 72.

11. Geoffrey Chaucer, *Canterbury Tales* cited in Frances and Joseph Gies, *Women in the Middle Ages* (New York: Thomas Y. Crowell, 1978), 59.

12. Rowling, *Life in Medieval Times*, 73.

13. Power, *Medieval Women*, 43.

14. Gies, *Marriage and Family*, 63.

15. Gies, *Women in the Middle Ages*, 55.

16. Gies, *Women in the Middle Ages*, 6.

17. Gies, *Women in the Middle Ages*, 204.

18. Gies, *Marriage and Family*, 61.

19. Philippe Aries, *Centuries of Childhood: A Social History of Family Life* (New York: Random House, 1962), 33.

20. Rowling, *Life in Medieval Times*, 138.

21. Ruth A. Tucker and Walter L. Liefeld, *Daughters of the Church: Women and Ministry from New Testament Times to the Present* (Grand Rapids: Zondervan, 1987), 141.

22. Gies, *Marriage and Family*, 106-107.

23. Karen Scott, "Catherine of Siena, 'Apostula,'" *Church History* (March 1992), 43.

24. Will Durant, *The Age of Faith* (New York: Simon and Schuster, 1950), 606.

25. Philip Schaff, *History of the Christian Church* (Grand Rapids: Eerdmans, 1979), V, 612.

26. Gies, *Marriage and Family*, 223.

27. Giovanni della Casa, *A Renaissance Courtesy-Book: Galateo of Manners and Behaviours* (Boston, 1924), 20, 26; Gies, *Marriage and Family*, 223.

28. della Casa, *A Renaissance Courtesy-Book*, 25.

29. *The Babees' Book*, 24-25.

30. Schaff, *History of the Christian Church*, VI, 731-733.

31. Henry Lucas, *The Renaissance and Reformation* (New York: Harper & Row, 1960), 143-144.

32. Gies, *Life in a Medieval Village*, 102.

33. Desiderius Erasmus, *The Religious Pilgrimage* cited in Lucas, *The Renaissance and the Reformation*, 511.

34. Gies, *Life in a Medieval Village*, 127.

CHAPTER 7

1. Roland Bainton, *Here I Stand: A Life of Martin Luther* (New York: Abingdon, 1950), 23, 26-27.

2. Jean Rilliet, *Zwingli: Third Man of the Reformation* (Philadelphia: Westminster, 1959), 32-33, 47.

3. Steven Ozment, "Re-inventing Family," *Christian History*, Issue 39, 23.

4. Bernard I. Murstein, *Love, Sex, and Marriage Through the Ages* (New York: Springer, 1974), 177.

5. Murstein, *Love, Sex, and Marriage*, 189.

6. C. Camden, *The Elizabethan Woman* (Houston: Elsevier Press, 1952), 102.

7. Murstein, *Love, Sex, and Marriage*, 178, 184, 185; Ozment, "Re-inventing Family," 24; Walther I. Brandt, ed., *Luther's Works*, 45 (Philadelphia: Fortress, 1962), 38.

8. Richard Friedenthal, *Luther: His Life and Times*, trans. by John Nowell (New York: Harcourt Brace Jovanovich, 1970), 438; Patrick F. O'Hare, *The Facts about Luther* (New York: Frederick Pustet, 1916), 353.

9. Murstein, *Love, Sex and Marriage*, 194.

10. Thea B. Van Halsema, *This Was John Calvin* (Grand Rapids: Baker, 1981), 113.

11. Ruth A. Tucker and Walter L. Liefeld, *Daughters of the Church: Women and Ministry from New Testament Times to the Present* (Grand Rapids: Zondervan, 1987), 179-186.

12. Murstein, *Love, Sex, and Marriage*, 183.

13. Steven Ozment, *When Fathers Ruled: Family Life in Reformation Europe* (Cambridge, MA: Harvard University, 1983), 55.

14. Ozment, *When Fathers Ruled*, 80-84.

15. Ozment, "Re-inventing Family," 26.

16. Cited in Murstein, *Love, Sex, and Marriage*, 199.

17. Paul Thigpen, "A Family Album," *Christian History*, Issue 39, 15.

18. E.G. Schwiebert, *Luther and His Times* (St. Louis: Concordia, 1950), 595.

19. Brandt, ed., *Luther's Works*, 45, 39-40.

20. Mary Ann Jeffreys, "Colorful Sayings of Colorful Luther," *Christian History*, Issue 34, 27.

21. Luther, *The Short Catechism* (1529) in Henry Bettenson, ed., *Documents of the Christian Church* (New York: Oxford, 1967), 203-204.

22. Cited in Ozment, *When Fathers Ruled*, 143.

23. Schwiebert, *Luther and His Times*, 595.

24. Ozment, *When Fathers Ruled*, 49.

25. Ozment, *When Fathers Ruled*, 134.

26. Philip Schaff, *History of the Christian Church* (Grand Rapids: Eerdmans, 1979), VIII, 489-492.

27. Ruth A. Tucker, *Private Lives of Pastors' Wives* (Grand Rapids: Zondervan, 1992), 45.

28. Cited in Ozment, *When Fathers Ruled*, 28.

29. Ozment, *When Fathers Ruled*, 216.

30. Menno Simons, *Reply to Micron*, 1556 in Elaine S. Rich, *Mennonite Women* (Scottdale, PA: Herald Press, 1983), 23.

31. Ozment, *When Fathers Ruled*, 107.

32. Patricia Gundry, "Why We're Here," in Alvera Mickelsen, ed., *Women, Authority and the Bible* (Downers Grove, IL: InterVarsity, 1986), 12-13.

33. Steven Ozment, *When Fathers Ruled*, 208.

34. Ozment, *When Fathers Ruled*, 55.

35. William J. Petersen, "Idelette: John Calvin's Search for the Right Wife," *Christian History*, 5, no. 4 (1986), 13.

36. Williston Walker, *John Calvin: The Organizer of Reformed Protestantism, 1509-1564* (New York: Schocken, 1969), 236.

CHAPTER 8

1. Leland Ryken, *Worldly Saints: The Puritans As They Really Were* (Grand Rapids: Zondervan, 1986), 74, 89.

2. Ryken, *Worldly Saints*, 44-48.

3. Eleanor Early, *A New England Sampler* (Boston: Waverly House, 1940), 4.

4. Lawrence Stone, *The Family, Sex and Marriage in England 1500-1800* (New York: Harper & Row, 1977), 524-525.

5. Elisabeth Dodds, *Marriage to a Difficult Man: The "Uncommon Union" of Jonathan and Sarah Edwards* (Philadelphia: Westminster, 1971), 24.

6. Early, *A New England Sampler*, 149-151.

7. Oscar T. Barck and Hugh T. Lefler, *Colonial America* (New York: Macmillan, 1958), 448.
8. Bernard I. Murstein, *Love, Sex, and Marriage Through the Ages* (New York: Springer, 1974), 320.
9. Amanda Porterfield, *Female Piety in Puritan New England: The Emergence of Religious Humanism* (New York: Oxford University, 1992), 34.
10. Ann Jones, *Women Who Kill* (New York: Holt, Rinehart and Winston, 1980), 34.
11. Edmund S. Morgan, *The Puritan Family* (New York: Harper & Row, 1966), 44.
12. Cited in Norman Foerster, *American Poetry and Prose* (Boston: Houghton Mifflin, 1957), 43.
13. Laurel Thatcher Ulrich, *Good Wives: Image and Reality in the Lives of Women in Northern New England, 1650-1750* (New York: Oxford University, 1980), 110-112.
14. Cited in Margo Todd, "Humanists, Puritans and the Spiritualized Household," *Church History* (March 1980), 29.
15. Murstein, *Love, Sex, and Marriage*, 256.
16. Murstein, *Love, Sex, and Marriage*, 318.
17. Dodds, *Marriage to a Difficult Man*, 4.
18. Dodds, *Marriage to a Difficult Man*, 40.
19. Dodds, *Marriage to a Difficult Man*, 45.
20. Brian L. Harbour, *Famous Parents of the Bible* (Nashville: Broadman, 1983), 30-31.
21. Ryken, *Worldly Saints*, 74.
22. Ryken, *Worldly Saints*, 80-81.
23. Early, *A New England Sampler*, 144.
24. Cited in Richard Lovelace, *The American Pietism of Cotton Mather* (Grand Rapids: Eerdmans, 1979), 130.
25. Lloyd deMause, "The Evolution of Childhood," in *The History of Childhood* (New York: Atcom, 1974), 9.
26. Alice Morse Earle, *Child Life in Colonial Days* (New York: Macmillan, 1924), 205.
27. Cited in Earle, *Child Life in Colonial Days*, 308.
28. Earle, *Child Life in Colonial Days*, 295-297.
29. Ryken, *Worldly Saints*, 82.
30. Henry W. Lawrence, *The Not-Quite Puritans* (Boston: Little, Brown, and Company, 1928), 96.
31. Lawrence, *The Not-Quite Puritans*, 172.
32. Lawrence, *The Not-Quite Puritans*, 120.
33. Lawrence, *The Not-Quite Puritans*, 54-81, 201.
34. Lawrence, *The Not-Quite Puritans*, 193-194.
35. Helen Evertson Smith, *Colonial Days and Ways* (New York: Century, 1900), 235-242.

CHAPTER 9

1. "Revival and Revolution," *Christian History*, vol. II, no. 1, 7.
2. J. Wesley Bready, *England: Before and After Wesley* (London: Hodder and Stoughton, 1939), 142-147.
3. Rebecca Lamar Harmon, *Susanna: Mother of the Wesleys* (London: Hodder & Stoughton, 1968), 37.
4. Bready, *England: Before and After Wesley*, 19.
5. John Kirk, *The Mother of the Wesleys: A Biography* (London: Jarrold & Sons, 1866), 44-48; 3, 6-16.
6. Kirk, *The Mother of the Wesleys*, 23.
7. Harmon, *Susanna*, 35.
8. Dale A. Johnson, *Women in English Religion, 1700-1925* (New York: Edwin Mellen, 1983), 241.
9. Harmon, *Susanna*, 45.
10. Ruth A. Tucker, *Private Lives of Pastors' Wives* (Grand Rapids: Zondervan, 1988), 53-54.
11. Robert G. Tuttle, Jr., *John Wesley: His Life and Theology* (Grand Rapids: Zondervan, 1978), 42.
12. *The Journal of John Wesley*, ed. by Percy L. Parker (Chicago: Moody, n.d.), 104-107.
13. *The Journal of John Wesley*, 108.
14. John W. Drakeford, *Take Her Mr. Wesley* (Waco, TX: Word, 1973), 19.
15. Harmon, *Susanna*, 57.
16. John Wesley Funston, *The Wesleys in Picture and Story* (Mount Morris, IL: Kable Brothers, 1939), 22.
17. Tuttle, *John Wesley*, 65.
18. Harry Stout, *The Divine Dramatist: George Whitefield and the Rise of Modern Evangelicalism* (Grand Rapids: Eerdmans, 1991), 157.
19. Stanley Ayling, *John Wesley* (New York: William Collins, 1979), 75-85.
20. Tuttle, *John Wesley*, 288-292.
21. Tuttle, *John Wesley*, 293, 309.
22. Tucker, *Private Lives*, 58.
23. L. Tyerman, *The Life and Times of the Rev. Samuel Wesley* (London: Simpkin, Marshall & Co., 1866), 125.
24. *The Journal of John Wesley*, 101.
25. Cited in *Christian History*, vol. II, no. 1, 33.
26. John Wesley, *The Works of John Wesley*, 13 vols. (Grand Rapids: Zondervan, 1958), 8:427-428.

CHAPTER 10

1. Walter Goodman, *Black Bondage: The Life of Slaves in the South* (New York: Farrar, Straus & Giroux, 1969), 26.
2. John W. Blassingame, *The Slave Community: Plantation Life in the Antebellum South* (New York: Oxford University, 1976), 78-79.
3. Blassingame, *The Slave Community*, revised and enlarged edition, 139-141.
4. Walter Fisher, ed. *Father Henson's Story of His Own Life* (New York: Corinth Books, 1962), 11-13; in Fishel and Quarles, eds. *The Negro American*, 87.
5. William Still, *Still's Underground Rail Road Records* (Philadelphia: William Still, 1883), 157-158.
6. *The Complete Poetical Works of John Greenleaf Whittier* (Boston: Houghton Mifflin, 1892), 177-179.
7. Blassingame, *The Slave Community*, 99.
8. Harriet Beecher Stowe, *Uncle Tom's Cabin* (New York, 1962), 297-298; in Fishel and Quarles, *The Negro American*, 188.
9. Bert James Loewenberg and Ruth Bogin, eds., *Black Women in Nineteenth-Century American Life* (University Park: Pennsylvania State University, 1976), 65.
10. Eugene D. Genovese, *Roll, Jordan, Roll: The World the Slaves Made* (New York: Random House, 1974), 469.
11. Harriet Jacobs, *Incidents in the Life of a Slave Girl* (New York: Oxford University, 1988), 87-89.
12. Genovese, *Roll, Jordan, Roll*, 506.
13. Jacqueline Jones, *Labor of Love, Labor of Sorrow: Black Women, Work and the Family from Slavery to the Present* (New York: Basic Books, 1985), 37-38.
14. Bernard I. Murstein, *Love, Sex, and Marriage Through the Ages* (New York: Springer, 1974), 307.
15. Stanley M. Elkins, *Slavery: A Problem in American Institutional and Intellectual Life* (Chicago: University of Chicago, 1959), 54.
16. Murstein, *Love, Sex, and Marriage*, 308.
17. Genovese, *Roll, Jordan, Roll*, 481.
18. Blassingame, *The Slave Community*, 99.
19. Elkins, *Slavery*, 54.
20. Blassingame, *The Slave Community*, 105.

21. B.A. Botkin, ed. *Lay My Burden Down: A Folk History of Slavery* (Athens: University of Georgia Press, 1945), 27.
22. Genovese, *Roll, Jordan, Roll*, 402.
23. Cited in Fishel and Quarles, *The Negro American*, 114.
24. Blassingame, *The Slave Community*, 60-61.
25. Amanda Smith, *An Autobiography: The Story of the Lord's Dealings with Mrs. Amanda Smith, the Colored Evangelist* (Chicago: Meyer & Brothers, 1893), 9-20.
26. Albert J. Raboteau, "The Secret Religion of the Slaves," *Christian History*, Issue 33, 42.
27. Cited in Rosalind Miles, *Women's History of the World* (New York: Harper & Row, 1989), 195.
28. Genovese, *Roll, Jordan, Roll*, 452.
29. Martin Luther King, Jr., Lincoln Memorial, Washington, D.C., August 28, 1963.

CHAPTER 11

1. Stanley Weintraub, *Victoria: An Intimate Biography* (New York: E.P. Dutton, 1987), 159-160.
2. Lytton Strachey, *The Illustrated Queen Victoria* (New York: Weidenfeld & Nicolson, 1987), 84.
3. Strachey, *The Illustrated Queen Victoria*, 88.
4. Betty A. DeBerg, *Ungodly Women: Gender and the First Wave of American Fundamentalism* (Minneapolis: Fortress, 1990), 19-23.
5. Colleen McDannell, *The Christian Home in Victorian America, 1840-1900* (Bloomington: Indiana University, 1986), 7-8.
6. Cited in McDannell, *The Christian Home*, 79-80.
7. McDannell, *The Christian Home*, 134-135.
8. Cited in Phebe Hannaford, *Daughters of America* (Augusta, ME: True and Company, 1883), 415.
9. McDannell, *The Christian Home*, 20-27.
10. Bonnie Angelo, "Clinton Family Values," *Time*, December 6, 1993, 38.
11. Cited in Margaret E. Sangster, *Fairest Childhood* (Grand Rapids: Zondervan, 1986, reprinted from 1906), 93-94.
12. Cited in Joan Evans, *The Victorians* (Cambridge: University of Cambridge, 1966), 111.
13. Mark Twain, "The McWilliamses and the Burglar Alarm," *Harper's Christmas Issue*, 1882.
14. Bernard I. Murstein, *Love Sex, and Marriage Through the Ages* (New York: Springer, 1974), 256.
15. Eleanor Early, *A New England Sampler* (Boston: Waverly House, 1940), 211-220.
16. C. John Sommerville, *The Rise and Fall of Childhood* (New York: Random House, 1990), 205.
17. McDannell, *The Christian Home*, 175.
18. Sommerville, *The Rise and Fall of Childhood*, 201-204.
19. Cited in Ralph L. Woods, ed., *A Treasury of the Familiar* (Chicago: Consolidated Book Publishers, 1944), 378-379.
20. Page Smith, *Daughters of the Promised Land: Women in American History* (Boston: Little, Brown, and Company, 1970), 209-210.
21. Paul Moody, *My Father: An Intimate Portrait of Dwight Moody* (Boston: Little, Brown, and Company, 1938), 82-83.
22. James F. Findlay, Jr., *Dwight L. Moody: American Evangelist, 1837-1899* (Chicago: University of Chicago, 1969), 382n.
23. B.J. Armstrong, *A Norfolk Diary*, cited in Evans, *The Victorians*, 157.
24. Cited in Woods, ed., *A Treasury of the Familiar*, 620.
25. Dale A. Johnson, *Women in English Religion, 1700-1925* (New York: Edwin Mellen, 1983), 170-171.
26. Cited in DeBerg, *Ungodly Women*, 47-48.

CHAPTER 12

1. Betty A. DeBerg, *Ungodly Women: Gender the and First Wave of American Fundamentalism* (Minneapolis: Fortress, 1990), 40.
2. *King's Business* (February 1921), cited in DeBerg, *Ungodly Women*, 43.
3. Cited in Alan Graebner, "Birth Control and the Lutherans," in *Women in American Religion*, ed. Janet Wilson James (Philadelphia: University of Pennsylvania Press, 1980), 231.
4. Douglas Frank, *Less Than Conquerors: How Evangelicals Entered the Twentieth Century* (Grand Rapids: Eerdmans, 1986), 185.
5. Mark Senter, III, *The Coming Revolution in Youth Ministry* (Wheaton, IL: Victor, 1992), 97-98.
6. James A. Warner and Donald M. Denlinger, *The Gentle People: A Portrait of the Amish* (New York: Grossman, 1969), 24.
7. Warner and Denlinger, *The Gentle People*, 24-25.
8. John A. Hostetler, *Amish Life* (Scottdale, PA: Herald Press, 1959), 20-21.
9. Ashley Montagu, "Can the Family Survive Free Love?" *Empire Magazine*, November 4, 1979, cited in Dolores Curran, *Traits of a Healthy Family* (Minneapolis: Winston Press, 1983), 8.
10. John R. Rice, *Bobbed Hair, Bossy Wives, and Women Preachers* (Murfreesboro, TN: Sword of the Lord, 1941), 79.
11. Curran, *Traits of a Healthy Family*, 6-7.
12. Marshall Frady, *Billy Graham: A Parable of American Righteousness* (Boston: Little, Brown, and Company, 1979), 28.
13. Frady, *Billy Graham*, 48.
14. Morrow C. Graham, *They Call Me Mother Graham* (Old Tappan, NJ: Fleming H. Revell, 1977), 27-28.
15. Edith Schaeffer, *What Is a Family?* (Old Tappan, NJ: Fleming H. Revell, 1957), 254-255.
16. Cited in *The Treasury of Inspirational Anecdotes, Quotations and Illustrations*, compiled by E. Paul Hovey (Westwood, NJ: Fleming H. Revell, 1959), 179.
17. Cited in *The Treasury of Inspirational Anecdotes*, 211.
18. Rosalynn Carter, *First Lady from Plains* (Boston: Houghton Mifflin, 1984), 19.
19. Margaret Jensen, *First We Have Coffee* (San Bernardino, CA: Here's Life, 1982), 40.
20. Edgar A. Guest, *Collected Verse of Edgar A. Guest* (Chicago: The Reilly & Lee Co., 1934), 569.
21. Rolf Zettersten, *Dr. Dobson: Turning Hearts Toward Home* (Dallas: Word, 1989), 93.
22. Cited in Ralph L. Woods, ed., *A Second Treasury of the Familiar*, 57.
23. Gloria Gaither in "What My Parents Did Right," *Today's Christian Woman* (September/October 1991), 48.
24. Tony Campolo, "A Dreamer for the Kingdom," in Gloria Gaither, ed., *What My Parents Did Right* (Nashville: Star Song, 1991), 36-38.
25. Amy Carmichael, *Toward Jerusalem* (London: S.P.C.K., 1936), 106.
26. Dale Hanson Bourke, "Ruth Bell Graham: "Tough and Tender Moments," *Today's Christian Woman* (November/December 1991), 53.
27. Bourke, "Ruth Bell Graham," 53, 129.
28. Joni Eareckson Tada in "What My Parents Did Right," *Today's Christian Woman* (September/ October 1991), 49.
29. E. Stanley Jones, *A Song of Accents: A Spiritual Autobiography* (Nashville: Abingdon, 1968), 346-47.

EPILOGUE

1. Ruth A. Tucker: *Women in the Maze: Questions and Answers on Biblical Equality* (Downers Grove, IL: InterVarsity, 1992), 9.
2. Ruth A. Tucker, *From Jerusalem to Irian Jaya: A Biographical History of Christian Missions* (Grand Rapids: Zondervan, 1983), 490.

Acknowledgments

I wish to express my grateful appreciation to cartoonists, poets, artists, and organizations for permission to use material in this book. For Cartoons: "Just Follow Me," Rich Bishop; "These Pictorial Church Directories," Dick Hafer; "The Children's Crusade," "Andrew and the Junior Highs," and "The Agape Meal," reprinted from *Less Than Entirely Sanctified* by Doug Hall (Copyright 1992 by Doug Hall. Used by permission of InterVarsity Press, P.O. Box 1400, Downers Grove, IL 60515); "I've Fallen and I Can't Get Up," Elizabeth Kramer; "We're moving to someplace called Ur," W. Miller (Copyright 1989, *The New Yorker*); and "Martin Luther and the 95 Theses," Tim Walburg. For Poetry: "The Gleaners," Alvin Ricklefs for the late Ruth Ricklefs; and the "The Carpenter" by Phyllis Hartnoll, Copyright: Christian Century Foundation (reprinted by permission from *The Christian Century*). For Photographs: "Tony Campolo with his family," Tony Campolo; "Rosalynn Carter at age six," University of Arkansas Press (201 Ozark Ave., Fayetteville, AR 72701); "Young James Dobson with his father," Focus on the Family (420 North Cascade Ave., Colorado Springs, CO 80903); "Billy Graham at six months," "The Graham family admiring the latest addition," Billy Graham Evangelistic Association (Photo Department, 1020 W. Magnolia Blvd., Burbank, CA 91506). For Illustrations: "Amish Men Talking," and "Amish Courtship," Beulah S. Hostetler from *Amish Life* by John A. Hostetler (Scottdale, PA: Herald Press, 1959); "Ruth gleaning," "The interior of a first-century Palestinian home," "The exterior of a first-century Palestinian dwelling," "A two-story first-century Palestinian dwelling," "A dwelling similar to Priscilla's and Aquila's house church," "Susanna Wesley, the home-school teacher," "Down on the farm—an Iowa barn in the 1950s," "The Stellrecht farm," Julie Stellrecht.

Selected Bibliography

General Sources

Aries, Philippe. *Centuries of Childhood: A Social History of Family Life.*. New York: Random House, 1962.

Cootz, Stephanie. *The Way We Never Were: American Families and the Nostalgia Trap.* New York: HarperCollins, 1992.

deMause, Lloyd ed. *The History of Childhood.* New York: Psychohistory Press, 1974.

Greven, Philip. *Spare the Child: The Religious Roots of Punishment and the Psychological Impact of Physical Abuse.* New York: Alfred A. Knopf, 1991.

Horie, Michiaki and Hildegard. *Whatever Became of Fathering? Its Rise and Fall and How Parents Can Rebuild It.* Downers Grove, IL: InterVarsity, 1993.

Lockyer, Herbert. *All the Women of the Bible.* Grand Rapids: Zondervan, 1985.

Murstein, Bernard I. *Love, Sex, and Marriage Through the Ages.* New York: Springer, 1974.

Noonan, John T. *Contraception: A History of Its Treatment by the Catholic Theologians and Canonists.* Cambridge, MA: Harvard University, 1986.

Phillips, Roderick. *Putting Asunder: A History of Divorce in Western Society.* New York: Cambridge University, 1988.

Pollock, Linda. *Forgotten Children: Parent-Child Relations from 1500-1900.* Cambridge: Cambridge University, 1983.

Rogers, Katharine M. *The Troublesome Helpmate: A History of Misogyny in Literature.* Seattle: University of Washington, 1966.

Stone, Lawrence. *The Family, Sex and Marriage in England, 1500-1800.* New York: Harper & Row, 1977.

Van Leeuwen, Mary Stewart. *Gender and Grace: Love, Work and Parenting in a Changing World.* Downers Grove, IL: InterVarsity, 1990.

Biblical Times

Daniel-Rops, Henri. *Daily Life in the Time of Jesus.* New York: Hawthorn Books, 1962.

Gaer, Joseph. *The Lore of the New Testament.* Boston: Little, Brown and Co., 1952.

Gaer, Joseph. *The Lord of the Old Testament,* Boston: Little, Brown and Co., 1952.

Hurley, James B. *Man and Woman in Biblical Perspective.* Grand Rapids: Zondervan, 1981.

O'Shea, Denis. *Mary and Joseph: Their Lives and Times.* Milwaukee: Bruce Publishing, 1949.

Phipps, William E. *Assertive Biblical Women.* Westport, CT: Greenwood, 1992.

Talmage, T. DeWitt. *From Manger to Throne: A New Life of Jesus the Christ.* New York: The Christian Herald, 1893.

Wagenknecht, Edward, ed. *The Story of Jesus in the World's Literature.* New York: Creative Age Press, 1946.

Warner, Marina. *Alone of All Her Sex: The Myth and the Cult of the Virgin Mary.* New York: Alfred A. Knopf, 1976.

Wiesel, Elie. *Messengers of God: Biblical Portraits and Legends,* trans. by Marion Wiesel. New York: Random House, 1976.

Apostolic Church and Early Centuries

Ewald, George R. *Jesus and Divorce: A Biblical Guide.* Scottdale, PA: Herald Press, 1991

Gorman, Michael J. *Abortion in the Early Church: Christian and Pagan Attitudes in the Greco-Roman World.* Downers Grove, IL: InterVarsity, 1982.

Heth, William A. and Wenham, Gordon J. *Jesus and Divorce: The Problem with the Evangelical Consensus.* Nashville: Thomas Nelson, 1984.

LaPorte, Jean. *The Role of Women in Early Christianity.* New York: Edwin Mellen, 1982.

Matthews, Shailer. *Jesus on Social Institutions.* New York: Macmillan, 1928.

Peabody, Francis, G. *Jesus Christ and the Social Question.* New York: Grosset & Dunlap, 1990.

Wirt, Sherwood E., ed., *The Confessions of Augustine in Modern English.* Grand Rapids: Zondervan, 1986.

Middle Ages and Reformation

Brooke, Christopher N.L. *The Medieval Idea of Marriage*. New York: Oxford University, 1989.
Gies, Francis and Joseph, *Marriage and the Family in the Middle Ages*. New York: Harper & Row, 1987.
Ozment, Steven. *When Fathers Ruled: Family Life in Reformation Europe*. Cambridge, MA: Harvard University, 1983.
Roper, Lyndal. *The Holy Household: Women and Morals in Reformation Augsburg*. New York: Oxford University, 1989.
Rowling, Marjorie. *Life in Medieval Times*. New York: Perigee Books, 1979.

Puritans to the Wesleyan Era

Bready, J. Wesley. *England: Before and After Wesley: The Evangelical Revival and Social Reform*. London: Hodder and Stoughton, 1939.
Dodds, Elisabeth D. *Marriage to a Difficult Man: The "Uncommon Union" of Jonathan and Sarah Edwards*. Philadelphia: Westminster, 1971.
Earle, Alice Morse. *Child Life in Colonial Days*. New York: Macmillan, 1924.
Early, Eleanor. *A New England Sampler*. Boston: Waverly House, 1940.
George, M. Dorothy. *London Life in the Eighteenth Century*. New York: Harper & Row, 1964.
Greven, Philip. *The Protestant Temperament: Patterns of Child-rearing, Religious Experience, and the Self in Early America*. New York: Alfred A. Knopf, 1977.
Harmon, Rebecca L. *Susanna: Mother of the Wesleys*. Nashville: Abingdon, 1968.
Lawrence, Henry W. *The Non-Quite Puritans*. Boston: Little, Brown, and Company, 1928.
Lystad, Mary. *At Home in America as Seen Through Its Books for Children*. Cambridge, MA: Schenkman, 1984.
Morgan, Edmund S. *The Puritan Family: Religion and Domestic Relations in Seventeenth-Century New England*. New York: Harper & Row, 1966.
Porterfield, Amanda. *Female Piety in Puritan New England*. New York: Oxford University, 1991.
Ryken, Leland. *Worldly Saints: The Puritans as They Really Were*. Grand Rapids: Zondervan, 1986.
Slater, Peter G. *Children in the New England Mind in Death and in Life*. Hamden, CT: Archon, 1977.
Smith, Helen Evertson, *Colonial Days and Ways*. New York: Century, 1900.
Ulrich, Laurel T. *Good Wives: Image and Reality in the Lives of Women in Northern New England, 1650-1750*. New York: Oxford University, 1982.

The Nineteenth and Twentieth Centuries

Andrews, William L., ed. *Sisters of the Spirit: Three Black Women's Autobiographies of the Nineteenth Century*. Bloomington: Indiana University, 1986.
Bentley, Nicolas. *The Victorian Scene: 1837-1901*. London: George Weidenfeld & Nicolson, 1968.
Blassingame, John W. *The Slave Community: Plantation Life in the Antebellum South*. New York: Oxford University, 1976.
Botkin, B.A., ed. *Lay My Burden Down: A Folk History of Slavery*. Athens: University of Georgia Press, 1945.
Brumberg, Joan J. *Mission for Life: The Story of the Family of Adoniram Judson*. New York: Macmillan, 1980.
Carter, Rosalynn. *First Lady from Plains*. Boston: Houghton Mifflin, 1984.
DeBerg, Betty A. *Ungodly Women: Gender and the First Wave of American Fundamentalism*. Minneapolis: Fortress, 1990.
Fox-Genovese, Elizabeth. *Within the Plantation Household: Black and White Women of the Old South*. Chapel Hill: University of North Carolina, 1988.
Frady, Marshall. *Billy Graham: A Parable of American Righteousness*. Boston: Little, Brown, and Company, 1979.
Frank, Douglas. *Less Than Conquerors: How Evangelicals Entered the Twentieth Century*. Grand Rapids: Eerdmans, 1986.
Gaither, Gloria, ed., *What My Parents Did Right*. Nashville: Star Song, 1991.
Genovese, Eugene D. *Roll, Jordan, Roll: The World the Slaves Made*. New York: Random House, 1974.
Graham, Morrow C. *They Call Me Mother Graham*. Old Tappan, NJ: Fleming H. Revell, 1977.
Heasman, Kathleen. *Evangelicals in Action: An Appraisal of Their Social Work in the Victorian Era*. London: Geoffrey Bles, 1962.
Hostetler, John A. *Amish Life*. Scottdale, PA: Herald Press, 1959.
Lystad, Mary. *At Home in America as Seen Through Its Books for Children*. Cambridge, MA: Schenkman, 1984.
Malone, Ann Patton. *Sweet Chariot: Slave Family and Household Structure in Nineteenth-Century Louisiana*. Chapel Hill: University of North Carolina, 1992.
McDannell, Colleen. *The Christian Home in Victorian America, 1840-1900*. Bloomington: Indiana University, 1986.
Rice, John R. *Bobbed Hair, Bossy Wives, and Women Preachers*. Murfreesboro, TN: Sword of the Lord, 1941.
Schaffer, Edith. *What Is a Family?* Old Tappan, NJ: Fleming H. Revell, 1957.
Stratton, Joanna L. *Pioneer Women: Voices from the Kansas Frontier*. New York: Simon and Schuster, 1981.
Warner, James A. and Donald M. Denlinger, *The Gentle People: A Portrait of the Amish*. New York: Grossman, 1969.
Weisberger, Bernard A. *They Gathered at the River: The Story of the Great Revivalists and Their Impact Upon Religion in America*. Boston: Little, Brown, and Company, 1958.
Zettersten, Rolf. *Dr. Dobson: Turning Hearts Toward Home*. Dallas: Word, 1989.

Index